From Colonial Warrior to Western Front Flyer

*I would like to thank Caroline Maxwell BSc MBA
for all her hard work in preparing the index for the book*

From Colonial Warrior to Western Front Flyer

The Five Wars of Sydney Herbert Bywater Harris

Carole McEntee-Taylor

Pen & Sword
AVIATION

First published in Great Britain in 2015 by
Pen & Sword Aviation
an imprint of
Pen & Sword Books Ltd
47 Church Street
Barnsley
South Yorkshire
S70 2AS

Copyright © Carole McEntee-Taylor 2015

ISBN 978 1 47382 359 4

The right of Carole McEntee-Taylor to be identified as the Author of this Work has been asserted by her in accordance with the Copyright, Designs and Patents Act 1988.

A CIP catalogue record for this book is available from the British Library

All rights reserved. No part of this book may be reproduced or transmitted in any form or by any means, electronic or mechanical including photocopying, recording or by any information storage and retrieval system, without permission from the Publisher in writing.

Typeset in Ehrhardt by
Mac Style Ltd, Bridlington, East Yorkshire
Printed and bound in the UK by CPI Group (UK) Ltd,
Croydon, CR0 4YY

Pen & Sword Books Ltd incorporates the imprints of Pen & Sword Archaeology, Atlas, Aviation, Battleground, Discovery, Family History, History, Maritime, Military, Naval, Politics, Railways, Select, Transport, True Crime, and Fiction, Frontline Books, Leo Cooper, Praetorian Press, Seaforth Publishing and Wharncliffe.

For a complete list of Pen & Sword titles please contact
PEN & SWORD BOOKS LIMITED
47 Church Street, Barnsley, South Yorkshire, S70 2AS, England
E-mail: enquiries@pen-and-sword.co.uk
Website: www.pen-and-sword.co.uk

Contents

Prologue: *France, June 1940* — vii

Chapter 1	Gold Fever	1
Chapter 2	From Liverpool to Skaguay	16
Chapter 3	The Gold Fields	28
Chapter 4	The Philippines Insurrection	38
Chapter 5	The Boxer Rebellion	45
Chapter 6	Arrival in China	53
Chapter 7	To Peking	64
Chapter 8	The Occupation of China	72
Chapter 9	Back to the Philippines: December 1900–1902	84
Chapter 10	Back Home	92
Chapter 11	Royal Flying Corps	110
Chapter 12	Off to France	123
Chapter 13	Action in the Sky	134
Chapter 14	Gun Spotting	143
Chapter 15	No. 2 School of Aerial Gunnery	149
Chapter 16	In Charge	157
Chapter 17	From Aircraft to Trains	169

Chapter 18	The Spanish Civil War	185
Chapter 19	Blitzkrieg	191
Chapter 20	The Long Road to Victory	201
Chapter 21	Adventures End	214

Epilogue: The View of a Grandson   218
Notes   221
Index   224

Prologue

France, June 1940

'You're getting too old for this, Harris old chap', a wry smile formed on Sydney Herbert Bywater Harris' lips as he realised what he'd said. Sydney never thought he would admit to his advancing age but at 58 he really was too old to be trying to outrun the German Blitzkrieg as it spread rapidly across France. With hindsight perhaps he should have been satisfied with the desk job they'd offered him, but no, he'd had to force his way into the action even though he really should have known better. On the other hand, he never felt more alive than when the odds were against him and, even though he was exhausted, a part of him was quietly exhilarated by the excitement. At the age when most men would be looking forward to their retirement he'd been given one last chance for some fun.

'Come on, Harris, we need to get a move on or they'll overrun us.' Sydney looked at his companions and nodded. The speed with which the Germans had closed the net was truly frightening. Word had reached them that the majority of the army had made it off at Dunkirk, but there were thousands, like him, stranded and making their way to places like Saint-Nazaire in the hope the navy would be able to rescue them.

It hardly seemed possible that the BEF had collapsed so quickly but now was probably not the time to think about it. He climbed into the staff car and the driver eased in the clutch and shot off. They had no idea how close the Germans were behind them and it wasn't wise to find out.

After the female ATS staff had gone back to England on 12 June it was fairly obvious that things were serious. With little else to do they had made plans to protect the camp. To start with they set up a tank trap on all the nearby roads by stretching steel wire at a 45-degree angle across them. To protect against parachutists dropping in they set up a Bren gun in one truck and twenty men in two other lorries to form a 'flying column'. But at 1pm on the 15th they were told they were leaving. French civilians were sent to other parts of the camp so they couldn't see what was going on and the men began packing up. The first convoy left at 6pm that evening.

As they headed towards Saint-Nazaire they passed other remnants of the BEF. There was little spare room in the car but they still pulled over to pick up a wounded infantryman who gratefully climbed aboard. There was a frightening sense of urgency in the air that intensified as they came closer to the town. The roads were soon crammed with stragglers and their progress slowed to a crawl. He looked round him with a feeling of disbelief. The sights that met his eyes had to be seen to be believed and his heart sank as they drove past an anti-aircraft battery towing two guns behind a tractor, which had obviously been commandeered from a French farm, and several ragged bands of men marching determinedly towards what they hoped was escape. Above their heads the skies were filled with Stukas who constantly menaced the retreating convoy, causing them to abandon their vehicles with increasing frequency and take cover wherever they could.

By the time Sydney reached Saint-Nazaire it was dark but even the lack of light could not hide the chaos that greeted him. On the outskirts of the town there were several fields full of British vehicles deliberately abandoned and wrecked by the escaping troops. Because of confusion as to what the Royal Navy could take, thousands of pounds' worth of serviceable equipment, guns, vehicles, tanks and much-needed ammunition would be abandoned in France. Distracted by the sight of so much destruction the sudden sound of anti-tank guns made him jump, but it was only soldiers firing rounds into British vehicles as a way of destroying them.

The town itself was a shambles with broken down and abandoned vehicles littering the roads. Everywhere he looked there were retreating soldiers and airmen. He spotted British, French and Polish within minutes of entering the town. Almost immediately they came to a road block and were told to leave the car and walk as all cars were being destroyed because they couldn't be rescued. All available space on the ships would be for the troops. Above his head he could hear the familiar sound of Stukas whining as they targeted the men on the dock and he looked skyward wondering if there were any RAF left in France or were they all being evacuated like him. A few moments later the reassuring sound of a patrol of Hurricanes could be heard above and he breathed a sigh of relief as they eventually chased the Stukas away.

The evacuation would never be successful if they couldn't control the skies above.

He climbed wearily out of the car, leaving it by the side of the road. The wounded infantryman leant on his arm and he helped him to the nearest First Aid Post. As they headed towards the port a group of drunken soldiers swept past them, the men laughing and shouting aggressively. He was about to intervene but they looked to be beyond reason and he thought better of it. The port was no less chaotic with men everywhere and eventually they returned to the town, settled down in an abandoned warehouse and tried to sleep.

The following morning, 17 June, they made their way down to the port where thousands of soldiers, airmen and civilians were queuing as they waited for transport to take them out to HMT *Lancastria*. Discipline seemed to have broken down with NCOs and men calling each other by their first names and men answering back when given orders. An air of every man for himself permeated the area and when one corporal tried to get Bren gunners to set up ready for the anticipated air attacks the men refused and threatened to throw him in the harbour. However, when the Luftwaffe flew over a few moments later every man who still had a weapon fired it at the German aircraft, although they appeared to have little effect.

Sydney turned his attention back to HMT *Lancastria*. From where he was standing it looked as if the ship was full with thousands of men already on board. Sighing heavily he resigned himself to having to wait until the next one. Then all hell broke loose. The banshee wail of the Junkers Ju-88 bombers shattered the air and his ears rang with the rapid bursts of the ack-ack guns mingling with the rattle of rifles and steady thudding of the Bren guns. Bombs began dropping everywhere catapulting debris into the air, demolishing buildings and creating large craters. Taking cover behind the nearest building, he frantically scanned the skies hoping to see the RAF, but there was no sign of them. The Junkers had used the cloud cover to their advantage and had the area to themselves. Despite the bombs falling all around him he continued to watch the destructive power of the Junkers, wishing he was up there to do something about them. This thought had only just gone through his mind when the frenetic rattle of machine guns caught his attention. In the distance he could see German aircraft machine-gunning the deck of the *Lancastria* and men scrambling for cover on the over-crowded ship. He felt sick as he imagined the carnage and for the first time that day he was glad he'd not been able to board the ship. Then something else caught his eye.

A lone Junkers was circling high above the *Lancastria*. As he watched it began diving rapidly towards the ship. To start with he thought it was going to crash onto the deck and he found himself holding his breath. But at the last moment it pulled up and he breathed a sigh of relief. If it had crashed on the ship thousands of men would have been killed. And then he saw the bomb. It was heading straight for the funnel.

Chapter One

Gold Fever

It was 3 March 1899 and 17-year-old Sydney Herbert Bywater Harris looked round with a satisfied smile. He had come a long way from Ilford in Essex to the Yukon in Canada and his adventure was only just beginning. He could hardly believe he had just purchased his Miner's Certificate from the Miners' Recorder for the princely sum of $5. It was valid for a year and would give him all the necessary rights as a free miner. The next step was to purchase the equipment he would need. He made his way quickly to McLennan, McFeely and Co.'s hardware store and began to list the items he would require to make the treacherous journey into the Canadian Yukon. The last items were a sled and a tent and as the man handed over the smaller purchases and Sydney loaded them onto his sled he felt a familiar frisson of excitement. He handed over his $31.65 and hastily joined the thousands of other prospectors as they left the city by steamer and headed towards Skaguay, the town from which they would travel to the gold fields.

It was under three years since enormous quantities of gold had been found in the Yukon in August 1896 and now here he was on the last leg of his journey. He was almost there. He found a place on the deck of the steamer and looked round with interest at his fellow passengers. Several languages assaulted his ears and although most of the other prospectors seemed like him, ordinary people out to make their fortune, he spotted some that looked more

Sydney Herbert Bywater Harris before he left for Canada.

2 From Colonial Warrior to Western Front Flyer

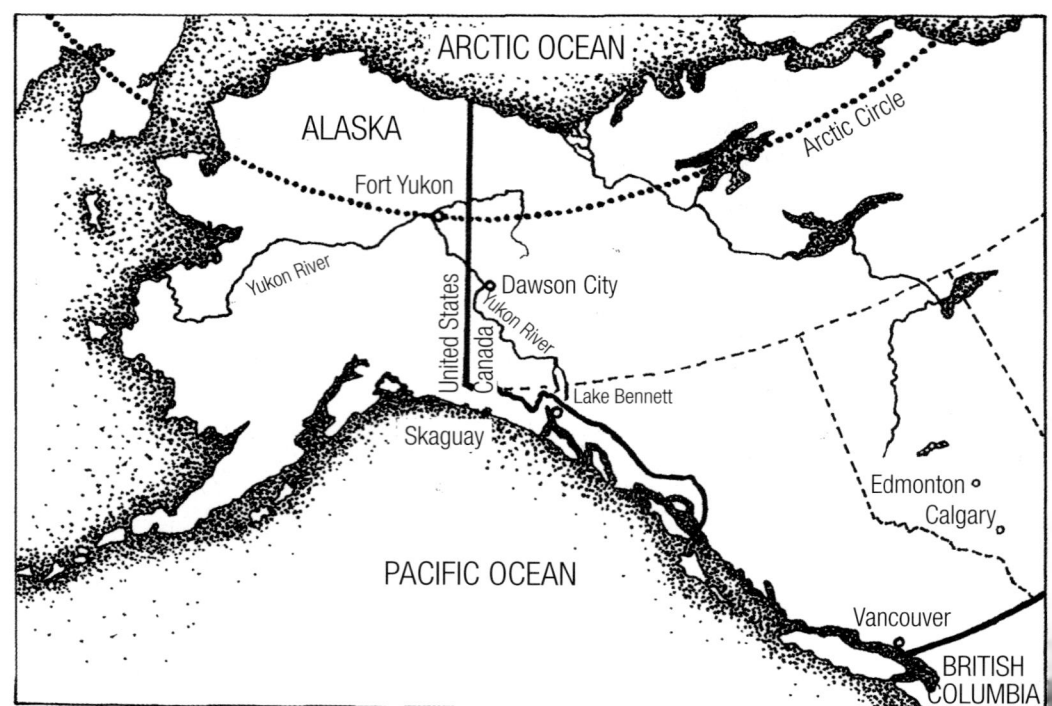

The main locations on Sydney's journey to the Gold Rush.

unsavoury. He pulled his supplies closer to him for safety and concentrated on looking out at the coast as it disappeared from view. He had arrived in Montreal in November 1898 and it had taken four months to get this far. He wanted to relish every moment.

The discovery of gold in the Klondike had been headline news for several months. The papers had been full of tales of those who had made it rich and it was this that had prompted him to undertake the long and dangerous journey. However, the newspapers had not mentioned the thousands who had trekked there in vain or those who had also lost their fortunes. So Sydney was convinced that once he arrived in the Yukon riches were his for the taking. With the optimism of youth the thought that he would not make his fortune never even crossed his mind.

Now they were out of sight of the coast there was little to see, but Sydney remained where he was, enjoying the fresh feel of the sea breeze in his face. With little to occupy him his mind strayed back to the disputed tales he'd

Sydney's Miner's Certificate, needed before he could start panning or mining for gold in the Yukon.

read about who really found the gold. These had persisted since the news of the gold find broke and centred round two men, Robert Henderson and George Washington Carmack. It was these stories that had really fired his imagination and fuelled his determination to seek his own fortune in the vast wilderness of the Yukon.

Robert Henderson was the son of a lighthouse keeper from Big Island off the coast of Nova Scotia and he had spent all his life looking for gold. As a child he searched Nova Scotia but found nothing other than white iron so, at the age of 14, he went off to seek his fortune elsewhere. Henderson was a tall, thin man with gaunt, chiselled features and a full moustache that drooped at the edges. His heavy eyebrows framed piercing eyes and a serious, intense expression. Wherever he went he wore his broad-rimmed miner's hat, a clear sign to the world that he was a prospector.

Henderson spent five years panning his way across New Zealand, Australia and other countries but did not find anything substantial so he finally returned

Sydney's receipt for the supplies he needed to make the crossing into Canada.

to the northern hemisphere. The following fourteen years also yielded little gold as he travelled through the Rocky Mountain states to Colorado. Eventually, he found himself heading towards Alaska. While others rushed to the gold finds on Fortymile or Birch Creeks, Henderson chose to press on into the unknown reaches of the River Pelly, but still he found nothing. Drifting aimlessly, virtually out of money and food, Henderson and his two companions finally arrived at Ogilvie, a small collection of cabins, tents and a two-storey trading post operated by Papa Harper and Joseph Laude.

Joseph Laude, known to all as 'Joe', was a stocky, swarthy man of French Huguenot descent. He had spent the last twenty years looking for gold because he needed to be rich to marry the love of his life, Anna Mason, whose wealthy parents considered him unworthy of their daughter. Like other prospectors, the slightest whisper of gold was enough for him to travel in search of his fortune but despite panning his way through Wyoming, New Mexico and Arizona he had failed to find anything substantial. He spent the next six years panning the creeks from Stewart to Nuklayaket but was still unsuccessful. Eventually, he gave up. But he still needed to earn a living so first he tried farming, but when that failed too he set up as a trader.

Joe was a confirmed optimist. He was convinced that sooner or later someone would find massive deposits of gold and, as it was often the merchants who made more money from a gold strike than the miners, once that happened everyone would be rich. He wasted no time in passing on this enthusiasm to all his customers and Henderson was no exception.

The trading post was situated about a hundred miles upstream from Fortymile and between these two settlements there were two rivers on the opposite side which flowed into the Yukon River. The Indian River was about 30 miles downstream from his trading post and the Thron-diuk River was a further 30 miles downstream from the Indian River. Joe had spent considerable time panning in the Thron-diuk River and was sure there was no gold there, but he was convinced that there was gold to be found in the Indian River.

It didn't take much to convince Henderson, but his two companions were less enthusiastic and decided to return to Colorado. Henderson offered to prospect for Laude who agreed. Now on his own, Henderson spent the next two years combing the Indian River and its tributaries for gold but, although he found some, it was never quite enough. As time went on the constant immersion in the icy waters and streams caused crippling leg cramps and the continual white glare of the snow-covered mountain slopes gave him snow blindness. But despite this he refused to give up, convinced that the next pan would be the one that would produce a massive gold find.

As he continued his search Henderson eventually found himself at the foot of a mountain nestling comfortably among several rolling hills that were considerably lower. He climbed slowly to the summit and then stopped. The view that met his eyes was breathtaking and for a moment he was stunned, the search for gold momentarily forgotten. As far as he could see row after row of rolling, moss-covered hills stretched endlessly into the horizon, their smooth contours intersected by numerous valleys and gullies. To his north snow-capped mountains disappeared into the far distance and from where he stood he could just make out three streams meandering lazily down to the Indian River. On the far side of the mountain a further three creeks glistened and glinted in the bright sunlight as they disappeared out of sight. Unknown to Henderson, these were six of the richest gold-bearing waterways in the world.

There was a deep gorge where he was standing and Henderson bent down slowly dipping his pan into the small creek. He carefully washed the sand and gravel away and then gasped in astonishment. In the pan, shining up at him, were about 8 cents of gold. Thinking he had finally found what he was looking for he returned quickly back across the mountain to the Indian River where he saw another twenty men who were also busy panning for gold. He scrambled down the mountain and quickly showed them what he had found. Although they looked at the gold with interest, only three of them could be persuaded to return with him. For the next few weeks they panned constantly and by the middle of the summer they had taken about $750 in gold. They were now running short of supplies so Henderson decided to go back to Laude's trading post to pick up some more. As the prospector's code encouraged a free exchange of information, Henderson told everybody he met on the way about the gold find and encouraged them all to head up there and stake their own claims.

Having filled his skin boat with supplies, Henderson drifted slowly back the way he had come. But it was now late summer and the water in the Indian

River was very low. Concerned that it would tear his boat to shreds if he tried to navigate it, Henderson carried on down the Yukon towards the Thron-diuk River, assuming correctly that the creek he had named Gold Bottom would flow into it. It was here he met George Washington Carmack, known universally as the squaw man. This meeting would change everything and would haunt Henderson for the rest of his life.

The Thron-diuk River was known as the finest salmon-fishing river in the Yukon. Its name is Indian and means 'Hammer Water'. It was called this because the Indians hammered posts across the shallow river mouth so they could spread their nets out to dry. As Henderson approached the mouth of the river he could see a white man moving about. Unable to believe that anyone would choose to fish when there was gold to be found, Henderson immediately presumed that this man must be someone who had failed to strike lucky so he immediately began to tell him all about the gold find.

George Washington Carmack was the complete opposite of Henderson. He was a plump, heavy jowled man who was rather lazy and invariably assumed that everything would work out well. His father had followed the gold rush of 1849 and he was born at Port Costa, across the bay from San Francisco. George wasn't the slightest bit interested in gold; his whole aim in life was to be an Indian. This was despite the fact that Indians were despised by the white men of the day and often called 'Siwash' as a term of abuse.

In pursuit of his goal George had married the daughter of the Chief of the Tagish tribe and, even though the line of descent in the Tagish tribe was through the Chief's sister, his aim was to be Chief. He had several children with his wife and he spent his time moving up and down the river with his Indian comrades. Like the Tagish, he was very easy-going and although he did boast about the odd gold find, no one really took him seriously as a prospector, including Carmack himself.

Several years after the gold strike Carmack would claim that he was also a mystic, stating that in May 1896 he had felt something unusual was about to happen. Having finished fishing in one area of the river, he had been unable to make up his mind whether to go back up the river or to go downstream. So he tossed a coin to decide. That coin determined his fate and he began the 200-mile journey to Fortymile.

As he slept that night he dreamed that he was seated on the banks of a stream when the graylings he was watching scattered in fright and two large king salmon appeared upstream and stopped in front of him. As he stared at them he realised that their scales were made of gold nuggets and their eyes $20 gold pieces. Carmack immediately decided this was an omen and he made the decision to go fishing for salmon on the Thron-diuk and sell it as dog feed.

Henderson found Carmack with several of his Tagish friends and began telling him all about his gold find. Carmack asked if there was any point relocating or had the area already been staked? Henderson agreed there was probably a chance for Carmack, but looking at the Indians he added that he didn't want any Siwashes on the creek.

A few days later Carmack and his friends headed slowly up the valley of Rabbit Creek. This eventually led them to the ridge which separated the Klondike and Indian watersheds. Carmack began panning in the mouth of the Rabbit and found the first signs of gold. Because they were only small amounts they decided not to stop but to continue on their way. Every now and then they halted and panned the river and they always found small traces of gold, but never enough to justify stopping. Carmack finally came to a fork in the river. Unknown to Carmack, this was actually the richest place in the world. There was gold in the stream and in the hills all around them. But he was totally unaware of this so they continued on until they saw Henderson's camp. What followed next is still disputed.

Carmack claimed he encouraged Henderson to come over to Rabbit Creek and stake a claim, while Henderson swore that he urged Carmack to prospect the creek and to let him know if he found anything. What was clear was that Carmack did promise to let Henderson know if he found anything and that Henderson promised to compensate him for his trouble. However, Henderson refused to sell the Indians any of his tobacco, claiming he was short of supplies. As Henderson adhered rigidly to the prospectors' code this would not have allowed him to refuse a fellow miner anything. It's therefore possible that his refusal was purely because of his attitude towards the Indians. It may have been this that sealed his fate.

Carmack and the Indians left Henderson and struggled back across the mountain. Their journey was long and tiring; their way was constantly blocked by fallen trees and they had to fight their way through particularly vicious thorn bushes and very thick undergrowth. Finally, they reached the other side but their problems weren't over. They soon found they had stumbled into swampland and were attacked by swarms of mosquitoes. Despite this Carmack pushed on and eventually they arrived at the fork of Rabbit Creek. This time they didn't stop but carried on for another half a mile before making camp. The date was 16 August 1896 and it was here they found the gold. However, there is also some confusion as to which member of the small party actually found it.

Carmack claimed he found a thumb-sized piece of gold protruding from the rim of bedrock. However, both Shookum Jim and Tagish Charley claim that Carmack was asleep and Jim was cleaning out a pan in the stream when he found it. To find a stream with 10 cents worth of gold in a single pan was considered very good, so to find ¼ ounce (about $4) in one pan was unbelievable and they knew they had finally struck it rich. That night they sat round their fire and celebrated, the Indians chanting and singing, while Carmack forgot about becoming an Indian and, instead, began dreaming of a large mansion, a trip round the world and gilt-edged securities.

The following day the three men staked their claim on Rabbit Creek. Under Canadian mining law the discoverer is allowed two stakes while everyone else is only allowed one. Carmack marked a spruce tree and claimed the 500ft running upstream from the notice; the claim also straddled the creek. He then measured off three more claims, one for himself, 'one above' for Shookum Jim and one below for Tagish Charley which was known as 'two below'. Carmack never again thought of himself as an Indian and in fact Jim later accused Carmack of taking his claim for himself after persuading Jim that an Indian would never be recognised as a discoverer.

The three men appeared to have forgotten all about Henderson and they began to travel down to Fortymile to record their claims. As they travelled they told everyone they met about the gold find. Within days the news was spreading like wildfire and Fortymile was soon deserted as the miners headed towards the swampy, weed-filled Rabbit Creek.

Three weeks later a group of men appeared on Henderson's side of the mountain. It was they who broke the news of the Carmack's find at Bonanza Creek, as it was now known. Henderson realised he would need to record his discovery claim to Gold Bottom before he was overrun by miners heading to and from Bonanza Creek. On his way back he met two other prospectors, Charles Johnson and Andrew Hunker. Hunker revealed that he had already staked a discovery claim on the other fork of Gold Bottom Creek and was panning $2.50 a time. This was obviously a much richer claim than Henderson's which was only yielding 35 cents a pan. Henderson had to make a choice. He could either claim the discovery claim to his part of Gold Bottom Creek which would give him 1,000ft of poor ground or he could forgo the discovery claim and stake 500ft next to Hunker's claim which was much richer. This creek would subsequently become known as Hunker Creek.

Still trying to decide which claim was likely to be most profitable, Henderson carried on down through the Klondike Valley where he met a Finn called Solomon Marpak. Marpak had just made a discovery on Bear Creek and Henderson decided to stake a claim next to him. He now had three claims to record, but when he reached Fortymile he found that the law had changed. He was told he could only make one claim and that had to be recorded within sixty days of the time it was staked. His protests were to no avail and Henderson ended up with just one claim, that on Hunker Creek.

Henderson was very ill throughout the winter of 1896 and unable to work his claim, but the following year he was back. However, instead of working the Hunker claim he continued to look for more gold. But his luck appeared to have run out and he was unsuccessful. Eventually, he decided to give up and return home to his wife and children who were living in Colorado. Saying goodbye to the Yukon and any further chance of making his fortune, Henderson boarded a steam boat and headed for home. But his bad luck continued and the boat became frozen at Circle City and he was trapped in the icy wastes for another winter. While trapped here Henderson became seriously ill and had no option but to sell his Hunker claim to pay his medical bills. He only received $3,000 for it. The royalty from that claim later paid $450,000 and was eventually sold on for another $200,000, of which Henderson received nothing. But his problems were not yet over. After finally reaching St Michael he boarded a steamer for Seattle with only $1,100 left. But Henderson had spent so many years in the wilds that he was completely unused to civilisation and by the time he arrived in Seattle all his money had been stolen.

Carmack left his Indian wife in 1900. She'd had considerable difficulty adjusting to the civilised world and had spent various periods in jail after drunken sprees with her Indian relatives. She was staying with Carmack's sister when he sent instructions for her to go home. She returned to Caribou Crossing on Lake Tagish and lived on a government pension. Although she wore clothes made of cheap cotton clothing, similar to those worn by other Indian women, around her neck was the necklace of gold nuggets taken from the original find on Bonanza Creek. She is believed to have died in 1917. Carmack remarried a camp follower and brothel owner, Marguerite Laimee, and they lived happily in Vancouver until Carmack's death in 1922. Carmack had invested his money in real estate and owned a hotel and apartment house in Seattle and operated a mine in California. He died a respectable member of the community leaving all his money to his wife, who died in 1949 in California.

Tagish Charley sold his mining properties in 1901 and lived in Carcoss operating a hotel, entertaining lavishly and drinking heavily, something that was only allowed because he was treated as a white man. He fell off a bridge and drowned after a drinking spree one summer.

Shookum Jim was also treated as a white man. Although his mining interests paid him $90,000 a year, he continued to live as a prospector, travelling ceaselessly across the north, sometimes going without food for days at a time as he sought more gold. He never really enjoyed his wealth and died in 1916.

Henderson outlived them all. He was belatedly recognised as co-discoverer of the gold fields by the Canadian government and awarded a pension of £200 a year. But he too spent the rest of his life looking for the one big strike that would make him rich. He continued his search on Vancouver Island, on the River Pelly and in Northern British Columbia. He never succeeded and died of cancer in 1932.

The row over who discovered the gold rumbled on and continues to be disputed, mainly on national lines with both the Canadians and English supporting Henderson while the Americans support Carmack.

Meanwhile, news of the gold finds took some time to reach the outside world. But once it did the stampede began as people from all over the world flocked to the Canadian Yukon, hoping to make their fortunes. The gold rush was fuelled by Canadian laws which allowed anyone to stake a claim in Canada and, after paying a small royalty, to take the gold out of the country.

At the time of the gold find the border area between the USA and Canada was already contested and it was probably only the presence of the Canadian constabulary that ensured a portion of the Yukon was saved for Canada. Charles Constantine,[1] an inspector in the North-West Mounted Police, originally came from Bradford, West Yorkshire. He was sent to the Yukon in 1894 because of government concerns about the influx of American miners and the rapidly expanding liquor trade. He returned the following year with twenty men and he was at Fortymile when news of Carmack's gold strike reached him. He immediately alerted the Canadian government in Ottowa which sent Inspector Scarth and a further nineteen constables to Fort Constantine on the River Yukon. They arrived on 12 June 1897. In October 1897 the new Commissioner of the Yukon, Major J. Walsh, and another detachment of constables arrived to be followed by further reinforcements during the winter of 1897–1898. By the spring of 1898 police armed with Winchester rifles and Maxim machine guns controlled both the Chilkoot Summit and the White Pass. Here they collected customs duties on all goods shipped across the border.

The situation along the disputed border was tense. The American authorities believed that under the treaty with Russia their Alaskan territory extended back to Lake Bennett and for a further 4 miles beyond it. Americans building their boats on the shores of Lake Lindemann considered that they were on American soil so were furious that they had to pay Canadian duty on any construction materials. The US Commissioner of Skaguay, Judge John Smith, began to organise a company of volunteers to cross the mountains and claim Lake Bennett by force. Washington sent four companies of infantry to Dyea and Skaguay under Colonel Thomas M. Anderson with instructions to control the unruly population and to show that the USA was prepared to back up their claims.

In 1898 Inspector Sam Steele had replaced Constantine. Colonel Anderson wrote to him demanding to know why the Canadians were exercising military and civil authority over American territory. Steele passed the note to Walsh who happened to be an ex-Mountie. Determined not to give an inch, he replied that Canadian territory actually extended all the way to Skaguay. However, the Mounties had decided not to exercise their control over it. Anderson reported back to his superiors that the Canadians were not going to give in and a lengthy period of arbitration began. The border today runs along the summit of the passes where the Mounties had their gun emplacements.

There were considerable differences in the way the two military forces controlled their territories. On the American side of the border there was little law or order. The Commissioner pocketed public funds, men were cheated, robbed and shot and the deputy marshal was little more than a gangster. Lynching, whippings and hangings were commonplace with little interference from the American authorities.

On the Canadian side of the border the opposite was true. The soldiers were also policemen and their job was to maintain order, which they did. In Canadian controlled areas packs of gold nuggets could be left on the trail for weeks at a time and not stolen, while boats could travel for hundreds of miles in virtually unknown territory in the security of the knowledge that the Mounties would protect them.

There were no guns in the town of Dawson and very little violence. Although the authorities here were Canadian, the businesses were mostly owned by Americans, so compromises were reached. Illegal activities were tolerated but not on Sundays. There were still plenty of places a man could lose his money, but they were controlled and on the whole, they were never conned or forced into these places in the same way they were in Skaguay.

By 1899 there were so many settlers arriving in the Yukon that the Federal Government negotiated a treaty with the northern 'Aboriginals'. Aboriginals was the term used to describe all indigenous people in Canada, including the Métis and the Inuit. The 1899 treaty was known as Numbered Treaty Eight and was signed so that the Federal Government could obtain Aboriginal lands to the north of Treaty Six (found in present-day northern British Columbia, Alberta, Saskatchewan and south-central Northwest Territories). The Federal Government had already taken land from the Aboriginals in the Prairies during the 1870s to enable European settlement and had deemed this enough. Despite Catholic missionaries in the area pleading with the government to sign treaties with the sick and starving northern Aboriginals throughout the 1880s and 1890s, the government only handed out small amounts of money. First, they had limited resources and did not want to be seen to be diverting large amounts of money to Aboriginals at the expense of Europeans. Secondly, they could not see that the northern lands would appeal to European settlers.

However, the Klondike Gold Rush changed this. Suddenly the land was attracting new settlers and yielding vast mineral resources. The government now decided they wanted to make treaties with the northern Aboriginals. The Han were already suffering from their contact with white men. Prior to the 1800s contact had been extremely limited so they immediately became prone to diseases like smallpox to which they had no natural immunity. These diseases moved through the tribe so quickly that they were soon driven to the brink of extinction.

The treaties were all very similar to each other but Treaty Eight introduced the creation of small family reserves for individual families. This was intended to meet the needs of some of the woodland Cree and Dene Tribes. Despite the fact that many of the tribes were suffering, they did not all want to sign the treaty. Many did not want to live on reserves like their southern counterparts, as they feared it would destroy their way of life. Others were concerned about the permanent nature of the treaties and virtually all were suspicious of the government, whose track record for keeping its word was not very good. Attempts to turn the Prairie Aboriginals into European farmers had not been very successful and many were starving and living in extreme poverty.

There were also serious concerns among the tribes that the government would eventually curtail their fishing and hunting rights as the land available to them shrank with each successive treaty. However, the government denied this and began providing extra money for fishing twine and gun ammunition as a means of allaying fears. Previous treaties had also included provision for the government to take a census of the Aboriginals living on reserves each year so they could pay them a lump cash sum in relation to the numbers. But the government had already lost track of how many Aboriginals there were in the Northern Territories so many tribes were sceptical of their intentions and were extremely nervous about signing any treaty.

American migration to the region finally began to slow down in 1898. There were two reasons for this. First, the news of a workers' strike in Alaska had reached the rest of the USA and this did little for the reputation of the Klondike which looked like a region with considerable problems. Secondly, in 1898 the Spanish-American War began and many of the young men who might have headed into Canada joined the state volunteer regiments instead.

By the time Sydney was on his way to the Yukon all the best land had been staked and those making the money were not the prospectors but the 'hangers on'. But for Sydney this would make little difference. He was about to embark on the biggest adventure of his life, an adventure that would change his life forever.

Chapter Two

From Liverpool to Skaguay

Sydney Herbert Bywater Harris was born in London on 15 June 1881 and baptised on 26 October of the same year. He was the second youngest of seven siblings. He had four older brothers, Frederick, William, Harold and Gordon, and an older sister, Mildred. His younger brother was Percival, to whom he was very close. His father, Frederick W. Harris, was born in 1851 in Bolsover, Derbyshire. In 1881 he was registered on the census as being a cigar importer and living at 215 Oxford Street, Marylebone. In 1891 the family had moved to 6 Trinity Villas, East Hastings in Sussex and Frederick was listed as a tobacco merchant. Sometime during the next ten years they moved back to London; on the 1901 census Frederick and his family were living in Paddington and he was listed as a 'South African Merchant of Dry Goods'.

Sydney's mother, Jeanette Harris (née Bywater), was a music teacher before she married Frederick. There appears to be some confusion about where she was born as the 1881 census says she was born in Abergavenny in Wales but all other census records have her birth place listed as Surrey.

The family were reasonably well off as Sydney attended the Lower School of the Merchant Taylors' School in 1894 and won a prize for

Sydney, aged 4.

mathematics and arithmetic in the Easter term of that year. The Merchant Taylors' School was an independent day school for boys founded in 1561 by Sir Thomas White, Sir Richard Hilles, Emanuel Lucar and Stephen Hales and was one of the nine English public schools investigated by the Clarendon Commission. The Clarendon Commission was set up in 1861 to scrutinise complaints about the buildings, management and finances of Eton College. The report looked into the life of nine schools including Merchant Taylors and led to the Public Schools Act of 1868. However, St Paul's and Merchant Taylors' day schools were subsequently left out of the Act, which only concerned itself with the seven boarding schools (Charterhouse, Eton, Rugby, Harrow, Shrewsbury, Westminster and Winchester).

In the 1890s it was considered just as honourable and respectable to seek one's fortune and to aspire to be rich as it was to be patriotic during wartime. The world had been in the grip of a deep depression since 1893. Known as the Panic of 1893, it had started in the USA after the collapse of the Philadelphia and Reading Railroad. The USA's rapidly expanding economy had been driven by railroad speculation which ensured that railroads were overbuilt and revenues failed to match expenses. Most of those who rushed to the gold fields of the Klondike were young men in their mid-20s who had no experience of climbing mountains, running rapids or crossing glaciers. Yet, like most young men, they considered themselves invincible and were carried forward on a tide of optimism, convinced of their ultimate success.

Thus it was that on 8 November 1898 Sydney said goodbye to his parents and took the train to Liverpool where he had previously booked a passage for 9 November on the SS *Lake Ontario* to Montreal. The SS *Lake Ontario* was a 4,502 gross ton ship with a length of 374½ft and beam of 43½ft. It had clipper bows, two funnels, three masts and a cruising speed of 12 knots. There was accommodation for 200 first-class passengers, 85 second-class passengers and 1,000 steerage passengers, one of whom was Sydney. It had been launched by the Beaver Line on 10 March 1887 and its maiden voyage to Quebec and Montreal took place on 10 June 1887.[1]

Sydney was due to arrive in Montreal on 20 November, but first he had the voyage to Canada to undertake.

Steerage was the cheapest form of accommodation and conditions varied according to the ship. Until the early 1860s the journey to the USA or

Canada was by sailing ship and took about thirty-five days. Emigrants were housed in a vast open space, rather like a dormitory, with bunks down the sides and tables in the middle. It was invariably overcrowded with very poor ventilation and seasickness was a common problem on the stormy North Atlantic route westwards. Diseases such as typhoid and cholera were rife and frequently became epidemics as they spread unchecked in such conditions. The situation only began to change after the 1855 Passenger Act laid down minimum standards for space, rations and sanitation.

Things had improved considerably by 1870 when virtually all journeys were by steamship. This cut the crossing time down to between a week and ten days. There was also plenty of competition between the steamship companies and this added to the improvements in steerage conditions. By 1900 steerage had become less common and third-class cabins gradually began to appear on some of the ships.

On arrival at Liverpool Sydney made his way to the steerage offices, which were in a basement of a large stone building near the docks. Once through the door, he went down the stone steps and into a dark tunnel. He carried on through the tunnel until he came to a dimly lit room. Here he found several other passengers waiting, most of whom were seated on stone benches round the edges of the room. Finally, the agent arrived and Sydney joined in the throng of people as they rushed forward, eager to make their final payment. Sydney handed over his ticket and inspection card which were stamped with his passenger number, 8129, and then handed back.

Sydney made his way back up the stairs and stood waiting for all the other passengers to finish. Eventually an officer of the shipping line appeared and led them all to the landing stage where the tender was moored. The passengers were left here while the numbers around them grew. Sydney was fascinated by the variety of different accents that surrounded him, but he was impatient to be off and the delay seemed interminable. Finally, all the passengers were closely packed aboard and it was time for the tender to puff its way slowly out to the steamship which was lying at anchor some way away. Sydney looked round at his companions, all were sitting stiff-lipped and bundled up against the cold wind that swirled round them. No one spoke yet he was sure he could feel a palpable air of excitement just below the surface. As he looked round his gaze alighted on a girl of similar age and he smiled.

She blushed and looked away but not before he had seen a brief smile on her lips. Sydney smiled to himself and hugged his coat round him to try and keep out the biting wind which was growing in intensity as they headed out towards the harbour mouth.

Half an hour later they reached the ship and Sydney had his first sight of what was to be his home for the next ten days. But he had little time to take it in before the gangplank was lowered and they began filing slowly onto the ship. As each passenger climbed aboard they were asked by a member of the crew whether they were second class or steerage.

While second-class passengers were politely shown in one direction, steerage passengers were offered no such courtesy. Stewards shouted at them rudely to move quickly as they were directed below and Sydney found himself swept along with the other passengers as they were separated into the various compartments that made up steerage accommodation.

On most ships the steerage accommodation was divided into three separate compartments. The front compartment would be for single men, the middle for married couples and families and the third compartment for single women. To Sydney's disappointment the latter was as far apart from the single men as possible. Meals were bought up from the galley and served on the long tables down the centre of each compartment. Each compartment was approached by a different entrance and each had separate toilets with an adequate water supply circulated by a pulsometer pump.

In the earlier ships there were row upon row of iron bunks with only a thin iron rod separating one sleeper from another. On each berth there was a thin straw mattress, a horse blanket, tin plate, pannikin, knife, fork and spoon. In later ships the steerage berths were made of canvas and could be stowed away when not in use, leaving space for tables and chairs during the day. Some later ships also had a hospital for every section and a separate one for infectious cases.

Feeling restless Sydney returned to the deck and watched as his trunk was loaded aboard and then, feeling more at ease, he wandered round the deck to see what was there. The main deck, fore and aft, provided a recreational area for steerage passengers while the other passengers had a special separate deck amid ships so that the classes were not mixed.

The telegram Sydney received from his family on the way to Canada.

Much of the deck was under cover and there was a rope to prevent them straying too near the saloon passengers. All access to the upper decks was guarded and he was disappointed there was no way of seeing what else was on the ship.

As he stood mulling this over a steward arrived and informed him he needed to see the doctor. Sydney was about to object when he realised this was compulsory for everyone, so reluctantly he followed the steward to the doctor's room and joined the long queue.

However, the long wait gave him time to make some new acquaintances as they were now united in a common cause, complaining about having to wait to see a doctor when they were not even ill. Sydney listened as others told him their plans for the future and he told them how he was on his way to the gold rush where he was absolutely convinced he was going to make his fortune. With the certainty and arrogance of youth he ignored the sceptical glances of some of his fellow passengers who shook their heads and muttered about it being a fool's errand. Instead, he concentrated his energy on impressing the young women in the queue who were hanging on his every word.

After what seemed an endless wait, he eventually reached the front of the queue and the doctor stared at him hard for several moments before nodding. He stamped Sydney's tickets, halved and then quartered them and then it was all over. Sydney was astonished that it had been so easy but he was also relieved that the doctor had passed him, even if he had no idea what the doctor had been looking for. It would never have done to be turned down after coming this far.

He was about to go back up on deck when a steward came along shouting out a name. Not expecting it to be him, Sydney paid no attention until suddenly he realised it was his name being called out. Stunned and not a little concerned, it took Sydney some time to react. Then he rushed after the steward who was almost out of sight. The steward handed him a telegram which he opened nervously. He needn't have worried. It was from his family wishing him well and he read it several times before putting it away carefully in his pocket.

For a few seconds a wave of homesickness overcame him and then it was gone as his natural optimism reasserted itself. He would soon be home and when he did come home he would be rich beyond his wildest imaginings.

He was still thinking about this when he felt the ship begin to move slowly. He rushed to look over the side and watched as two tug boats guided her gently towards the landing stage, the gangway was lowered and the saloon passengers began climbing aboard. Sydney was fascinated as the well-dressed men and women streamed aboard and then the warning bell sounded, the gangway was drawn up and the ship began to move sideways away from the pier. As they pulled away a great cheer went round, a cheer of hope tinged with the sadness of those who knew they were never likely to see their family or friends again.

Sydney joined in, waving madly at the people waiting on the quayside. He didn't know any of them but that didn't matter. His earlier homesickness was completely forgotten and all he could think of was the excitement ahead.

While his fellow passengers gradually dispersed he remained on deck in the biting cold as the lights of Liverpool faded and they pulled out into the Irish Channel. The wind was stronger now and the ship began to pitch and roll as the swell of the open sea caught her. Sydney breathed in the fresh, bracing air and smiled. Not long and he would be in Canada. He wondered what Canada was really like. He couldn't wait to arrive and find out. He patted the pocket that contained his wallet and made a mental note not to let it out of his sight. The money it contained was all that stood between him and starvation. It had to pay for him to travel right across Canada from Montreal to Vancouver, unless he could find work of course. It also had to pay for any supplies he might need. Just thinking about it sent a tingle down his spine and he shivered with anticipation.

The darkness was complete and there was nothing to see on deck so reluctantly he headed downstairs to his bunk. But seasickness had already taken hold with some of the passengers and the stench quickly sent him back up on deck. Even the biting cold was better than the smell of sick and people retching. Once there he found a quiet place to sit down, huddled into his coat and there he remained as the ship headed towards its next stop, Queenstown, now known as Cobh, in County Cork.

Of the 6 million adults and children who emigrated from Ireland between 1848 and 1950, over 2½ million had left from Cobh. It was here the SS *Lake Ontario* collected the mail and took on some Irish emigrants. As before, Sydney watched as they came aboard in the darkness, their lilting voices carrying on the wind to where he was sitting.

He listened for a while and then, as they dispersed to their accommodation, silence fell again and all he could hear was the sound of the waves as they crashed against the ship. Finally, they were out into the Atlantic and the sea grew rougher as the ship began riding the giant waves. Sydney closed his eyes and leant back, just out of reach of the cold sea spray that was crashing on the deck in front of him. He smiled as he thought about the gold he knew he was going to find. The rolling of the ship had no effect on him, if anything he found it exhilarating. As the night wore on he gradually dozed off, waking only as dawn broke on the horizon behind him, lighting the sea in a golden hue that he felt augured well for the future.

The rest of the Atlantic crossing was uneventful, although there were several squalls and storms. These threw the ship around, leaving it teetering precariously on the crests of enormous waves and floundering in the inky depths. But each time they resurfaced and the ship sailed on, ever closer to its destination.

Sydney arrived in Montreal on 20 November 1898 and then made his way across Canada to Vancouver. Anecdotal evidence suggests he went via Winnipeg. This would have been the natural route across Canada and would have also taken him through Edmonton, Alberta which earlier had advertised itself as the back door to the Yukon. However, by the time Sydney was making his pilgrimage, the best route was still via Vancouver to Skaguay, across the White Pass to Lake Bennett and down the river to Dawson.

In March 1899 Sydney left Vancouver by steamer and made his way to Skaguay. From Skaguay he joined thousands of others as they made their way to the Yukon via White Pass. The White Pass crossing had considerably improved by now, thanks to the construction of a wagon road along the mountain sides which was completed by the winter of 1898. But back in 1897 traversing the White Pass was so difficult and dangerous that it became known as Dead Horse Trail. The Skaguay of 1899 was also a very different place from the earlier town of 1897.

Built at the foot of the pass where the Skaguay River entered the flat wooded area of Skaguay Bay, the name was derived from the Indian word 'Skagus' that means 'the home of the north wind'. In 1888 Captain William Moore built a cabin at the foot of the pass. He was convinced that there was gold in the Yukon and that when it was found this would be the main entry point to the gold fields. His predictions also included that roads and a city would be built there and that steamers would sail the upper Yukon loaded with passengers and freight.

The bay was the northern tip of the Lynn Canal, a straight 90-mile stretch of crystal clear water surrounded by snow-covered mountains that were reflected in the translucent stillness of its waters. Initially, Moore was alone other than John J. Healy's trading post on the Dryea Inlet, 3 miles to the west. But once the first gold-rush steamer arrived in the bay on 26 July 1897 Moore's peace was shattered. The steamer had bought the first of thousands of dogs, horses and prospectors and gradually the semblance of a town grew. By August it was big enough to elect a local government and a committee began to plan the town properly. As a result, 60ft streets emerged offering neatly parcelled lots for sale, each 50ft by 100ft. Those who wished to buy land were charged a $5 registry fee and rule was by committee. Although Moore protested that the land was his, he was completely ignored and totally overrun. Miners who had already built properties in the way of the neatly drawn up streets found they were demolished without any form of redress. This also included the cabin Moore had originally constructed. But Moore refused to give in without a fight and he applied to the courts for compensation. Although the courts took a long four years to find in his favour, he then received 25 per cent of the assessed value of all the lots built on the original town site. He had also had the foresight to build a mile-long wharf over the tidal flats so boats could moor properly and this made him a fortune.

The anarchy and lawlessness evident when Skaguay was first established continued. Rule of law was by committee. Hangings and lynch mobs became the normal way of dealing with theft, murders and any other crimes. And all the while thousands of prospectors continued to arrive. By the autumn there were so many ships, steamers and other craft that they began anchoring a mile off shore. Scows were used to transfer goods from ship to shore, horses and men were often dumped in the shallow sea, the horses in special boxes that opened at the bottom plunging them into the icy waters. The main street in Skaguay became a river of mud along which men, horses and dogs ploughed continually in an attempt to cross the White Pass before the winter set in.

White Pass consisted of a 46-mile trail that began gently enough, but then plunged through bogs and mires and over ground strewn with massive boulders and shale. It skirted steep cliffs with sheer drops and crossed and re-crossed rivers. It made its way through canyons and across mountain summits, through valleys and across slopes until it finally reached the beaches of Lake Bennett where the River Yukon began.

White Pass began along a relatively wide wagon trail which first wound its way across flat land surrounded by acres of trees and then through mosquito-infested swamplands. After that it gradually began to climb up a series of steep hills, each of which was separated by wet, muddy riverbeds and very narrow pathways that zigzagged along them.

The first major hill was called Devil's Hill. At this point, as it wound its way like a corkscrew round the slippery, slate-covered cliffs, the path was barely 2ft wide in places. There was a sheer 500ft drop to the side and for those who missed their step, a fall to certain death, a frequent occurrence for many a packhorse.

The next major obstacle was Porcupine Hill, so-called because the trail was littered with massive, closely packed 10ft boulders through which the heavily laden horses and their packs had to squeeze. A further 1,000ft climb took the prospector up Summit Hill, where the trail was little more than liquid mud. This part of the trail was also littered with sharp rocks which tore the feet and flanks of the horses and large impenetrable slabs of granite which blocked their way. But there was an even worse horror for the men and their horses to face.

Yawning mud holes were everywhere, sometimes up to 10ft deep, into which horses, packs and men disappeared forever. Major J.M. Walsh, on his way out to the Klondike to take over as the new Commissioner of the Yukon, also crossed through the White Pass during the autumn of 1897 and he was horrified by the thousands of dead horses he saw. Some had fallen off the cliffs and were lying in groups at the bottom, still with their packs on. Others filled the mud holes and provided the only footholds for successive travellers to walk on. It was only as he crossed one mud hole that one of the horses moved and he realised it was still alive.

In places the trail was not wide enough to let two horses pass each other so movement often stopped completely. While they were halted the prospectors lit fires and huddled round them to keep warm. The horses, however, would be left standing for hours with their heavy packs on their backs as no one would risk unloading them in case they had to move again. In this way a horse could remain loaded with a heavy pack for 24 hours. Virtually none of the 3,000 horses used to cross the pass in 1897 survived. Many were already old when they were bought in Seattle or Victoria for ridiculously inflated prices. Some were not even broken in while others had never had a pack on their backs. Many of those who bought them had never handled horses before and it would often take two partners a full day to load a single horse. Horses that cost $200 in Skaguay were invariably worthless by the time they reached the summit. Of the 5,000 men and women who attempted to cross the pass in the autumn of 1897 only a handful reached the Yukon before the winter freeze-up.

Samuel H. Graves, who was to play a leading role in building the railway over the pass, recalled passing a horse that had broken its leg while trying to squeeze through two large boulders. Its pack had been removed and the horse knocked on the head with an axe. Then people and other pack animals continued to walk over it. By the end of the day the carcass of the horse had been completely trampled into the ground leaving only its head and tail on either side of the trail.

In the winter of 1897 the Canadians introduced new regulations for those wishing to cross into Canadian Yukon Territory. No one could enter without a year's supply of food, the equivalent of 1,150lb. In addition to this they had to carry a tent, cooking utensils and tools which amounted to about a ton of goods in all. Food included lime juice to prevent scurvy, lard, black tea, chocolate, salt, sauerkraut, string beans, cornflour, baking powder, mincemeat and dried potatoes. In addition, they took candles, rubber boots, lamp chimneys, saws, files, overshoes, mukluks, everything to keep them going for a year. All this had to be loaded on pack animals, dragged by sleds or carried by the men themselves. A man on his own would carry about 65lb for 5 miles, leave it secured and then go back for the next load. It could take him thirty round trips to move his entire outfit to Lake Bennett and he would cover about 2,500 miles.

About a quarter of a mile from the Canadian border the miners stopped and removed the packs from the horses' backs and covered the running sores with blankets in an attempt to fool the Canadian Mounties, who would shoot any injured animals on sight.

The summit marked the border between Canada and Alaska after which the trail continued through a network of tiny lakes and then to another 1,000ft climb up Turtle Mountain. Once at the summit the trail descended into Tutshi Valley and then through yet another mountain pass before finally reaching Lake Bennett.

However, by the time Sydney reached Skaguay in 1899 things had changed considerably. It had slowly become a law-abiding town of around 1,600 people, with electric lights and a water supply, and it is unlikely Sydney would have seen much of its lawless past. The White Pass was also much improved and 35,000 men were now working on the emerging railway between Skaguay and Whitehorse Rapids. It was even possible to cycle from Dawson to Skaguay in around eight days.

Sydney put the tow ropes of his sled over his shoulder and began the slow passage across the pass. The sun was warm on his back and he could hear the continuous trickle of water as the surrounding snow and ice began its slow thaw. The journey across the pass was not without its dangers at this time of year, the worst being that of avalanches as large areas of thick frozen snow began to melt, leaving dangerous overhangs just waiting for something to tip them into movement.

It wasn't long before Sydney left the flat swampland and began the sharp climb up the first of the hills. As he climbed higher the temperature dropped and the way became more difficult. It was soon very steep and he had difficulty picking his way through the boulders, rocks and other obstacles on the heavily worn track. Despite the sun and the exertion of the climb, as he left the tree line the wind was icy, cutting through his clothes and freezing the sweat on his skin until he shivered with cold. The sun was now shrouded in an incessant grey soulless drizzle and Sydney peered anxiously into the thick fog trying to identify the stakes that had been driven into the edges of the trail. As he neared each one he breathed an inward sigh of relief that was quickly gone as he searched for the next. The snow was much thicker here and the wind whirled round him freezing his breath into droplets that fell onto his coat and froze instantly.

It was growing dark and he knew he would have to stop soon. He glanced around and saw an area that had obviously been used by previous travellers. Relieved he stopped and pitched his tent, lit a fire and began to heat some coffee and beans. As the fire warmed the snow around him he frowned. He could see something appearing in the gloom, glistening white in the light from the fire. He carefully made his way to the other side of the small fire and leaned forward to get a closer look. As he finally realised what it was he stepped back and gasped in horror. In front of him the snow continued to melt and as it did so the skeleton of a dead horse began emerging from its icy grave. Sydney shivered, wondering briefly if it was some kind of warning, then, smiling at his own fertile imagination, he turned and made his way back to the fire. He was still smiling to himself while he poured some more coffee. Obviously it was one of the horses that had given the pass its name, but it was nothing for him to worry about. He hadn't come all this way to die before he even reached the Yukon. This brief uncharacteristic attack of nerves was probably just a combination of being tired and the almost unnatural silence that surrounded him. He poured the dregs of his coffee away and decided it was time for bed. He left the fire, crawled into his tent, snuggled down into his sleeping bag and closed his eyes. In the distance a lone wolf howled its haunting cry and horses and dogs of other prospectors shifted restlessly, but Sydney slept on, dreaming of the gold that was just over the other side of the pass.

Chapter Three

The Gold Fields

The following day Sydney continued his journey, each step taking him closer to his goal. With luck he should reach the Canadian border in a couple of days. He passed several miners coming back the other way and they either showed him their haul, which gave him hope, or discouraged him by telling him he was wasting his time and they were going to try elsewhere. At first he refused to believe that the gold fields were all staked out. How could they be sure? Just because one area was mined out it didn't mean that other places weren't just waiting to be discovered. His natural optimism refused to be dismayed by their reports and he would soon convince himself that they had just given up too easily. After all, the Yukon covered thousands of square miles.

But as successive days wore on his doubts began to increase and he seriously contemplated turning back, Then, suddenly, out of the gloom, he spied the Union Flag. Rejuvenated that he was now within reach of the Canadian border and his fortune, he put his head down and quickened his pace.

The flag appeared to be on the same level as the snow from a distance, but as he drew closer he turned into a passage that had been cut through the mountains out of snow. Here he could see a Mountie standing in front of a large tent. Only the entrance could be seen, the rest hidden by snow. This was the customs post and general quarters. There were 24-hour police patrols as the Mounties were paid $2 a day to stand in the blizzards and bitter cold guarding the entrance to the Yukon.

When the Canadians had first set up the post it had been the depths of winter. It wasn't until they had pitched camp, erected their tents and started their heaters that they realised they were actually on top of a lake. Given the proximity to the American border it had been quite difficult to identify firm land on which to relocate to and it had taken them some time. But eventually they found some and were finally able to erect the camp safely. The Union Flag acted like a beacon to all nationalities as it was a welcome sight that they had at last reached the border. Not only was this a landmark on the difficult crossing, it was also a sign they had crossed from the lawless American side into the law-abiding Canadian area.

Sydney passed through the customs post, paid his dues and had his goods receipt stamped with the White Pass custom stamp. It was dark by the time he'd finished so he pitched his tent and made himself something to eat.

The next morning he continued on towards Lake Bennett. On arrival at Lake Bennett Sydney spent the night at the Yukon Hotel. This was a large tented structure with roaring heaters throwing out a very welcome heat after the freezing cold journey. Sydney joined several other prospectors and gratefully downed a couple of whiskies, relieved he had survived this far. The following day he made his way to Dawson, a journey that was also nothing like as difficult as it had been only a year earlier.

In the spring of 1898 all those who had survived the winter descended on the Yukon River. With various craft, ranging from rafts to boats, they began the next stage of their journey towards the gold fields. But first they had to run the gauntlet of Miles Canyon and the two sets of rapids that followed it.

Their first sight of Miles Canyon came as they arrived at a turn in the river and saw a piece of red calico. This was followed by a board on which was scrawled one word 'CANYON'. In the distance they could hear the roar of the rapids, but this meant little to most of the prospectors who had no experience of fast-moving water.

In front of them lay a deep gorge lined on either side by 100ft sheer black basalt cliffs. These acted like a funnel on the river, reducing it to a third of its size and creating wave crests 4ft high. As the boats tried to steer round the various obstacles that blocked their way they found themselves hoisted onto small geysers that seemingly erupted out of nowhere. The water rushed on leaving them teetering precariously while their helmsmen frantically fought to avoid the jagged reefs, drifting timber, boulders, sand bars, twisted tree roots and sharp rocks that could tear the bottom out of their unstable craft.

Eventually, the river broadened out but their ordeal was nowhere near over. Now they were approaching a rapid, churning whirlpool in the centre. Having successfully navigated this, most thought they had overcome the worst but they hadn't. The river again narrowed to a mere 30ft as they were rushed through the other side of the gorge and deposited roughly into the Squaw Rapids, a series of jutting, sharp-edged rocks over which the river raced. Having survived this, they hardly had time to catch their breath before they were hurled over the White Horse Rapids, so-called because the foam crashing across the rocks resembled white horses leaping and dancing in the sunlight.

The first attempts to ride the river caused so many deaths that the Canadian authorities intervened. Sam Steele refused to allow any more craft to cross unless they adhered to strict rules. He placed a Mountie, Corporal Dixon, in charge. Dixon would have to verify that any craft crossing the canyon and rapids had enough freeboard to allow it to ride the waves safely and that the crew were competent to do so. No women or children were allowed on the boats, instead they were made to walk the 5 miles across the grassy banks to the foot of White Horse and any who broke the rules were fined $100.

Realising there was a way to make money, enterprising Norman Macaulay built a tramway with wooden rails around the rapids and used horse-drawn cars to move a boat and outfit round the fast water for the princely sum of $25. Of the 30,000 who travelled that way to Dawson after this only 23 drowned, thanks to the Mounties who ushered them from checkpoint to checkpoint, often against the will of American citizens who found it very irritating not to be allowed to drown themselves if they so wished.

Once the prospectors had navigated the rapids they proceeded down to the next section called The Lewes and having reached the end of this they reported in to the Lake Laberge police post. The next stage entailed avoiding icebergs and blocks of floating ice, down 30 miles of windswept river to the next lake. This led onto Thirtymile, a swift-flowing, clear blue stream which, after the previous hazards, appeared safe, but the banks of which were littered with the crafts of those who had not given it sufficient respect.

The next obstacle was Five Finger Rapids where the river split into five channels, rather like an outstretched hand, around four piles of rocks. Here the Mounties were stationed to warn them all to the take the right-hand channel. This took them through a whirlpool that threatened to smash them on the rocks, but at the last minute swept them clear. As they raced through the rapids and the treacherous whirlpool most were too occupied to notice the small cabin on the left bank, the door of which bore the inscription 'G.W. Carmack'.

From here they carried on past Fort Selkirk where during the summer temperatures reached the mid-90s and the forests were full of thick clouds of mosquitoes, gnats and blackflies. This was often the last straw for the miners who had endured so much and the place names reflected the rows and arguments that took place as tempers frayed and best friends became implacable enemies. The prospectors continued on past Split Up Island and on to Split Up Town at the mouth of the Stewart River where the Yukon became a confusing tangle of channels and islands. For the prospectors their goal was almost in sight, only a few more hours and they would arrive in the Klondike. Then, as they swept round a rocky bluff, they heard the sound they had been waiting for. On the right of the Yukon River the Klondike River came roaring in. Beyond it they could see a gently tapering mountain and at its foot, sprawling into the nearby hills, lay Dawson with its thousands of cabins, shacks, tents, hotels, some complete, others in the process of construction, saloons, markets, shops and brothels.

Prior to July 1898 Dawson was little more than an overgrown frontier town characterised by a community of numerous shacks and tents. It sprawled across several square miles, crossed two rivers and reached up the edges of the surrounding hills. It was a long way from civilisation and was the only occupied settlement of any size in hundreds of thousands of square miles. Despite this it had a telephone service, running water and steam heat. There were dozens of completed hotels and even motion picture theatres. In the restaurants string orchestras played, men wore tail coats, ate pâté de foi gras and drank vintage wines. The shops had fashions from Paris, there were churches, hospitals, more than seventy doctors, vaudeville and drama societies.

The busiest part of the town was Front Street where gaming houses, dance halls and saloons snuggled together over three or four blocks. The dance halls were all two-storey buildings with similar layouts. The saloon was a small, dark room dominated by a sheet-iron stove. It had a large plate-glass window that faced the street and a long, polished bar with mirrors behind. These reflected the bartenders in their starched white shirts, aprons, white waistcoats and diamond stick pins.

Behind the saloon was a smaller room where the men could play faro, poker, dice and roulette. This was open all day and all night except Sunday. Behind this there was a theatre with a ground floor, balcony and small curtained stage. Above this were a few bedrooms which could be rented from an hour to all night and could be used for any purpose, even sleeping.

The dance halls were also open every day except Sunday. They usually came alive after about 8pm when the evening began with various entertainments, drama, vaudeville acts, etc. and was followed by dancing at midnight. Once the final curtain fell the dance girls mixed with the miners and charged them one dollar to dance a single lap round the room. As soon as the music stopped they rushed them to the bar and encouraged them to buy drinks. The girls were given a circular disk for each dollar the miners spent. This represented their share of the profits so they secreted them in their stockings, ready to claim the next day. There were also occasional prize fights on the dance-hall stages.

Life in Dawson was very confusing. Tents, cabins and buildings were constantly moving and with no street addresses people often lost track of their friends. Often the only way to find people was to post a notice on the A.C. Store on Front Street.

In April 1898 there was a massive fire which completely destroyed the most expensive section of the town. This was not the first fire to engulf Dawson, but it would be the one that changed the face of the town completely. April began with a strike by the newly established fire brigade which was asking for better wages and conditions. Then, on 26 April, with the temperature 45 degrees below, the fire broke out, destroying 117 buildings at a cost of $1 million dollars.

As before, the town immediately began to rebuild. This time sewers were installed and roads were constructed properly using the techniques pioneered by Scottish engineer John Louden McAdam in around 1820. As proper pavements were built and the roads became lined with shops, full of fancy goods displayed behind plate-glass windows, Dawson became known as the San Francisco of the north.

Gone were the log cabins and tents, so long characteristic of the town. In their place houses were built with dressed lumber and plate glass, carpeted parlours and equipped with pianos. Schools quickly followed and steamboats lined the riverbank, up to eleven at a time. Men shaved off their facial hair, polished their boots and began wearing white shirts. The streets no longer ran with mud, and instead horses moved freely along dry roads drawing heavy dray wagons behind them.

But, as Sydney had already experienced, by the spring of 1899 a sense of anti-climax had begun spreading through the prospectors. This was fuelled by rumours of another gold find elsewhere. Of the approximately 100,000 people who set out for Dawson only about 30,000 to 40,000 had actually arrived. Of those who did, around 20,000 looked for gold and of those only about 4,000 found any. Of these a few hundred found enough gold to call themselves rich, but only a handful managed to keep their wealth. The gold 'stampeders', as they were known, found that virtually all the good claims had been staked long before they arrived by the prospectors who were already in the area. On finding themselves penniless in Dawson they began to look for alternative employment, and often this entailed labouring on the claims of others. To start with there was plenty of employment and they were paid well. But as the number of men continued to rise, wages dropped away and by the spring of 1899 labourers' wages had fallen from $15 a day to $100 dollars a month. As the rumours of another gold find elsewhere continued to trickle through and the disillusioned left to go back to civilisation, there was less and less work available and shops, saloons and dance halls began to close down.

Unknown to Sydney, who was still making his way to the gold fields, the word Klondike, once synonymous with adventure, wealth and excitement, was rapidly becoming a word of derision. It was even used as an insult in the USA as people were told 'ah, go to the Klondike!'. By July 1899 previously expensive hand axes and gold pans were being sold at bargain rates and $1,500 worth of Klondike groceries and hardware could be bought for virtually cost price.

Dawson would be a bustling city for just one year because in July 1899 the rumours that gold had been found in None, just across the Bering Strait from Siberia, were finally confirmed and the exodus began. In a single week in August over 8,000 people left Dawson to chase their dreams elsewhere.

By August Sydney had been in the Klondike for a few months and his earlier enthusiasm had waned considerably. The first problem had been trying to find a gold-rich area that wasn't already staked out. In desperation he had travelled further north, but had still found nothing. Refusing to be beaten he had been determined to stake a claim somewhere so he and his companion stopped panning the creeks and rivers and went further inland. Here they staked their claim and began panning for gold. After about three weeks they had accumulated a small pile of gold dust. Unfortunately, this was to be as close as Sydney came to finding his fortune as his companion accidently knocked the whole pile back into the river! His money quickly began to run out leaving him reliant on the odd labouring job with other prospectors, but it was obvious he was not going to make his fortune here. He reluctantly returned to Dawson and knew his only option was to move on somewhere else and try something different. Mining for gold was hard work. He didn't mind that, but he expected some reward and having realised that wasn't going to happen he soon decided prospecting was not for him. He could go further north to None and join the stampede for gold there, but he had lost interest. All he really wanted now was to go back to civilisation. Unfortunately, to do this, he needed money and there was virtually no employment to be had in a town that was shrinking visibly every day. The answer to his prayers came in guise of the Arctic Express.

The Arctic Express was originally part of the Bennett Lake and Klondike Navigation Company (BLKN). The BLKN was founded by Otto Partridge who had emigrated to San Francisco from England and fought with America in its war with Mexico. In 1898 he became one of the gold stampeders but never made it as far as the Klondike. Having heard stories of men arriving in San Francisco with suitcases full of gold, he knew his boat-building skills would be in demand in the north. So at the age of 42 he went to Skaguay and then onto Bennett via the Chilkoot Pass.

In Bennett he founded the BLKN and built the first three stern-wheelers in the Yukon. The BLKN then acquired a charter to build a light railroad from the McClintock River to the mouth of the Hootalingua River. The manager of the BLKN was given the job of managing the Arctic Express, a new venture that would be responsible for carrying American and Canadian mail from the upper reaches of the Bennett back to Skaguay. He began by setting up posts every 30 miles or by making arrangements with someone located 30 miles from another post.

Unfortunately, there were problems. Prior to setting up the Arctic Express the BLKN had carried mail bags for the police and government free of charge, but they mistakenly assumed that the Canadian government would see the advantages of having its mail delivered to Dawson and beyond and would therefore be happy to pay. The American government, determined to see that its mail was delivered as promptly and expeditiously as possible, paid accordingly. However, the Canadian government did the exact opposite. As far as they were concerned the Arctic Express should also carry its mail free of charge. After all, they had already granted it the privilege of carrying American mail across Canadian territory.

Because of the arduous conditions that faced the men who delivered the mail the company was offering to pay large sums of money to those prepared to take on the task. Their money was guaranteed so, for many, including Sydney, it was the lifeline they needed to allow them to travel away from the gold fields and back to civilisation.

Large sums of money were also spent building the posts and scows and on buying the necessary provisions. Even more money was spent on purchasing suitable sleds and dogs as well as employing fishermen to catch the fish to feed them and to build the facilities to dry the fish.

But it appeared the BLKN had under-estimated the costs. Suddenly word came down that payment of all wages was to be stopped and everything that could be salvaged was to be saved and transferred to another company called the Relay Company.

It took a long time to find the men who had already gone down the river, although it was easier to stop those still in Dawson. Rows ensued over unpaid wages and legal action was threatened but never happened. Eventually, some of the men were hired out to the new company, more posts were built and the new company was formed. Others took their wages and left completely, having had enough of the frozen north.

Sydney had made friends with some Americans and together they made the decision that they would join the new company just long enough to carry the mail back to Skaguay. It was now late summer and the winter would soon be upon them. Sydney had experienced one winter in Canada and that was further south. He had no intention of spending another winter in the frozen northern wastes. It was time to go somewhere warmer. The wages from carrying the mail should give them enough money to catch a boat back to San Francisco.

Having left Dawson, Sydney picked up his canoe and the supplies left by the Relay Company. Everything he needed was there, a fur cap, sheepskin coat, moccasins, mukluks and provisions to keep him fed until he reached the next station. He packed the sled with the mail and set off with the dogs provided by the company. His orders were not just to carry the mail, but to make charts and map any short cuts that avoided long detours due to the winding river. It was expected to take between twenty-five and thirty days.

The journey would push him to the limits of his endurance. Winter was already setting in and the temperature well below zero as he began the 600-plus miles down to Skaguay. The dogs were well trained and covered the snow-covered trails easily. It was a new experience for him and to start with he enjoyed himself. Despite the icy cold, he loved the wilderness, its serenity and the sound of the sled as it swished its way through the snow. He had always loved dogs so he treated them well, making sure they had adequate food and they didn't pull too hard and fast for too long. He even enjoyed the frozen nights, staring up at the vast, star-filled skies, listening to the eerie howls of the wolves as their cries echoed across the snow-filled world. But after a few days his enjoyment began to pall, the weather had deteriorated and there were frequent blizzards, blinding them and covering the dogs in damp snow which clung to their fur. Sydney wiped his goggles again with his thickly mittened hands and began to wish they were at their destination. The route he had travelled over in the spring was now unrecognisable and following the map became more and more difficult as the snow continued to fall. He greeted each outpost with a sigh of relief, another step closer to safety.

His biggest worry was crossing the frozen lakes and he was genuinely fearful of the ice breaking without warning, plunging him and the dogs into a watery grave. But by the time he reached the largest of them, they were covered in such thick snow that he realised his fears were probably unfounded.

As they reached the end of the trail and Skaguay finally came into view Sydney stopped and turned round. He looked back up the trail from where he'd come and wondered if he'd every return. Somehow he thought it unlikely. Although the cold, vast wilderness had a beauty and majesty that was unique, he'd had enough snow and ice to last him a lifetime. He turned towards Skaguay and yelled at the dogs to mush. The Klondike was behind him, he would keep his snowshoes as a souvenir, but the rest he would sell and use to fund his steamer trip back to San Francisco. He had no idea what he was going to do once he arrived there but he was sure something would turn up.

Although he did not know it yet San Francisco would offer him a new opportunity, one that would allow him to earn some money and provide the adventure and excitement he craved. He was going to fulfil a boyhood dream and join the US Cavalry.

Chapter Four

The Philippines Insurrection

When the Spanish-American War started the US Army consisted of only 28,183 officers and men. Congress immediately raised the regular strength to 56,688 and President McKinley also requested that all states recruited 125,000 volunteers for 1 year's service.

The Spanish–American War began in 1898, initially because the Americans wanted to free the Cubans from Spanish rule. The Spanish Fleet was anchored in Manila Harbour so Commodore George Dewey and the US Asiatic Fleet headed to the Philippines. At 5.45am on 1 May 1898 they opened fire and destroyed all but one of the Spanish ships. The Spanish suffered 371 casualties, while the American casualties were 9 wounded and 1 dead from heatstroke.

However, although the Americans had sunk the Spanish Fleet, the Spanish still occupied the Philippines, as they had for the past 300 years. But, their occupation was not without its problems. At the time of the war the Spanish were embroiled in the problem of trying to defeat a native uprising led by 27-year-old provincial Mayor Emilio Aguinaldo y Famy. Aguinaldo was of mixed Tagalog and Chinese ancestry and a talented guerrilla leader who had already managed to throw the Spanish out of Cavite Province, albeit temporarily. Once he had successfully engineered the execution of his main rival, Andreas Bonifacio, Aguinaldo became the undisputed leader of the Philippine independence movement. But while the infighting had weakened the independence movement, the Spanish began to increase their attacks. They finally retook Cavite but Aguinaldo escaped and established an impregnable stronghold in the mountains north of Manila.

Unable to defeat Aguinaldo, the Spanish decided to try and buy him off. They offered him 800,000 pesos to leave the country which he accepted. However, he had no intention of giving up his fight for independence. He simply relocated to Hong Kong with a couple of trusted aides and used the

The Philippines Insurrection 39

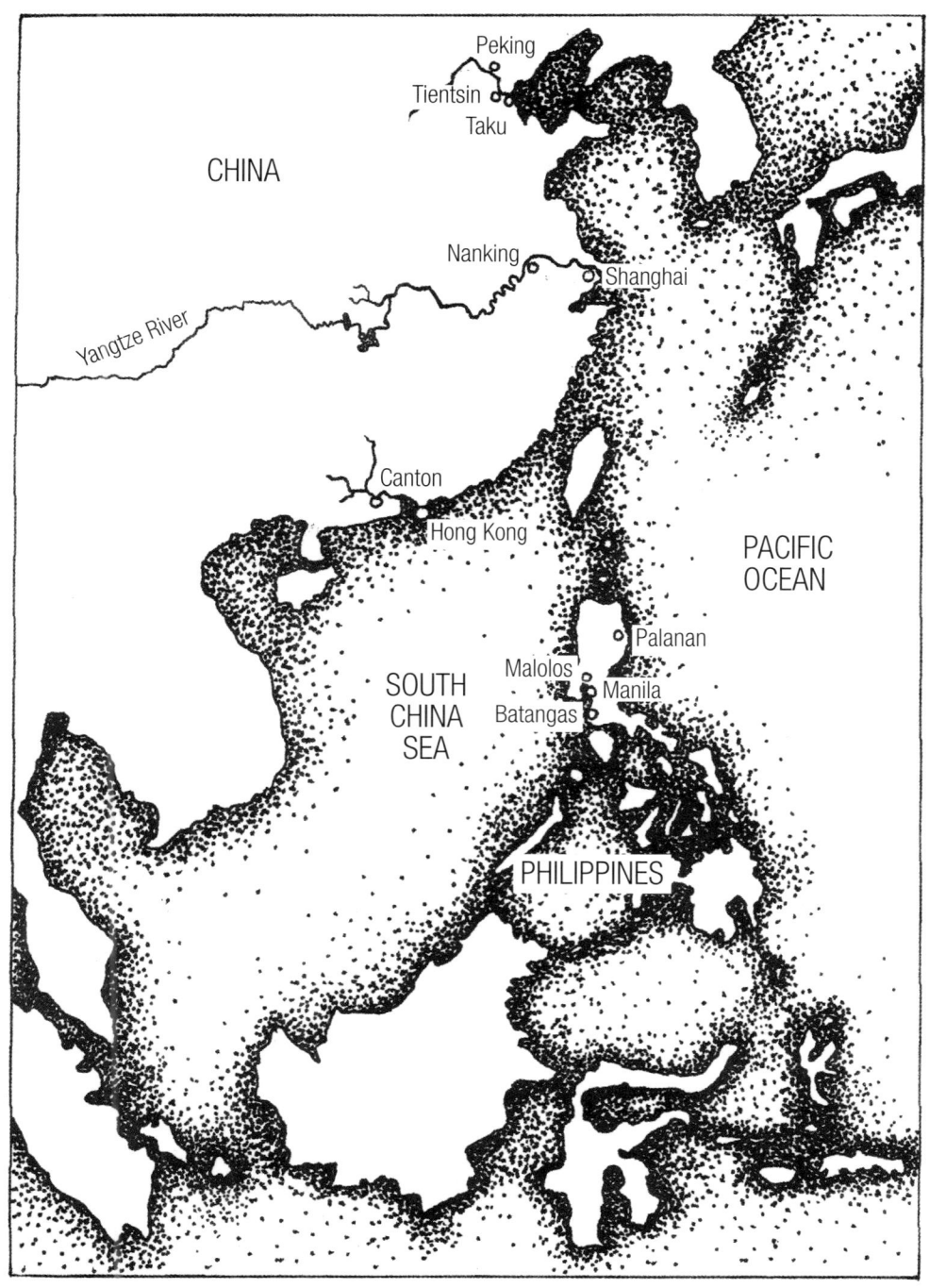

The main locations for Trooper Harris in Asia.

Spanish money to buy more arms. He also approached the American consuls in Hong Kong and Singapore, offering to help them in their war against the Spanish. The American consuls were very enthusiastic about the idea, but clearly stated that they had not promised American support for Philippine independence, something Aguinaldo was convinced they had done.

Once the Spanish Fleet had been sunk Dewey sent a cutter to Hong Kong and invited Aguinaldo to a meeting on his flagship, the *Olympia*, which was anchored in Manila Harbour. After the meeting accounts differed as to what took place with Dewey adamant that all he had asked was for Aguinaldo to engage the Spanish Army until the US Army arrived. Aguinaldo saw things differently and was convinced Dewey had pledged American support for Philippine independence.

The Filipino Army had been very active anyway before this meeting and they continued to be so. It was not long before they had taken the whole of the Philippines except Manila, which held a garrison of 15,000 Spanish soldiers. They immediately issued a Declaration of Independence, based on the American model. Dewey did not attend or give any recognition to the new government, instead he waited for the arrival of the US Army which began at the end of June.

Dewey's first problem was to deploy his troops on the Philippines. The Filipino Army was already well entrenched around Manila and it took some rather delicate negotiations for them to allow the American troops to pass through their lines. The commanders of the Spanish Garrison inside Manila had no will to fight, but they did not want to be seen to surrender without making some token gesture. Finally, Dewey brokered a deal with them. He would lob a few shells on Manila and then the Spanish could surrender, honour intact. Unfortunately, no one bothered to tell the ordinary Spanish soldiers. When the first few shells came over they panicked and immediately began firing back. As a result, forty-nine Spanish troops and six Americans died before the Spanish commanders regained control of their men and Manila was finally surrendered. American troops proceeded to occupy Manila but they now found themselves having to keep the Filipino Army out at gunpoint. To add insult to injury, they then gave the Filipinos no part in the surrender ceremony despite the fact that it was they who had done virtually all the fighting and dying. Understandably, the Filipinos were not pleased.

The USA had found itself unexpectedly in possession of Manila, but President McKinley had no idea what to do with it. Eventually, he decided that the USA should take the whole of the Philippines. His argument, that the USA could 'civilise and Christianise them', ignored the fact that most Filipinos were Catholic, therefore Christians anyway. But it was very much in tune with America's protestant piety and jingoistic attitude which characterised much of its foreign policy during the turn of the century and beyond. There were, of course, also practical reasons to take the whole of the Philippines.

The race for colonies had been ongoing for some time and America feared it would be shut out of the lucrative Asian markets if they did not have some colonies in the area. Britain's naval base in Hong Kong gave them access to China and US strategists argued that Manila would be a perfect base for the USA. But both the Navy and Army Departments argued that it would not be practical to hold Manila if a European or Japanese army took control of the Philippines. It would only be possible if they held the whole of the islands. Their argument was backed up by the knowledge that the Kaiser's German Fleet was already shadowing the US Fleet.

Another factor was Dewey's own intelligence which, scant though it was, suggested Aguinaldo was unpopular with non-Tagalogs. This raised the possibility of conflict between the competing ethnic groups, something that could lead to chaos.

McKinley listened to all the arguments and made his decision. He sent a telegram to the American envoys who were meeting with the Spanish envoys in Paris to draw up a peace treaty. In it he demanded all of the Philippines, Guam and Puerto Rica. The Spanish agreed and the treaty was signed on 10 December 1898. The USA paid the Spanish $20 million and received the titles to the Philippines with its 7,108 islands and 7 million inhabitants. It was described by McKinley as a 'benevolent assimilation'. But the acquisition of the Philippines was not universally supported in the USA.

There was considerable opposition to its annexation. Several prominent Americans joined the Anti-Imperialist League, among them Grover Cleaveland, Samuel Gompers, William James, Jane Addams, Mark Twain and Andrew Carnegie, who offered $20 million dollars to buy the Philippines himself and then set them free. As with all oppositional alliances, they were joined by some rather strange bedfellows including southern Democrats like Senator 'Pitchfork Ben' Tillmann. His reason for joining the alliance was that he was against Americans mixing with what he considered were inferior races and Asiatic hybrids.

Opposing them and in favour of the annexation was another powerful lobby led by Theodore Roosevelt and other imperialists. Their argument was not only based on the USA's commercial and security interests. They also put forward an idealistic argument that God had been preparing them for several hundred years to administer, govern and civilise the savages of the world. They were even supported by Rudyard Kipling, who wrote a poem called *The United States and the Philippine Islands* to help further their argument. The treaty was finally ratified by the Senate but it was a close-run thing with only one vote more than was needed, 57–27.

Meanwhile, back in the Philippines the American troops set to work, cleaning up Manila, improving the sanitation, vaccinating the population and building schools. This was not entirely altruistic as it made life more comfortable for the troops to live in and also kept them occupied while they waited for the American government to tell them what to do next. But despite the improvements in their living conditions tensions continued to rise. Most Filipinos had no desire to be 'benevolently assimilated' and there were several incidents between the soldiers of the rival armies, the Americans inside Manila and the Filipinos outside. But despite the tension between them neither side was in any rush to begin fighting. The President hoped that if he waited long enough the resistance would eventually crumble. The Filipinos hoped that if they waited long enough the Senate would refuse to ratify the Treaty of Paris.

The insurrection finally began on 4 February 1899 with the Battle of Manila. The 11,000 American soldiers in the Philippines were mainly volunteers and their lack of numbers meant they were very thinly deployed. Opposite them were 20,000 Filipinos, well dug in and with much better equipment. However, appearances were deceptive. Many Filipinos had received even less training than their American counterparts. They were also short of shoes, there were not enough rifles to go round and some of those who had rifles had no idea how to use the sights. As the sun rose on the morning of the 4th American warships began firing their heavy guns onto Aguinaldo's men and Major General Elwell S. Otis ordered the American advance.

In the first day 700 Filipinos were killed, while American casualties were 44 killed and 194 wounded. Reinforcements were requested and on 28 February 1899, the 9th US Infantry Regiment was dispatched to the Philippine Islands. Immediately upon arrival in Manila, the regiment moved on to the front line. Its remit was to eliminate insurgents on Luzon Island.

By the end of March the Americans had taken the Filipino capital of Maldos, 20 miles outside the American held capital of Manila, and Aguinaldo and his men had retreated northwards. But, despite the increase in manpower to 30,000 troops, the Americans did not have enough men to garrison the Philippines, so they were unable to consolidate their position. Instead, they advanced, took territory and then retreated back to Manila. The Filipinos moved back in and retook the area. More than half of the American troops were volunteers who were due to finish their service in April 1899 and this, together with advent of the rainy season, meant the American offensive had more or less petered out by the spring. By then the roads were impassable and cholera, dysentery, malaria, heatstroke and venereal diseases had incapacitated virtually 60 per cent of the remaining troops. Although the war in the Philippines had already lasted longer than that against Spain, the USA had only managed to take and retain control of a 40-mile perimeter round the outside of Manila.

But the Filipinos were in just as much disarray as the Americans. Ethnic and class rivalries were causing major divisions. The constitution had been drawn up by the National Assembly on September 1898 in Malolos. But the upper class Filipinos, known as Ilustrados, had controlled the meeting and only given the vote to the landed gentry. Aguinaldo was made President with the powers of a dictator. But General Antonio Luna, the army commander with a reputation for being hot tempered, and Apolinario Mabini, the Prime Minister, wanted to win the support of the peasants by challenging the power of the ruling elite. However, Aguinaldo refused to support them. Instead, he took the side of the wealthy landowners. It was this decision that probably went some way to preventing the mass mobilisation of the ordinary people against the Americans.

By the end of March, having suffered two months of defeat, the majority of the Malolos Congress voted for an end to the armed struggle and in favour of some kind of accommodation with the American occupiers. General

Luna was furious. He was an upper class Ilocano who had gone to Spain to study chemistry and had instead learnt military strategy. The majority of the members of Congress were Tagalogs so Luna had them arrested for treason. But Aguinaldo immediately overruled him and released them.

On 5 June 1899 Luna was murdered. Although those who committed the murder were Aguinaldo's soldiers, it was never proved that he had ordered the assassination. While some prominent members of the Congress did travel to Manila to surrender to the Americans, Aguinaldo took control of the army.

By November the American state volunteers had been replaced by 35,000 men from the Federal Volunteer Regiments, authorised by Congress. With more troops at his disposal, General Otis drew up a three-pronged attack designed to capture Luzon, the main island, and Aguinaldo and his men before they could retreat into the mountains to the north.

Among those volunteers was a young Englishman. Sydney had joined the 6th US Cavalry at the end of 1899 and was among those shipped out to the Philippines.

Chapter Five

The Boxer Rebellion

But it was to be some time before Sydney reached the Philippines. Instead, he found himself unexpectedly en route to China as part of an international force to rescue foreign embassies and their citizens from the uprising known as the Boxer Rebellion.

The Boxers were a secret society whose aim was to expel foreigners from China. Its Chinese name was I Ho Chuan, which was translated into English as 'Fists of Righteous Harmony'. The movement began in the north

The front of an envelope containing a letter to Sydney that followed him from San Francisco to China and the Philippines and back again to the USA.

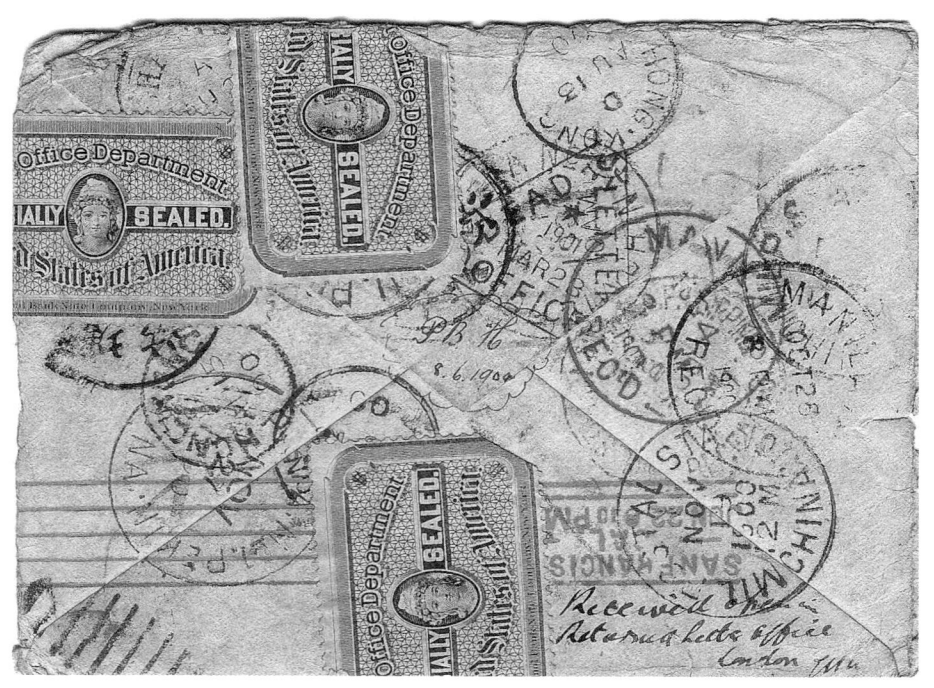

The back of the envelope overleaf.

Chinese provinces of Shantung and Chihli where a severe drought had led to a terrible famine. This, together with mass unemployment, was blamed on the foreigners who had intruded into Chinese life. The rebellion was peasant based and its members were easily recognisable by their red banners and colourful clothing with red sashes and turbans. New recruits to the Boxers were given this distinctive uniform before taking part in exotic ceremonies in which converts were supposedly endowed with supernatural powers that made them invincible.

The word 'Boxer' first appeared in Western correspondence in May 1898 but it wasn't until January 1900 that there was widespread concern within the Western community. By then Boxer placards had begun appearing in towns and villages across Northern China, all proclaiming: 'Protect the Empire, Exterminate Foreigners'. Although it wasn't specifically anti-Christian, it was the missionaries in the interior cities who were the first to feel its effects as bands of lawless peasants roamed the countryside harassing missions and Chinese Christian converts. They were also to become its first victims. Realising that Boxer fanaticism and their belief in special powers made them a dangerous enemy, missionaries began drawing it to the attention of foreign ministers in Peking. In turn, the ministers asked the Tsungli Yamen (the Chinese government office that dealt with foreigners) to outlaw the movement. But nothing happened and although some provincial governors did fight against the Boxers, others supported them, either actively or silently.

Tientsin was an important commercial centre situated at the junction where the Pei-ho River met the Grand Canal. On arrival in China travellers to Peking would moor off the coast in the Gulf of Pechihli, about 10 miles off shore. Passengers and cargo would then transfer to lighters and small steamships as only small ships could cross the sandbar across the mouth of the Pei-ho River. The crossing was normally turbulent even when the weather was good. In the frequent bad weather high winds made it much worse and it often took over 2 hours to reach the sandbar. On the south bank was the city of Taku and on the northern bank the city of Tongku.

Passengers disembarked at Tongku and made the train journey to Tientsin, about 30 miles away and a travelling time of about 2 hours. When they reached the Tientsin terminus they crossed the river to reach the Foreign Concession. This comprised about 500 people, half of whom were missionaries, the rest were businessmen and their families. There were three distinct Western communities in the Foreign Concession: French, British and German and the buildings were of good quality and design. It had an excellent road network and gas lighting as well as parks, churches, clubs and theatres. It was completely separate from the walled city of Tientsin where approximately 1 million Chinese lived.

The railroad went from Tientsin to Peking via Langfang and Fengtai and took about 5 hours to travel the 80 miles. The train stopped at Machiapu, which was a few miles outside the rectangular shaped walls that enclosed Peking. One of these walls was also a wall for the adjacent square-shaped city of Tartar. Inside Tartar was the Imperial City which contained all the government buildings and offices. The Forbidden City, the location of all the royal palaces, was also within Tartar City. Adjacent to the Forbidden City was the Legation Quarter where all the foreign legations were housed, each legation with its own walled compound within the quarter. The numerous missionary societies also had their own walled compounds but these were spread throughout Tartar City and many were a long way from the Legation Quarter.

The legations within the quarter were housed in Western style accommodation with proper sanitation and their social life was totally separate from their Chinese neighbours in Peking. They had their own dinner parties and dances, produced their own theatricals, took picnics in the countryside and even had their own racing track. By contrast, Peking itself was considered by visitors to be very crowded and unsanitary with dirty streets. There were about 500 foreigners living in Peking, about half of whom were diplomats while the rest were missionaries.

On 31 December 1899 an Anglican missionary, the Revd Sidney Brooks, was murdered in Shantung Province. The British Minister immediately demanded the execution of the murderers as well as the punishment of any officials involved and the suppression of the Boxer Society. The two men who carried out the murder were beheaded and some of the lesser officials were reprimanded. Yu-hsien, ex-Governor of Shantung and head patron of the Boxers, was ordered to Peking. However, when he arrived he was received with honour by the Empress-Dowager. He was then given the Governorship of Shan-his where he continued to foster the Boxer movement. Although an edict was published ordering the suppression of seditious societies, it was worded in such a way that it not only exonerated the Boxers but also encouraged them to continue their fight against foreigners. The Viceroy of Chi-li, Yu-lu, recognised the need to keep the Boxers in check but on 22 May 1900 a party of his cavalry were ambushed at Lai-shui and completely wiped out.

Gradually, the movement spread from Shantung to the Province of Chihli until by the spring of 1900 Boxers were active on the outskirts of both Tientsin and Peking. Attacks on Chinese Christians grew more frequent and the London Mission chapel at Kung-tsun, 40 miles to the southwest of Peking, was destroyed. The Boxers had even set up a centre for recruitment and training at Tung-Chow, just 13 miles outside Peking.

After a warning by Pere Favier, the Roman Catholic Bishop of Peking, that the situation was becoming serious, foreign ministers demanded that the Tsungli Yamen suppress the Boxer movement. The Tsungli Yamen assured the ministers that they were doing everything in their power and that the Chinese government considered the Boxers to be outlaws and rebels and that the safety of the legations was paramount. While they gave these assurances to the foreign ministers, the Manchu Party continued to encourage the Boxers and assure them of the favour of the Empress-Dowager.

On 28 May Western ministers were grudgingly given permission by Tsungli Yamen to summon legation guards from the warships anchored off Taku Bar. As a consequence, 350 soldiers and sailors travelled the 80 miles to Peking, arriving without incident on 31 May and the various legations breathed a sigh of relief believing they were now safe. But the situation began to deteriorate rapidly. Boxers destroyed the railway station at Fengtai, 6 miles outside Peking, the main junction for trains to both Tientsin and Peking. The British legation began notifying its citizens in Tartar City that they could seek refuge in the legation if they felt threatened.

The crisis continued to deepen during the first week in June. General Nieh's troops who had been protecting the railway line between Tientsin and Peking were ordered back to their camp at Lu-ta, although they remained in the neighbourhood for a few more days. By 7 June all communication between the legations and the outside world had been cut off and the Boxers were drilling their recruits openly in Peking itself. On 9 June Tung Fu-hsiang's Kan-su troops, who had been withdrawn during the winter of 1898–1899 at the request of the Foreign Ministers, arrived back in the capital. They were Muslims who were fiercely anti-foreigner and with them came hoards of Boxers, armed with swords and spears. They began parading through the capital declaring death to all foreigners. Sir Claude MacDonald sent an urgent telegram to Vice Admiral Sir Edward Seymour and the Allied Fleet, which was anchored off the Gulf of Pechihli, requesting he advance on Peking.

Senior naval officers held a council of war on HMS *Centurion* on 9 June under the leadership of Vice Admiral Seymour. They decided to send a naval brigade, consisting of seamen and marines, under Seymour's personal direction to Peking. The 2,072 men, including 116 officers, were from all the nations present and were made up of 921 British, 450 Germans, 305 Russians, 158 French, 112 Americans, 54 Japanese, 40 Italians and 25 Austrians. They quickly assembled and by the early hours of 10 June they were on their way to Tongku. Here they disembarked and began the journey to Tientsin where 5 engines and more than 100 railway cars were ready to take them to Peking. They were divided into five sections with train 1 carrying half the British force, all the Americans and Austrians plus coolies and supplies to repair the railways. Train 2 carried the remainder of the British, the Japanese and some of the French. Train 3 consisted of Germans and train 4 the Russians, the rest of the French and the Italians. The fifth train was the supply train which would run back and forth between Tientsin and Peking. The Seymour Expedition, as it was known, never reached Peking.

Expecting to be in Peking by the 11th, they had only taken enough rations for three days. The first day was spent repairing railway tracks, the second fighting Boxers who were destroying the railway at Langfang. Finding his rations and the supplies for repairing railway line running low, Seymour sent the fifth train back to Tientsin to pick up some more. Unfortunately, the train only went as far as Yang-tsun. Here it met heavy Boxer activity and the track was destroyed between there and Tientsin so it returned to Langfang on the 15th. Seymour decided to retreat back to Yang-tsun but the crossing across the river had been badly damaged and was unsafe to cross. The troops detrained and began the long march along the banks of the Pei-ho River. They eventually managed to capture some junks and loaded the wounded, the artillery and the supplies onto these, but the river was so low they had to ditch the artillery because the boats kept grounding. After three days they came across a building that was only lightly protected by Chinese troops. They captured the building and decided to wait there until help arrived. The building was well supplied with food, water, arms and ammunition. But they were not rescued until 25 June when 1,000 Russian Cossacks and 600 British troops arrived to escort them back to Tientsin.

Meanwhile, back in Peking, on 11 June the Japanese Chancellor, Mr Sugiyama, was murdered by Tung Fu-hsiang's troops as he went to the station to meet the expected relief column. The Boxers attacked the legations on 13 June and on the same day began massacring Chinese Christians.

By 16 June all foreigners and Chinese Christians in Peking were either in the Legation Quarter or the Catholic Cathedral Pei-t'ang. The same day the Boxers set fire to the area of the city that housed foreign shops and businesses and those that dealt with foreigners, destroying over 4,000 premises. Three days later the Foreign Ministers were issued with an ultimatum to leave Peking within 24 hours as the Tsungli Yamen could no longer guarantee their safety. They were offered safe transit to Tientsin provided they were ready to move on the morning of 20 June 1900.

The Foreign Ministers agreed unanimously that they would not leave Peking and to delay the ultimatum they requested a meeting with the Tsungli Yamen for the 20th which was ignored. The German Minister, Baron von Ketteler, set out for the Tsungli Yamen with his interpreter on the morning of the 20th but was shot dead by a member of the Imperial Army. At 4pm the Chinese opened fire on the Legation Quarters which were defended by the troops who had come up from Tientsin. Three days later the Chinese attempted to burn down the legations by setting fire to the adjacent buildings. During the following days American and German Marines attacked Manchu Bannermen and Chinese troops successfully. There were more successful attacks by the Allies at the beginning of July but then, on 13 July, the French Legation was blown up by Chinese mines.

It was not only in Peking that the situation was critical. Other towns within Chihli Province were also under threat. The Chinese section of Tientsin was under Boxer control and the legations were in danger, as were the railway towns of Tong-shan, Pei-tai-ho and Shan-hai-kuan. When Rear Admiral Bruce discovered that the Chinese were about to attack the forts in Tongku and Taku another landing party was sent ashore to occupy them, this time led by Commander C. Craddock of HMS *Alacrity*. The landing party of 35 officers and 869 men was made up of all the nations present, with 321 British, 244 Japanese, 159 Russians, 133 Germans, 25 Italians and 22 Austrians. Both attacks were successful, although the British suffered casualties, three men killed and thirteen wounded, on their assault on the South Fort.

The attacks continued on Tientsin and by 18 June all rail communications had been cut off. There were now 10,000 Chinese troops including those from the Imperial Army facing a defence force of only 2,400 men. But reinforcements were arriving. The British sent HMS *Terrible* with 382 men from Hong Kong, and the French had already sent 600 marines and 400 seaman from Marseilles. The Russians arrived on the 11th with 1,746 men with artillery, cavalry and transport at Taku and on the 18th a further 12,000 men at Taku.

On 21 June Major General Stessel headed towards Tientsin with a strong detachment of Russians, Americans and Italians. He was followed by a further three detachments. They all met up at the railhead 10 miles from Tientsin and at dawn on 23 June they advanced towards Tientsin. They came under intense fire from the Chinese defenders 6 miles from the city, but they continued to advance slowly until finally they reached the last bridge before entering the settlement. Here the resistance was considerable but eventually, aided by American field guns, they entered the settlement.

By 25 June HMS *Terrible* had silenced the guns of Tientsin and at Taku HMS *Fame* had captured the Hsin-ch'eng Fort. The International Force, now numbering 12,000 men, was made up of 3,752 Japanese, 3,735 Russians, 2,300 British, 1,340 German, 421 French, 335 American, 138 Italians and 26 Austrians. They completed the relief of Tientsin and communication with the sea was once again restored.

Back in Peking things had deteriorated. The last communication had been three weeks earlier and the legations had reported that they were under constant bombardment and only just hanging on. Then rumours began circulating that there had been a massacre. But the International Force in Tientsin had its own problems. First, they could not agree about when to advance. The Kaiser wanted to wait for the arrival of General Albrecht Graf von Waldersee, who he had named Commander in Chief of the International Force. But he had not left Germany yet. The British under General Gaselee were in favour of moving quickly so as to start before the rainy season began.

However, there was also a manpower shortage. General Gaselee had been expected to arrive with 10,000 troops but he only brought 6,000. The Japanese, under Lieutenant General Yamaguchi, considered this to be too small so offered to make up the shortfall by providing 10,000 troops. The Americans wanted to wait for the arrival of their artillery which was still on its way to Taku and the Russians were distracted by events in Manchuria.

Chapter Six

Arrival in China

It was 1 July 1900 and Sydney watched from the deck of the US Army Transport *Grant* as the shoreline of San Francisco disappeared into the distance. He was wearing his new khaki cotton uniform and his rather drab campaign hat. Others were still wearing their 1895-pattern forage caps and some of the officers were wearing their Ulster overcoats, while others had the 1883-pattern brown canvas, blanket-lined overcoats. The 6th US Cavalry traditional dark-blue uniform was optional, although very few were wearing it, but the full dress uniform remained dark blue. The new khaki uniforms were very popular with the men as they reflected the heat much better than the dark blue and were more comfortable. They also allowed the soldier to blend in more with his surroundings, making him less of a target. The men were also kitted out with brown leather campaign shoes and khaki canvas leggings instead of boots.

They had just been informed their destination was to be China and not the Philippines, as expected. Like the rest of the men, Sydney didn't mind at all. Although he had been expecting to go to the Philippines, he was just as excited about going to China. He had joined the 6th Cavalry in San Francisco after the call for volunteers to fight in the Philippines in the hope of finding some excitement and also earning some money. But as the regiment sailed from San Francisco to the Philippines the situation in China deteriorated and they were told that two squadrons were going to be diverted to help quell the Boxer Rebellion. On board with them was General Adna Romanza Chaffee,[1] who was to become the Commander in Charge of the China Relief Expedition.

Just 15 miles outside the harbour the ship ground to a halt, turned round and steamed back to San Francisco. A small break in one of the steam pipes had been discovered and as this was likely to prove quite serious the ship had no option but to return to harbour and effect repairs. Being cooped up on the ship for the next two days in the heat of summer was very uncomfortable and

Sydney was becoming increasingly disgruntled. Like his fellow troopers he couldn't wait to visit such an exotic location as China and he was concerned that if they delayed too long, the rebellion would be over and he would miss his chance. So the news that the ship was finally ready to leave for Japan on 3 July at 6.45pm was received with a considerable degree of relief, by Sydney and the rest of the 6th Cavalry.

Fortunately, the rest of the journey was uneventful and there were no further incidents. Sydney spent as much time on deck as he was allowed, gazing out onto the vastness of the Pacific Ocean, hardly able to believe that he was really going to the Far East. On 24 July the ship arrived in Nagasaki to take on coal and Sydney had his first glimpse of a completely different country. From the deck he looked out at the harbour. It was bordered by jagged mountains on either side, the sprawling city overlooked on the southern side by Mt Kazagashira. Although the flat land available for expansion was limited, the original fishing village had grown steadily, finally becoming a city on 1 April 1889.

The city itself was crowded with traditional style wooden buildings and the harbor was bustling with ships. A small artificial island, Dejiima, could be seen in the middle of the harbour, separated from the mainland by a waterway.

On the Bund in Oura-Sagarimatsu he could see the large white building that was the Nagasaki branch of the Hong Kong Shanghai Bank and next to it a large brown building, the Nagasaki Hotel.

Away from his immediate view were the 'tea houses', a rather misleading name for the Nagasaki brothels that were very popular with the crews of foreign ships. At the height of their popularity the Maruyama and Yoriai districts had no fewer than 54 brothels with 766 prostitutes. They were also popular with soldiers who were lucky enough to be given shore leave while their transports refuelled with coal. Unfortunately, venereal diseases were rife and many a customer ended up in the local cemetery.

Taking on coal in Nagasaki was an event not to be missed and Sydney joined the other troopers on deck to watch the spectacle. As soon as the ship entered harbour hundreds of men, women, girls and boys swarmed round it. Many were wearing little other than loin cloths and head bands as protection from the burning sun.

Before the ship had even settled at anchor the large coal barges also bore down and in a very short time there was a scaffold of poles tied in place reaching from the ships sides to the water's edge. A young girl stood on each rung of the improvised ladder, leaving a long line of girls stretching from the barge to the dock and they began passing the coal up the ladder to the ship's bunkers.

On the barges men shovelled up a small amount of coal, a little less than half a bushel, and placed it in shallow baskets. The baskets were passed from hand to hand until they reached the ladder. Here the first girl took it and swung it over her head to the girl above who passed it to the girl above her. It continued, without stopping, in this vein until it reached the ship's bunkers. Once the basket was empty it was passed onto a line of small boys who passed the empty baskets back to the barges to be refilled.

This went on for several hours as barge after barge was unloaded and then replaced by a full one. Eventually, the ship's bunkers were full and the scaffolding was removed as quickly as it first appeared. The whole process resembled that of a well-oiled machine and coal could be transferred at an average of 353¾ tons per hour, nearly 6 tons a minute.

It is not known whether Sydney was granted shore leave but given their relatively short time in port it is probably unlikely. While there General Chaffee received Washington's instructions to proceed to China and assume control of the US Forces there. Before leaving Nagasaki there was a conference on board the *Newark* with Admiral Kempff, the American Consul Mr Harris and Mr J. Hattori, Governor of Nagasaki Ken.

At daybreak on 29 July the *Grant* finally arrived at Taku Bay in China and Sydney looked around with interest. There were already several other warships and transports from other countries in the bay. These included several American ships: the *Brooklyn*, Admiral Remy's flagship, army transport *Indiana*, which was busy unloading the 14th Infantry Regiment from Manila, and the *Port Albert*, which had unloaded the 9th Infantry Regiment, but still had about 500,000ft of lumber on board. Because there was an urgent need for other stores the *Port Albert* was directed to sail immediately to Nagasaki with the lumber still on board.

The Light Battery, Fifth Artillery commanded by Captain Henry J. Reilly and two companies of the 14th Infantry Regiment had arrived two days earlier from Nagasaki on the *Flintshire* but they were still on board, and the *Solace*, a hospital ship, was busy tending to the wounded from the previous day's battle for Tientsin.

Sydney watched as various tugs and river boats with the flags of other nations travelled up and down the bay unloading their transport. It seemed the Americans had very few boats at their disposal and he could see the Quartermaster and his assistant energetically trying to acquire the much-needed boats without which they would be unable to unload the American ships.

The only boat that appeared to have been chartered was the *Pechili*, although there were also two scows and a tug. These were able to carry about 75 tons each and were already busy unloading the stores from the *Indiana*. But the draft of the *Pechili* was so deep that it could only cross the bar at high tide. This happened to be at 5pm that day and once across it could not come back again until 5am the following morning when the tide was high again. However, the situation improved over the next few days and soon cargo and stores were being unloaded with little difficulty.

General Chaffee hurried off to Tientsin accompanied by his Adjutant General, Captain Grote Hutcheson of the 6th US Cavalry, and his aide, Lieutenant Roy B. Harper of the 7th US Cavalry. They arrived at the beleaguered city at 11.40am on 30 July to find the 9th Infantry under the command of Lieutenant Colonel Charles A. Coolidge were already there. However, over 200 men were sick and the regiment was in physically poor condition. Fortunately, the 14th Infantry under Colonel A.S. Daggett were in much better condition with only a very small sick list. They were joined two days later by a further two companies from the 14th Infantry who had finally disembarked from the *Indiana*. There was also a small battalion of Marines under Major Littleton W.T. Waller. On 1 August a further battalion of 920 Marines arrived from the *Grant* under the command of Major William P. Biddle. There was very little transport available at Tientsin, only 19 wagons, 4 ambulances and 1 Dougherty wagon which belonged to the 9th Infantry. The transportation belonging to the 14th Infantry had been delayed and did not arrive until several days later.

On 1 August the various generals held a conference to decide whether their armies were ready to move on Peking. Present were the commanding general of the Russian Army and his chief of staff; Lieutenant General Yamaguchi of the Japanese Army and his chief of staff, Major General Fukushima; Lieutenant-General Gaselee of the British Army and his chief of staff, General Barrow; General Frey of the French Army; an officer of the German Navy; General Chaffee, Major Jesse M. Lee, 9th Infantry, and Lieutenant Louis M. Little of the Marines, who spoke French.

The Japanese, who together with British and American forces, were currently occupying the right bank of the river in and around Tientsin, reported that the Chinese were massing in force near Pei-tsang, about 7 miles away. They also reported that the Chinese were strengthening their position by extending their earthworks about 3 miles westwards on the right bank and that the area from the left bank to the railroad embankment was also being reinforced. The Japanese believed there were around 12,000 Chinese in the vicinity of Pei-tsang and behind that there were even more massing at Yang-tsun, their main line of defence.

It was agreed by all except two of those present that they should move immediately. The two dissenters were not against taking action, but they were concerned their forces might not be strong enough to overcome the opposition. They were overruled.

It was decided that the attack would begin on 5 August. The Japanese, British and Americans were already occupying the right bank and the Russians were on the left so it was agreed to continue the assault without any changes to these positions. In addition, the British were asked to send four heavy guns to help the Russian column. The strategy on the right bank was left to the commanders of the forces occupying it. After more discussion it was decided they should make their way to Yang-tsun where the roads and railway went directly to Peking. The Foreign Force was made up of 8,000 Japanese, 4,800 Russians, 3,000 British, 2,100 Americans, 800 French, 200 German and a mixed group of about 100 Italians and Austrians. Their first objective was to secure Pei-tsang.

Reilly's battery made it to Tientsin by 3 August and quickly assembled their guns. The Marines and the 6th Cavalry were finally disembarked from the *Grant* and made it to Tientsin by 4 August. They would initially be used dismounted because the horses had not yet arrived. The other squadrons remained at Tientsin with the British, French, Japanese and Russian troops to keep the port open while the others pushed on to Peking under General Chaffee. But this enabled Chaffee to take all available men from the 9th and 14th, only leaving one company of 100 men behind to help the civil government of the city. The civil government had been established prior to the arrival of the 6th Cavalry and would have a mixed military force of which the American contribution was 100 men.

On 4 August Captain De Rosey C. Cabell of the 6th Cavalry arrived at Pehmoon with M Troop, consisting of two officers and seventy-six men. There were still over 200 men from the 9th and 14th Infantry who were unfit to march. All the troops except the company of Marines were put under the command of Lieutenant Colonel T.J. Wint of the 6th Cavalry.

At 3pm that afternoon there were 2,500 men ready to march, although transportation was limited with only 18 4-mule wagons and 1 pack train. There were 100 rounds of ammunition per man on 5 heavily loaded wagons, but once the pack train arrived they were able to transfer ammunition to that. The men were carrying haversacks with one day's rations, there were a further four in the wagons and ten days in the junks which were to follow the Army up the river. Major Waller of the Marine battalion had secured Chinese carts and packs to carry four days' rations for the Marines which alleviated the load on the wagons and there were a number of Chinese coolies carrying cooking utensils, water and other essentials that would not fit on the wagons.

Sydney looked around as they moved out of the city. It was late afternoon and they marched some distance before bivouacking near the Siku arsenal. Ahead he could see that the road branched westward and made its way round to the right of the entrenched Chinese position. The force was divided into two with the Japanese, British and Americans operating on the right bank of the Pei-ho River and the remainder on the left bank. The plan was for the Japanese to march along the road at 1am on the 5th followed by the British and Americans. They were to envelope the Chinese right and take the powder house that formed the right of the Chinese position. Once that had been accomplished the three forces were to turn to the right, force the Chinese out of their entrenchments and head to Pei-tsang. They knew there was a strong Chinese outpost on the road, about a mile in front of Pie-tsang and the plan was for the Japanese to assault this with a battalion backed up by a battery at 3am.

The attack started during the night to avoid the heat of the day and before long the Japanese had captured Kanochia-ju, Liu-chia-pei and Tang-chia-wan. The Chinese began retreating, first towards Pei-tsang, then on to Yang-tsun.

The plan was working perfectly but there was not enough room for three forces to enter combat and once the Japanese had taken the Chinese arsenal they spread out along the bank preventing the British and Americans from getting into positions in which they could render assistance. By 5am the Japanese had cleared the arsenal and were pursuing the Chinese back towards Pei-tsang. They requested that the British and Americans move northward from their positions which both forces did. But in order to help the Japanese the Americans needed to pass round the British and this took some time. In fact, by the time they had completed this manoeuvre, the Japanese had cleared the Chinese back to the river at Pei-tsang and the fighting was all but finished.

Sydney and the rest of the 6th Cavalry continued northwards round the British and eventually arrived at the river about a mile to the north and west of Pei-tsang. Although they had not taken any casualties, the heat was intense, the lack of air magnified by the dense cornfields through which they marched and Sydney was exhausted. They could go no further as their way was barred. The British forces were on their right and the Japanese had possession of the whole of the river front. The bank had been cut and the only way forward was via a narrow road alongside the river and that was flooded. By now the Chinese had retreated up the river towards Yang-tsun so, much to Sydney's relief, the Americans decided to make camp at Too-wa-she, a small village north of Pei-tsang.

Because the front of the Chinese positions on the left bank was flooded, the Russians were unable to advance any further so they gradually crossed over to the right bank. As no one was able to march any further forward on the right bank the Japanese made the decision to construct three 40–50ft-wide bridges. A pontoon bridge had already been erected by the Japanese at Pei-tsang and the decision was made by the British, Americans and Russians to march up the left bank of the river to Yang-tsun. The Japanese informed them all that the bridge would be broken at 6am the following morning so they needed to start early to ensure they all crossed safely.

Sydney and the rest of the 6th Cavalry were woken early. They were still exhausted through lack of sleep and from the intense heat but by 4am they were ready to go. They were about to leave when they were told that the bridges would not be ready until at least 9am so they shouldn't leave Pei-tsang until 6am at the earliest. The men groaned and muttering under their breath sat down and waited for another 2 hours while the temperature gradually rose.

The Americans finally moved at 6am, marching briskly along the railway embankment which was between 10 and 20ft high. On either side there were stones and rock ballast. The railway track itself had been completely removed, the ties burned or carried away and rails scattered alongside the road. Much to their relief the country they marched over was reasonably level and although it was cultivated, the crops were stunted due to the severe drought. This made marching much easier but the heat was just as intense and Sydney longed for some cold water to quench his thirst. He could feel the sweat on his body and he thought with longing of the ice cold of the Yukon. For the first time since he'd joined the US Army he began to think he'd made a mistake.

Once they were across they marched to the railroad where they halted and watched as the Russians, British and French crossed on the pontoon bridge. They then marched along the river road which was parallel to the railroad and located about a mile and a half from it.

It was 4 hours later, at around 10am, when they finally reached the village of Hsin-chuang, about a mile and a half outside Yang-tsun. But there was no time to rest as they could see the Chinese positions. They were occupying a section immediately in front of the bridge and the bend in the road where the railroad and river road converged. Sydney readied himself and then they were given the order to advance. But as the British and Americans went forward they came under very heavy fire. General Chaffee consulted with the British commander, Lieutenant General Gasalee, and then placed the 14th Infantry in a position to attack along the west side of the railroad where they connected with the British line. The Russians were in a column at the rear of the British to the left. Sydney and the 6th Cavalry, together with the 9th Infantry, Marines and Reilly's battery, crossed to the east side of the railway embankment where they could support the 14th Infantry and

British troops. On the right of the American troops was a squadron of British cavalry protecting the right flank.

As the 14th Infantry headed in the direction of Pei-tsang the enemy opened up with artillery on the right flank. The British commanding officer reported that there were eight companies of Chinese infantry and three guns in the village directly to the right of the Americans. The Americans immediately changed tack and moved against it. The guns were soon silenced and the village set on fire. However, before this was completed General Chaffee received a request from the British commander, asking that they bring their artillery to bear on the embankment and the village that the 14th Infantry were attacking because they were struggling against strong resistance.

General Chaffee had not yet secured the villages on his right so he was reluctant to do this. His forces were still coming under artillery and infantry attack from the right. He also considered the British had sufficient artillery and with the Russians immediately to their left he was concerned about the concentration of too many artillery batteries in a small area. However, he then received a second message requesting urgent support and reluctantly moved his guns into a position to assist the 14th Infantry. He was intending to fire over the railway embankment which was about 20ft high.

The battery had now unlimbered and was about to open fire when General Chaffee noticed the men of the 14th Infantry climbing the embankment directly in the line of fire. He ordered Captain Reilly not to fire. This gave the Chinese infantry, hiding in the surrounding cornfields, the chance they had been waiting for. They immediately attacked the battery, forcing Captain Reilly to open fire with shrapnel. He was only able to disperse them with the help of the Marines.

The 9th Infantry, coming up on the right of the battery, mistook the Chinese flag for the French flag and held back from firing, thus missing a valuable opportunity to inflict damage on the Chinese troops. In part this was due to repeated messages from the Russians warning that the French and Russians were likely to pass through the American front. Neither French nor Russian troops were actually in advance of the American line, but because of the messages all commanders and officers were extra careful.

The 14th Infantry and the British, who because of the contracted ground were now mixed up, assaulted the Chinese position vigorously and soon overcame it. The 14th Infantry took several casualties with seven killed and fifty-seven wounded. Some of these casualties were probably the result of 'friendly fire' from the British and Russians and happened after the British and 14th Infantry had succeeded in taking the Chinese positions. The 14th Infantry halted at the railroad embankment while the 9th Infantry and Marines continued northward through the villages east of Yang-tsun until they reached the railroad bridge. The heat had increased and the men suffered terribly from dehydration and heatstroke with two of the men dying due to the heat and lack of water.

Eventually, the Chinese were in full retreat back through Yang-tsun to Peking. The Japanese, who were on the extreme right, were able to march unopposed into Yang-tsun and by 7 August the entire International Force came to a halt in Yang-tsun. This had been agreed at the first conference in Tientsin. Here they buried the dead and sent the wounded back in boats to Tientsin. At the same time the commanders took the opportunity to decide how to proceed. While they reconvened their conference the men were able to rest. Even though Sydney had seen little action so far, he had been close enough to hear the noise of the shells and experience the heart-stopping moments when bullets and shrapnel ricocheted off the buildings, ground and surrounding areas. Like the others, he was also suffering from heat exhaustion and the lack of water.

The next day the French remained to garrison the town while the Japanese, British and Americans moved forward. The Russians stayed behind too as they were waiting for more supplies. It was intensely hot so after a short while they abandoned the march and camped at Nan-tsai-tsun, where they waited for their junks which were loaded with artillery and other supplies to reach them. That evening the Russians also arrived, as did a Christian messenger from Peking. He bought with him a cipher from Sir Claude MacDonald to General Gaselee suggesting he attack Peking from the south. That way they could enter through Tartar City via the Sluice Gate under the wall and to the south of the Legation Quarter. The cipher also said the legations were holding out and had enough provisions to last until 16 August.

The International Force set out again on the 9th. Their progress was agonisingly slow, the way choked with stifling dust and intense heat. They were also hampered by the continual need to be on the lookout for danger from the Chinese. The conditions were so bad that, having marched only 11 miles, the British and Americans decided to camp at the village of Ho-hsi-wu. Here they were joined by two companies of French troops, ready for the assault on Peking.

The commanders held their conference in the early afternoon at the headquarters of the Russian commander. They all agreed that they should continue moving forward the following day and once they reached Tong-Chow they would halt, reconvene and plan the assault on Peking. Therefore, all the forces would concentrate at Tsai-tsun the next day and the march would resume that morning at 4am. The Japanese would lead followed by the Russians, the Americans and the British.

Chapter Seven

To Peking

Their departure was staggered and because the Japanese did not set off until 4am it meant the Americans could not leave until 7am. By this time the heat was rising rapidly, as was the humidity. As in previous days, the march was agonisingly slow and as the heat rose so did the number of casualties. Men began dropping out by the side of the road, hoping to regain camp when the sun went down and the temperature was lower.

The next five days to Tong-Chow continued to take their toll on the Americans who had not had sufficient time to acclimatise to the conditions. Even the fittest and healthiest suffered in the intense heat as their tongues swelled up and they became confused and developed headaches and fevers. Desperate for water, many drank from polluted streams and other water courses which led to bad stomachs. As the dreary march to Tong-Chow continued and casualties continued to rise, Sydney was no exception. He had thought he much preferred the heat to the icy cold of the Canadian north, but even he'd had more than enough by the time they reached their destination.

The Japanese, who were in the lead, came up against some limited opposition at Shang-shia, a walled town not far from Tong-Chow, but they soon overcame it and by that night one brigade had reached their objective.

At 3am on the 12th the Japanese blew in the south gate of the wall of Tong-Chow only to find the Chinese had deserted the town. The rest of the armies arrived by noon of that day. Much to Sydney's relief, the day was cloudy and the cooler conditions made the march considerably easier than the previous few days.

Now they had reached Tong-Chow the Russians wanted to remain there and rest their troops for the day. The other generals did not agree and at 6pm that evening they visited the Russian commander to try and change his mind. But he would not be swayed. Instead, he insisted that he was not moving the next day as he must rest his troops.

After considerable discussion a compromise was reached and it was finally decided that the 13th should be devoted to reconnaissance. The Japanese had already advanced some of their troops 6 miles towards Peking so it was agreed the Japanese would reconnoitre the two roads to the right and north of the paved road which was north of the canal. The Russians would reconnoitre the paved road itself, the Americans the road south of the canal and the British a parallel road just over a mile to the left of the road occupied by the Americans. On the 14th the armies would concentrate on the advance line held by the Japanese and then hold another conference to determine the details of the attack on Peking.

On the morning of the 13th Sydney and the rest of M Troop, 6th Cavalry together with Reilly's battery and the 14th Infantry moved off to reconnoitre the road up to 7 miles from Tong-Chow. They advanced cautiously but all was quiet. They found no opposition and eventually General Chaffee directed the remainder of his force to march out and catch up with the advance guard. As the Russians were still resting the Japanese reconnoitred both their own and the Russian sections.

However, the Russians had other ideas and at the same time Sydney, the 6th Cavalry and the rest of the advanced guard were cautiously exploring their own front the Russians were leaving the camp. They followed the road assigned to them and at 9pm heavy fighting was heard in the vicinity of Peking. It appeared that despite their insistence on resting their troops the Russians had, in fact, made alternative plans. Instead, they had moved forward the previous evening and were attacking the Tung-pien-men gate, on the east of the city where the Chinese wall joined the Tartar wall. The small arms fire and heavy artillery continued throughout the night but the Americans had no idea it was the Russians who they thought were still in Tung-Chow. They assumed it was the Chinese making a last attempt to destroy the legations. It was only at daybreak the following day when a Japanese staff officer asked General Chaffee if he knew where the Russians were that suspicions were raised. To start with General Chaffee replied that he assumed they were either still in Tong-Chow or on his right flank on the opposite side of the canal. The Japanese officer replied that they were definitely not on the opposite side of the canal.

As it had been agreed the forces would all concentrate on the line 7 miles from Tong-Chow there were no operations planned, other than a small reconnaissance by the 6th Cavalry Troop at 5am. Captain Cabell led the troop, leaving the rest of the equipment in the camp. General Chaffee had originally intended to send a battalion of infantry with him but changed his mind. Not long after the 6th Cavalry troop had left General Chaffee was passed by a 200-strong column of French troops who stated that they wished to cross the bridge about 3 miles ahead so they could join the Russian troops. General Chaffee was surprised as he had no idea any troops were in front of him except the cavalry troop that had just left. He was still under the impression that the Russians were on his right.

Meanwhile, Sydney and the rest of the advanced guard had run into trouble. About a mile and a half forward, as they approached a village, they came under attack from Chinese cavalry. They immediately dismounted and took up positions on the left bank of the road. Lieutenant Guiney and six men, including Sydney, went ahead to draw the enemy fire. They were immediately fired on by up to a dozen mounted cavalry and a number of dismounted men, leaving them no option but to retreat back to the left of the main force where there were also twenty French infantry. They opened fire on the Chinese and for the next 20 minutes volleys of rifle fire and other small arms ricocheted round Sydney as they returned fire. There was little difference in the numbers on each side, but the 6th Cavalry slowly began to overwhelm the opposition. As they prepared to advance they received orders to remain where they were and hold until relieved so, instead, they eased forward and began taking up positions in the walled enclosures of the village houses.

Warned of approaching Chinese reinforcements by the interpreter, Mr Lowry, who had accompanied Captain Cabell's troop, General Chaffee immediately sent for the 14th Infantry. The French reluctantly allowed the Americans to take over their road and once they were forward the 14th Infantry found Cabell's men occupying houses and firing from roofs in a village further forward.

Now they had some reinforcements the 6th Cavalry moved into a position so they could cover the left of the line and began moving forward again. They encountered some more light opposition, but they were soon in possession of the village.

Having cleared the opposition, the Americans pressed forward, hoping to get as close to the walls of the city as possible without moving their whole force forward, which was contrary to the agreement with the other forces. Although they were fired at by Boxers in villages on their left and to their front, they didn't face any serious opposition and they soon reached the northeast corner of the Chinese city.

Once again the 6th Cavalry dismounted and took up positions so they could cover the left flank of the line. Firing on the three bastions protecting the walls of the city, they took up positions close to the wall and set up a steady fire on the bastions for over an hour. Before long they had silenced two of them and helped the artillery to silence the fire from the gate tower on their left.

On the night of 13/14 August the British had also woken to the sound of firing coming from Peking. Thinking the legation might be under attack, the British left Tung-Chow at about 2am and marched towards Peking. On arrival they discovered that the firing had come from the Russians who had inadvertently found themselves in the position that had been allocated to the Americans. They had marched on the Tung-pien-men (gate) and then come under heavy fire from the Chinese on the Tartar wall which forced them back to the suburbs.

By 9am the Japanese troops with their fifty-four guns were in position at Chih-ho-men and Tung-chih-men and were waiting for the order to fire. By 10am General Chaffee had realised that the Russians were in action on their right and he could also hear the Japanese artillery farther to the right. His left flank was uncovered apart from a small force of British cavalry as the main British force had not left Tong-Chow until the 14th because of the agreement. As they marched forward to the concentration area they found the Americans preparing to advance on Peking. At 11am two companies of the 14th Infantry scaled the walls of the northeast corner of the Chinese city and raised their flag on the walls, the first flag of a foreign power to be unfurled on the walls of the city.

By noon one of the British batteries was busy firing on the city from a position a mile to the rear and left of the American forces. Meanwhile, the Americans arrived at Tung-pien-men at 12.30pm, and with the help of the two companies on the wall and those assaulting from the outside they soon managed to break through into the Chinese city. At the same time the British broke through the relatively undefended Shau-huo-men. The Americans arrived at Tung-pien-men to find the Russians in disarray. Their artillery was facing in both directions and they seemed to be making no effort to extricate themselves from the confusion and gain entry to the city.

One company of the 14th Infantry deployed into the buildings on the right of the gate and began pouring effective fire onto the Tartar wall. At the same time Captain Reilly managed to get two guns through a very narrow passage on his left. He tore down some walls and having found a position a few yards to the left of the road he began to enfilade section by section of the Tartar wall with shrapnel.

Meanwhile, the 14th Infantry crossed the moat and, having taken up positions parallel to the moat along the street facing the Tartar wall, they and the artillery cleared it of all Chinese forces. They moved slowly westward along the wall removing opposition all the way to and beyond the Hait-men gate. The 9th Infantry were given orders to follow the 14th and the artillery as soon as the wall was cleared of Chinese forces. The Marines were also given orders to follow them, but later these were changed and they were sent to protect the train instead.

By 3pm the advanced party arrived opposite the legations. The Chinese opposition had virtually ceased and after finally overcoming the defenders on the Tartar wall they gained access to the legation grounds. The 14th Infantry entered by the water gate while Reilly's battery went through the Chien-men gate which was opened by the American and Russian forces of the besieged legation. The British entered through the Shahuo gate and followed a road through the centre of the city to the legations, arriving through the water gate in advance of the American troops. As they entered the Legation Quarter, they received a rapturous welcome by those who had been besieged there.

Having communicated with Minister Conger, General Chaffee withdrew the troops from the legation and they set up camp for the night just outside the Tartar wall. American casualties were light. They had suffered 8 wounded in the 14th Infantry, 1 wounded in F Battery, Fifth Artillery and the Marines had 1 officer and 2 men wounded.

At 7pm M Troop entered the city as the guard to the wagon train. They had been waiting outside Peking for some time by the Avenue of Statues near the Ming tombs so Sydney was relieved to be finally moving again. He looked at his surroundings with interest. All around him he could see evidence of the siege. Barricades built from every conceivable type of material blockaded the streets. The majority incorporated native brick and were topped with sandbags made from sheets, pillowcases, dress materials and curtains. Many of the legations were in ruins and although the Russian, British and American ones were still standing, the walls were pitted with bullet holes from small arms and there were large holes from shell fire.

The children looked pale and wan due to the lack of proper food, but most of the adults seemed cheerful. Their daily rations were very tiny and had included a small piece of horse or mule every day. The Christian Chinese had resorted to killing dogs for meat. It was obvious that they had suffered greatly, not least from not knowing whether they would be rescued.

The Chinese had used the part of the Imperial City opposite the Chien-men gate to fire on the legations and this was General Chaffee's next target. Early on the 15th he placed four guns on the Tartar wall at the Chien-men gate. From there they could fire on the walls to the west of the next gate where there was some opposition supported by poor artillery. At 8am the Chinese opened fire on the Chien-men gate from the second gate of the Imperial City, north of the Chien-men gate. The Americans immediately retaliated with fire onto the first gate. Within a short while Lieutenant Charles P. Summerall of Reilly's battery had cleared the opposition and opened the gate and the American troops poured through. They were met with a hail of fire from the next gate about 600yd away. They returned fire on the second gate with the artillery and as many infantry as could be elevated on the Tartar walls and side walls of the Imperial city. It took half an hour but eventually all Chinese fire died away and Colonel Daggett led his regiment forward to the second gate. Lieutenant Summerall directed his artillery on the second gate and the Americans soon silenced any opposition. They continued with this strategy for four gates and the Chinese were driven from each gate in turn. The final gate was close to the palace grounds and was defended by Imperial Guards.

The commanders held a further conference at which it was decided not to occupy the Imperial City. General Chaffee withdrew the main body of his troops back to the camp they had occupied the previous night while maintaining his position on the Tartar wall at the Chien-men gate. However, not everyone agreed with this decision and the following day they held another conference. This time the generals decided they should occupy the Imperial City. The Americans immediately proceeded to reoccupy the grounds they had won on 15 August and the 9th Infantry was placed on guard at the gate where the attack had halted.

The assault had not been without casualties. The 9th Infantry had 2 men killed and 4 wounded, the 14th Infantry 3 men killed and 14 wounded and Captain Henry J. Reilly, 5th Artillery, was shot in the mouth and killed instantly while standing at the general's side observing the effects of his artillery barrage.

By the evening of the 14th all the forces had reached their own legation and a plan was formed to retake the Pei-t'sang cathedral which was still under siege by the Boxers. The small force that had defended it, including several priests, had held out against all the odds and had saved the lives of 2,500 nuns and native converts. They were finally relieved on the 16th.

At 7am on 15 August the 6th Cavalry followed the artillery into the square within the Tartar City gate. They had been there about 2 hours, awaiting further orders, when they were suddenly attacked by Chinese sharp shooters. One horse was killed and another two wounded. Spotting the snipers in trees about 300yd to their left, the troop commander ordered four or five of his best shots to open fire on them. Sydney had already shown himself to be an accurate shot and he needed no more encouragement. Within moments the snipers had fallen from the trees and the men ceased fire.

The next conference on 16 August divided the Chinese and Tartar cities between the various forces so they could effectively police and protect the inhabitants. The Americans were assigned the west half of the Chinese city and the section of the Tartar City that lay between the Chien-men gate and Shun-chin gate of the south wall of the Tartar City and north to the east and west through the Tartar City. The border was the east wall of the Imperial City.

It was important to safeguard the Pei-ho River so that boats could continue to carry supplies and transport the wounded and sick to Tientsin. To ensure this, troops were left at several points along the way. At Pei-tsang 400 men including G Company from the 9th Infantry were left. At Yang-tsun 800 French were left, and at Ho-shi-wu 100 Japanese, 50 British and 50 Americans (C Company, 9th Infantry) were left under command of a British officer. At Matow 50 Americans and 50 British were left under an American officer along with a further 150 men who were physically unable to continue. They were under the command of Captain Alfred Hasbrouck from 14th Infantry.

At Tong-Chow 800 Japanese (1 battalion), 400 Russians, 50 British and 50 Americans (Marines) were deployed. A further 50 Marines were detailed as guards at the river in conjunction with 100 British troops.

However, the relief of the Peking legations and the cathedral did not signal the end of the Boxer Rebellion. Trouble continued in other cities throughout September and October and Sydney was to see more action in China before leaving for Manila at the end of the year.

Chapter Eight

The Occupation of China

The foreign powers were now garrisoned in Northern China so, to keep American troops out of trouble and to uphold the honour of the country, on 29 August Captain Cabell of the 6th Cavalry issued orders to prevent looting of property and ill treatment of Chinese citizens. There was at least one court martial for rape during this time as the Americans sought to keep order and foster friendly relations with the Chinese. Orders were given that the men were also to ensure they remained healthy and as such all precautions against epidemics were to be taken, including the requirement that all drinking water should be boiled. No vegetables that matured on the surface or immediately below the surface were to be bought with Army funds and if they were bought in an emergency they were to be boiled thoroughly before being eaten. Soldiers were to abstain from eating uncooked vegetables such as lettuce, radishes, turnips and tomatoes.

By the beginning of September further orders stipulated that no troops of soldiers should leave the city without an officer and that no enlisted men should discharge weapons unless in personal danger. It was the duty of all officers to arrest any soldiers violating this order and to deliver them immediately to the commanding officer of the nearest American troops. Enlisted men were not allowed to leave camps or quarters, whether individually or in groups, with arms except when on duty. Those stationed

A photograph Sydney had taken of himself in Hong Kong, 1900.

in Peking were not allowed to leave the American sectors or the direct road connecting them without a written or printed pass signed by a commissioned officer that specified the objective of the bearer.

The trouble continued but the Boxers were no match for a properly trained army and they did not have the support of the Chinese people. The troops of the International Force, except the British and American, proceeded to ransack the Forbidden City and many treasures found their way back to Europe.

On 19 August the 6th US Cavalry, mounted with carbines and pistols, left camp after receiving orders to make a reconnaissance with a force of British troops which they would meet at the Racetrack gate at 5am. The reconnaissance was to locate a possible force of Imperial troops which had been reported west of Tientsin. Their orders were quite specific. They were not to engage with any Imperial troops they came across, other than to gauge their strength; they were to walk the horses and not cover more than 15 miles including the return back to camp and they would only be supplied with one day's rations. However, things did not work out as planned.

Two squadrons of the 6th Cavalry composed of A, C, D, I, K and L Troops with all the available men, plus a detachment from the hospital, left the camp near Taku at 4am and marched to the Racetrack gate. They crossed the canal there at about 4.30am. Lieutenant Gaussen with twenty-five men of the Bengal Lancers and an officer and twelve men from the Japanese cavalry also accompanied them. As the Bengal Lancers were familiar with the country for several miles in the direction of their intended march they were appointed to accompany the advanced guard, which was Captain Blocksom's squadron consisting of A, C and D Troops. They were followed closely by the Bengal Lancers and then Forsyth's Squadron of I, K and L Troops.

Shortly after 6am, about 3 miles west of the Racetrack gate, they began to take heavy rifle fire on their right and front from long range and Private Hartsfield was severely wounded in the hand.

Captain Blocksom immediately dismounted the entire First Squadron including the advanced guard and formed a skirmish line. The 25th Bengal Lancers under Lieutenant Gaussen formed up on their left. They advanced slowly forward, driving the enemy through a large cornfield for nearly a mile, until they reached an open plain which was full of hills. It was impossible to tell how many Chinese there were in front of them, but it was easy to see that the main body was in a line parallel to them and overlapped both their left and right flanks by nearly a mile. The enemy formed the arc of a circle about 4 miles in length facing east, southeast and south. The Americans estimated that there were about 4,000, entrenched in front of three or four villages. They appeared to be armed with both large- and small-bore rifles and several old-fashioned field pieces shooting slugs and scrap iron. Several horses in C Troop were hit.

As the dismounted cavalry pushed forward the Chinese began abandoning weapons, including the improvised field pieces known as 'jingals'. This was the name given by the British to Chinese rampart guns from the 1700s to the Second World War. Originally muzzle loaded, they had exceptionally long barrels and were used as a kind of precision artillery. The jingals they found in the cornfield had their barrels thrust through the back of a rickshaw. From a distance the gun appeared to be a rapid fire gun with a shield.

Opposite the left flank there was a battery of nine guns which fired volleys every so often. Fortunately, they were nearly always ineffective, although two men and three horses were struck. Trumpeter Corrigan was wounded seriously in the head and Private McCormick through the left side. The Squadron Commander's trumpeter was also wounded at the same time. Afterwards they discovered that these were jingals attached to rickshaws.

Although they managed to advance slowly for another mile, they were soon halted by the ferocity of the opposition and the number of bodies blocking their way. Captain Blocksom halted the line after a further 800yd into the plain and tried to find the correct range for the guns. Although this ranged from 900 to 1500yd, it was hard to tell which was the most effective as the enemy were continually jumping up and down with their banners, of which there were about a dozen. This made it difficult to see where the artillery shells were landing. The Boxers tried several times to charge the American forces, but were never able to get closer than 700 or 800yd.

When the initial fire fight broke out Lieutenant Forsyth was ordered to dismount two of his troops and get them into action as soon as possible. He extended the right of the line with two of the dismounted troops and left the third in reserve and as a guard for the horses. He left L Troop under Lieutenant Scales and took R and I Troops under Captain Paddock and

Lieutenant Karnes forward through the cornfield to a small village. K Troop were sent round to the right and I Troop to the left and on the west formed a skirmish line. Once in position they began moving forward towards the sound of the firing. But the cornfield was so dense and the corn so high they couldn't see anything in front of them at all.

The village on the left front was still occupied by the enemy who were successfully preventing any advance so Captain Blocksom halted and waited for reinforcements. For the next hour the line hardly moved forward at all and they kept firing to a minimum as they waited for the Japanese and British infantry to assault the enemy on the right flank. He knew the Japanese and British infantry had arrived before he saw them as the enemy began moving quickly towards their left flank.

As soon as Lieutenant Forsyth emerged from the cornfield he realised the enemy was massing on their left front so he moved his squadron up to connect up with the First Squadron. The enemy were still busy trying to work their way round his right flank so he had to keep moving his squadron to the right. He eventually reached the firing line at about 7.15am.

Once the reinforcements arrived Lieutenant Colonel Wint ordered Blocksom to advance on his left flank. While the fighting raged all around them, they continued to rain down heavy fire on the village and on the enemy who were still trying to pass on their right.

Earlier Captain Blocksom had bought the horses of the First Squadron up to the firing line so they were ready if needed for a charge. Lieutenant Marshall now asked for permission to do this, which Captain Blocksom readily gave. He was to follow himself with two other troops.

At about 8am the men drew their pistols and readied themselves for the charge. The majority had never been in a charge before, even in drill, but they steadied themselves and waited for the signal.

The three troops charged forward using their pistols and reached the first line of the enemy after about 500yd. Once they had emptied their pistols the men drew their sabres and the hand-to-hand fighting began with several of the enemy fighting to the end. Private Van Sickle was wounded in the back and the right thigh with a lance.

They charged through them for about a mile, killing about 150 and capturing 601, of whom 3 were wounded. Only about a third of the enemy had rifles, the majority were carrying swords and spears and although they put up a spirited resistance at first, they soon broke and ran back to the rear on the left. The third squadron, back on the skirmish line, killed a considerable number of those fleeing across its front during the charge. More prisoners might have been taken if they'd followed them, but the horses were not yet acclimatised to the heat and the day was very warm.

Lieutenant Forsyth and his squadron remained on the firing line until the First Squadron charged then they were ordered by Lieutenant Colonel Wint to send one troop to occupy and hold the village on their right and for the other two troops to follow and support Captain Blocksom. K Troop under Captain Paddock was sent to hold the village and Lieutenant Forsyth took I and L Troops to follow Blocksom. But by that time the First Squadron had been recalled so they halted and waited for further orders.

The Americans set fire to the hostile villages and remained in the area of the burning villages for another hour, but the Chinese did not return so they rode slowly back to camp, arriving at about 1.30pm. They had captured all the flags as well as some breech-loading rifles, swords, lances and several large jingals mounted on wheelbarrows. Most of the arms were captured by individuals who took them as souvenirs. Huadshiadsh and Yanshitsuai and four other villages were burned to the ground and there were between 350 and 500 dead Boxers, over 150 killed by the cavalry in their charge. The 6th US Cavalry had 12 officers and 890 men engaged in the action of whom 6 were wounded. Enemy forces in the area were estimated to have been in the region of 20,000 and those engaged by the 6th US Cavalry to have been between 5,000 and 7,000.

The action relieved Tientsin from the considerable Boxer force building up on the outskirts that was increasing daily and made the supply and communication lines more secure. Several awards were made to the 6th US Cavalry for their bravery in the action. Lieutenant Colonel T.J. Wint was brevetted Colonel for gallant conduct and Captain Blocksom was brevetted Major for gallant conduct for his part in the battle.

Of the 202 men who started out in the First Squadron only 8 were wounded, 2 seriously. There were 4 horses killed, 1 of these under Lieutenant Marshall. A further 10 were wounded and 2 were lost in the charge after throwing their riders and running away.

On 26 August I and K Troops were ordered to make another reconnaissance westward and locate supplies, visit coal mines and gather information about the country in the surrounding area. They left at 6am on 27 August by the northwest gate of the Chinese city. Their interpreter, Mr Robert Coltman, doubted they would be able to cross the Hun Ho (Muddy River) so they went southwest to Lu-kou-chiao, a walled city, and crossed the Hun Ho at the Marco Polo bridge. Because of the detour it was impossible to reach the coal mines and return back to camp in one day. At Lu-kou-chiao, the place where the railroad from Peking to the capital of the province crossed the river by means of a substantial iron bridge, they found about 200 tons of fine coal and 50 tons of lump coal. The only damage they could see to the railroad and bridge was the removal of the ties. The rails were lying alongside the roadbed and were undamaged.

The interpreter spoke to the local inhabitants who informed them that the coal mine was northwest of Lu-kou-chiao, so they set off in that direction. The country they travelled through was all cultivated with vegetables and corn and the local inhabitants were busy about their work, showing little fear of the troops. They frequently offered them tea and fruit and there did not appear to be any Boxers in the area.

They eventually reached the coal mine at about 2pm. It was not being worked and the coal there was of a poor quality. The mandarin from the village informed them through the interpreter that the coal mines that supplied the city of Peking were located 7 miles north of the village. However, they weren't being worked either and it was unlikely there was any coal there as the coal companies only worked the mines when there were coal orders to fill. The coal, once mined, would then be transferred over the Hun Ho, a distance of 16 miles by the ferry road. They never stockpiled coal in anticipation of orders. The troops turned and headed back to Peking, reaching camp at 9pm that night.

On 28 August three troops of the 6th US Cavalry, I, K and L, were ordered to the Chinese hunting park southeast of the city to forage for some white rice that was supposed to be located close to the park, about 6 miles from the southern gate of Peking. The 14th Infantry volunteered to go with them and they also took a Chinese man who knew the exact location of the rice. Reports stated that the rice was being guarded by about a thousand

Boxers so the real purpose of the expedition was to ascertain whether there were any Boxers in the vicinity. They took two interpreters, Mr Lowry and Mr Coltman, and the Chinese guide. On approach to the southern wall of the park, K Troop, which was the advance guard, was fired on by a small group on horses and from an old Buddha temple directly in front of them. One of the sergeants of K Troop reported back that there was a party of about 200 Boxers a mile and a half ahead on the left. There were about seven flags and twenty of the Boxers were mounted.

L Troop dismounted and was sent forward to fight on foot in support of the advance guard. By the time Lieutenant Forsyth had reached them the Boxers had fled southwards out of the park, either through the gate or by scaling the walls. However there was still a group of about fifteen or twenty inside the temple. A detachment was sent to chase them out while the rest of L Troop was ordered after those who had fled the park. But by then the Boxers had scattered in all directions so orders were given to burn the village, just inside the South Gate, in which they had first taken refuge.

Back at the temple the fighting was still raging, but eventually the detachment took it killing fourteen Boxers. Outside the park three others who had escaped by scaling the walls were killed. A further seventeen were killed near the buildings east of the park and four in a village outside the park. The cavalry had taken no casualties as the opposing fire was high and wide and those inside the temple were only armed with swords and lances. They found 200,000–250,000lb of rice stored in the palace as well as some old-fashioned firearms, 1,000lb powder, some flags, lances and swords. All the weapons were destroyed. They also discovered a herd of thirty-nine head of cattle which they took back and handed over to the subsistence department. Virtually all the buildings in the vicinity of the rice store were destroyed. The Chinese guide informed them that this was the home of a Boxer general.

The troops marched 2 miles further east and then turned northwards to the granaries. They were hoping to find a party of Boxers that had been seen on their left, but they were nowhere to be seen. The granaries were in a group of fortified barracks previously occupied by Imperial troops but there was no rice there either. Lieutenant Buchan searched the buildings and then prepared a report considering their possible suitability as a quarter for the troops. The central part of the park was a large plain, slightly undulating and unobstructed by buildings, walls, trees or shrubs. However near the wall on the southeast there were inhabited buildings and large fields of corn.

On 5 September a further patrol was sent out as men from K and M Troops scouted the country to the southeast of the city for about 10 miles. They found no Boxers in the vicinity at all and the inhabitants were friendly as they tended to their crops of corn, millet and vegetables. The roads were dirt, though, and would prove troublesome in heavy rain.

Finally recognising they were unable to defeat the foreign powers the Dowager-Empress called Li Hung-chang[1] to Peking to negotiate a settlement with the foreigners. Peace was finally established after considerable discussions and on 7 September the Boxer Protocol was signed. This laid out the terms and conditions for peace between China and the powers of Germany, Austro-Hungary, Belgium, Spain, USA, Great Britain, Italy, Japan, Netherlands and Russia.

The main points of the protocol included paying reparations of 450,000,000 taels (approximately $335 million) over thirty-nine years with an interest of 4 per cent per year and agreeing to the Legation Quarter remaining under exclusive control of the foreign powers and each legation having its own defence force. The foreign powers were given the right to occupy Huang-tsun, Lang-fang, Yang-tsin, Chun-liang, Tong-ku, Lu-tai, Tong-shan, Lan-chou, Chang-li, Chin-wang Tao and Shan-hai Kuan. Those they considered as instigators of the uprising were to be punished. Tsai-Hsun, Prince Chuang, Ying-Nien and Chao-chiao were sentenced to commit suicide. Tsai-li, Prince Tuan, Tsai-Lan and Duke Fu-kuo were sentenced to execution or deportation to Turkestan and life imprisonment. Kang Yi, Hsu Tang and Li Ping-heng received posthumous degradation. Chinese control over their own internal administration and national defence was also affected as was the economy which had to levy enormous taxes to pay the reparation. Including interest, over thirty-nine years, China paid out over 900,000,000 taels.

The third squadron of 6th US Cavalry set out on 14 September to Tong-Chow. They rode 27 miles and camped the first night on the Uhinng Kan River. With them were Robert Holtman, the interpreter, and six Chinese guides.

They crossed the river about a mile above the city after having to tie stringers to poles with rope and laying down boards to make the road bed. About a mile further on they forded the Pei-I-Io. The banks were very muddy and the current fast flowing. In some parts of the river the water was 4ft deep but the bottom was hard so the crossing was not that difficult. While they were crossing the river one of the horses from K Troop became excited and unsaddled its rider. The horse became tangled in its halter strap and bridle reins and began floating downstream. He ended up on the nearby bank where he was rescued by Private John Rudy of K Troop riding bareback on another horse. Private Rudy bought both horses back to the ford and led them into the water but as they neared the far bank one of the horses began to plunge and dragged the other down with it, trapping Private Rudy between them. Fortunately, Private Rudy and both horses were unhurt.

In the village near where they camped, Chu Dten, the missionary Mr Ament searched a house whose owner had fled. He found a quantity of ammunition, firearms and characteristic Boxer swords. The house was burned down and the arms thrown into the river.

The following day they marched northeasterly for about 16 miles to Hsuch-chuang-tsz. At about 9am, while passing through the village, Captain Cabell spotted several Chinese with guns disappearing round the corner of a wall and the troops gave chase. They were fired on from the wall of a large enclosure containing several houses owned by a rich Boxer leader. The men quickly returned fire and then dismounted to chase the enemy as they dispersed. Unfortunately, as they returned fire one of the Chinese guides was also killed. He was armed and had climbed onto the roof of one of the buildings in the enclosure. But as he was dressed no differently from the Boxers one of the troopers shot him, mistaking him for the enemy.

Directly across the street from where the shots had come from was another building owned by the same Boxer chief. They forced the gate and after a careful search they found a pile of new Boxer uniforms, a number of rifles, Boxer lances, swords, bows, arrows, pistols, powder and cartridges. The Chinese guides began to pillage the properties of the Boxer chief and the troops asked Mr Ament to intervene to stop them. He had little influence so eventually he was told that if they did not stop and return the property they had stolen, the American forces would immediately return to Peking.

This threat appeared to have the desired effect as the property was put back. The troops set about removing a Chinese lady who was said to be mad and then set fire to the buildings. As soon as they were sure the buildings would be destroyed the troops mounted up and resumed their march. A few miles further on the air shook with an enormous explosion indicating the buildings had contained considerable amounts of ammunition they had missed.

At noon the advanced guard was fired on from a small village near the foothills of the Emtern Mountains and in the skirmish that followed one Boxer was killed, another wounded and the third escaped. The others scattered. At about 8pm they reached Yongkichon where they had been told one of the rich Boxer leaders lived. However, they encountered no opposition and the inhabitants were very friendly. The house of the reputed Boxer leader was searched but there was nothing to show he was a Boxer or a rich man. According to the villagers, the man himself had fled taking his riches with him. The leaders of the village were called together and Captain Forsyth explained that they had not come to harm innocent people but that Christians should not be persecuted and should be afforded the same rights and protection as everyone else and that they, the leaders, would be held responsible that this was done.

They finally reached Wastz at 5pm. It was here they were expecting to find some more Christians, but they were informed by the two who had joined them on the road that the Christians could be found at Sunkochuani or Hsinchuani, about 6 miles on the Sanho road from Wastz. Sanho was about 30 miles via Pingku and it was about 17 miles to Sanho via Sunkochuani or Hsinchuani. They were further informed that there were Boxers, Imperial troops and cannon at both places and that there was a company of Boxers about 2 miles away at Choochiaying and they were were anxious to fight.

Captain Forsyth decided that there was not time to visit both places, especially as when they did meet them they would spend several hours speaking to them. He decided to abandon the idea of going to Pingku and instead go to Chochiaying and disperse the Boxers there. From there they could go to Sunkochuang and then to Sanho.

On the morning of the 16th they headed for Choochiaying and on to Sunkochuang but did not find any Boxers there. They did find 12 Christians,

5 males and 7 females, who they placed in 2 carts and took with them. They reached Sanho by 2pm but there were no Boxers, Imperial troops or Christians, however the people were friendly, the stores were open and everything seemed normal. The mandarin was sent for and given the same message as the leading men of the Yongkichon.

The march continued through Po-fu-tu-wah, Hsiatien and Yneyu where the populations were friendly, everything was normal and the streets were full of Chinese going about their everyday business. It was market day in Yneyu and the streets were impassable with stalls selling vegetables, fruit and other food stuffs. They rescued four more Christians in Chaoli, about 5 miles east of Tung-Chow and finally reached the Pei-ho at about 1pm. They forded the river and then made camp at Tung-Chow. Here they sent for a boat for the Christians who boarded it the following day and went back to Peking.

The troops remained at Tung-Chow all day on 18 September, making the 18-mile journey back to Peking on the 19th after receiving a telegram ordering their immediate return. During their patrol they did not see any sheep and only a few rather old cattle.

After the foreign powers entered the Forbidden City the Dowager-Empress, Tz'u-hsi, fled the city to Sian and although she returned a year later the Ching Dynasty had lost its power forever.

As the situation stabilised the men were given some leave. Many chose to go to Hong Kong where like Sydney they would have had their photos taken.

Sydney also had two tattoos while he was in China. On one arm he had a Chinese lady and the other he had a snake curling round his arm. Its tail was on his upper arm and its head was on the back of his wrist. He complained that tattooing the tendons on the back of his wrist had been extremely painful. The tattoo was hidden by the cuffs of his shirt and only those who knew him well would have realised it was there. He also bought back another souvenir from China, a pigtail of one of the Boxer rebels who had been executed. Fortunately, this appears to have disappeared, probably thrown away at some point! The men in the family were always interested in Sydney's tales of adventures including macabre details such as soldiers betting on how many times the eyes would blink after the head of a rebel had been severed from his body.

The two squadrons of the 6th US Cavalry remained in China until the end of November when they were recalled to the Philippines. They had seen little action, but the experience was one Sydney would never forget.

The successful conclusion of the Boxer Rebellion gave the Allies a foothold in Northern China and access to its natural resources. For the Chinese it was a disaster that led to the eventual fall of the Manchu Dynasty in 1912 and reduced their prestige as a world power. It also placed them second to Japan as an Asian power. Japan would go on to defeat the Russians in the Russo-Japanese War (8 February 1904–5 September 1905) and further increase their dominance in the Far East.

Chapter Nine

Back to the Philippines: December 1900–1902

The plan called for Major General Arthur MacArthur to keep the Filipino Army on the Plains of central Luzon while Major General Henry Lawton's cavalry moved northeast and closed the mountain passes. At the same time Brigadier General Lloyd Wheaton would land his force 150 miles north of Manila at Lingayan Gulf. Unfortunately, Wheaton and Lawton failed to link up in time to stop Aguinaldo from fleeing into the mountains, although he was nearly caught by Brigadier General Samuel M.B. Young's 1,100 cavalrymen who had moved north extremely quickly.

On 2 December 1899 a battalion of the 33rd Infantry Regiment under Major Peyton C. March reached the Tila Pass where the commander of Aguinaldo's bodyguard, Brigadier General Gregorio del Pilar, was waiting. The Filipinos opened fire killing several men from the 33rd and blocking their advance. They were on a narrow trail with a gorge one side and a 1,500ft-high mountain on the other so March ordered a company to climb the mountain and outflank the Filipinos. This they did and when they finally opened fire from the summit, successfully killing del Pilar, March led the rest of the men in a frontal charge. Aguinaldo had escaped again, but by February 1900 the American troops had scattered his forces and broken the back of his army.

Realising they could not defeat the Americans head on, Aguinaldo and his top commanders resorted to guerrilla warfare. However, it was very difficult for Aguinaldo to coordinate an effective offensive from his remote hideaway in the mountains leaving his generals with almost complete autonomy. This meant the intensity and nature of the resistance varied from place to place. The south and Central Luzon were the major centres of unrest. Bands of guerrillas, thirty to fifty strong, lived in the hills, cutting telegraph wires, attacking army patrols and supply wagons and firing into towns.

The Americans tried to overcome this by setting up Filipinos in positions of government such as police chiefs and mayors, but in some areas the Filipinos set up parallel structures, often using the same people already selected by the Americans. Even those not involved in resistance would not help the Americans, either by passing on information or giving up sympathisers, for fear of violent retribution by the nationalist movement which was known as the Katipunan Society.

Early in 1900 General Arthur MacArthur had replaced General Otis and he was determined to make it more difficult for the guerrillas to operate. At his disposal he had 70,000 combat-experienced men, two-thirds of the whole army, and they were supported by locally recruited soldiers from ethnic groups already suspicious of the Tagalogs, such as the Macabebes and Illocanos.

General MacArthur frequently clashed with William Howard Taft who had been sent to oversee the transition from military rule to civilian rule in the more peaceful areas. Under Taft soldiers built schools, improved sanitation and vaccination, set up native courts and municipal elections. In these areas, despite the harsh treatment meted out to the guerrillas and their supporters, most Filipinos were friendly toward the American troops. By the end of 1900, encouraged by William Taft, several well-known Filipinos set up the Partido Federal and began touring the country campaigning for statehood for the Philippines.

On 20 December MacArthur declared martial law and invoked General Orders 100 (GO 100). This required the occupying army to behave humanely in its dealings with civilians and at the same time put a duty on civilians not to resist. If they did resist they would be treated harshly and those combatants not in uniform would be treated as highway robbers or pirates and subject to the death penalty.

By the end of December 1900 the two squadrons of the 6th US Cavalry which had deployed to China arrived in Manila where they were reunited with the rest of the regiment. The next two years would be spent fighting the insurgents who were still active despite the introduction of martial law. Sydney viewed his new surroundings with interest. It had taken him slightly longer than expected to reach the Philippines, but he was much more experienced now and looking forward to seeing some more action.

Now martial law had been introduced the Americans extended their operations to Southern Luzon and the Visayan Islands of Leyte, Samar, Panay, Negros and Cebu. The command viewed everyone as either a guerrilla or a supporter so before long the Navy began shelling the coastal villages on the Visayan Islands as a prelude to invasion. In the first two months of 1901 the whole 51,000 population of the Marinduque Islands were ordered into 5 'concentration' camps. These camps had been used by the US Army against the Indians, although in America they were called reservations and the British were using the same tactic to defeat the Boers in South Africa.

On 8 January 1901 at his HQ in San Isidro, Northern Luzon, Brigadier General Frederick Funston received a telegram informing him that some of Aguinaldo's couriers, together with despatches, had surrendered to an American garrison and told them where Aguinaldo was hiding. Funston was delighted, but the approaches to the remote village of Palanan in the Sierra Madre Mountains were well guarded. This made it almost impossible for the Americans to get close enough to capture Aguinaldo without his receiving warning and escaping.

Funston hatched a plan that entailed using Macabebes scouts posing as Aguinaldo's reinforcements and Funston and four other American officers posing as their prisoners. This way they could get close to Aguinaldo without alarming him and then capture him. On 6 March 79 Macabebes scouts, 4 American officers, 4 renegade rebels and 1 Spanish intelligence officer left Manila Bay aboard a US Navy gunboat. To avoid suspicion they landed 100 miles south of their objective and began the long hike north. It rained continually as they hacked their way through thick jungle and overflowing streams and because they had not bought enough rations they eventually resorted to eating snails and limpets. When they were 10 miles from Palanan they received a letter from Aguinaldo telling them not to bring their American prisoners to the hideout, instead he would send men to take custody of them. Determined not to turn back, the Americans drew back from the Macabebes and followed some way behind them. The Macabebes were soon welcomed into the insurgent camp and then they struck, taking Aguinaldo and his men so much by surprise that there was little resistance. The rebel leader even asked Funston if it was a joke.

Aguinaldo was well treated by his captors and on 19 April 1901 he issued a proclamation asking his fellow guerrillas to give up and accept American sovereignty. Over 4,000 guerrillas surrendered in the next few months, however, the fighting continued. Sydney and the rest of the US 6th Cavalry did not take part in any major battles, however, they were continually on their guard when they left the confines of the garrison. The heat and humidity, the flies, mosquitoes and ever present danger soon became wearing and it was not long before Sydney began to look forward to returning to the American mainland.

Diseases were rife, including venereal diseases and many men regretted their choice of entertainment. There was also the constant threat of isolated guerrilla action which also took its toll on the Americans.

On 28 September 1901, 48 men of the 9th US Infantry were killed in a surprise attack on their garrison at Balangiga on Samur Island. There had been extensive fraternisation between the Americans and local civilians in Balangiga until on 22 September two drunken American soldiers tried to molest a Filipino girl in a local store. She was rescued by her two brothers who attacked the soldiers. In retaliation Captain Thomas Connell, the Company Commander, rounded up 143 male residents and made them clean the town in preparation for an official visit by his superior officers. They were kept overnight without food in the town plaza under tents that could only accommodate sixteen people. He then ordered the confiscation and destruction of all stored rice which only served to increase tensions. The townspeople plotted their revenge, masterminded by Valeriano Abanador, the local chief of police. He was helped by two guerrilla officers, Captain Eugenio Daza and Sergeant Pedro Duran, Sr, and Casiana 'Geronima' Nacionales. Feelings against the Americans were so strong that nearly all the families in Balangiga were represented in the 700-strong attack force.

On the 27th Private Adolph Gamlin reported that all the women and children had left the town, but no one took any notice of him. At 6.45am on 28 September Abanador grabbed Private Gamlin's rifle and knocked him unconscious. He then turned the rifle on the men in the Sergeants' Mess, wounding one man. As he shouted attack, the church bells rang signalling the start of the assault.

The guards outside the municipal hall were killed as the Filipinos stormed the building. The guards outside the convent were also killed and the Filipinos in the church, who were dressed as women in an attempt to disguise the evacuation of the women from the town, broke through into the convent. Here they hacked the soldiers to death before they could grab their weapons. However, although they had now successfully occupied the municipal building and the convent, they did not have sufficient forces to overrun the mess tent and the barracks. Company C troops retook these buildings and Private Gamlin recovered consciousness and began shooting Filipinos (Private Gamlin survived the assault and died, aged 90, in 1969).

Although Abanador ordered a retreat, the surviving Americans escaped by native canoes to Basey, about 20 miles away. The townspeople quickly buried their dead and then abandoned the town. Captain Bookmillar, Commander G Company of the 9th US Infantry, commandeered a civilian steamer and headed to Balangiga. When he arrived he found it deserted, except for the dead and wounded of C Company. Of the 78-man contingent, 48 men were dead and 22 were severely wounded. The guerrillas suffered 28 dead and 22 wounded and they managed to capture 100 rifles and 25,000 rounds of ammunition.

Retribution was swift and brutal. Captain Bookmillar burned the town to the ground and General 'Howlin' Jake' Smith ordered his men to kill all those over the age of 10 during the vicious Samur campaign that followed.

On 27 December 1901 the Americans approached a village in Samur and were told to kill everything that moved. The shooting began when they spotted a small boy coming down the mountain path. The bullet missed, but the sound of the shooting brought the villagers out of their homes in alarm. Although they were unarmed, they were all shot, those that fled were pursued and shot and those that remained in their houses died in the flames as the Americans burned the village to the ground.

Samur was not the only place to cause the Americans problems. In Batangas province in Southern Luzon they were faced with dogged resistance from General Miguel Malvar. Malvar was originally a businessman who joined the Katipunan to fight the Spanish. After the Spanish arrested his father in retaliation for Malvar's successful raid in Talisay, Batangas, Malvar immediately led another raid and successfully rescued his father. He then moved to Cavite and joined up with Aguinaldo. After successfully leading his troops in several battles he was soon promoted to General and then commanding General of Batangas.

When the Pact of Biak-na-Bato bought about temporary peace he left for Hong Kong with Aguinaldo as treasurer of the revolutionary funds. He returned to the Philippines with 2,000 rifles. When the insurrection broke out in 1898 he took part in several more battles and was soon in charge of all the provinces in Southern Luzon. After Aguinaldo's capture on 23 March 1901 he assumed command of all the Filipino forces and the fight continued.

E Troop of the 6th US Cavalry had several skirmishes with insurgents between 28 March and 16 May 1901 and on 26 April Lieutenant Anderson with a detachment of 6th US Cavalry attacked insurgents near Talisay, Batangas. They killed one man and captured eight Filipinos.

To try and put an end to the resistance in Batangas General Chaffee, fresh from the successes in China, appointed Brigadier General J. Franklin Bell to deal with the problem. Beginning in early December 1901 he forced all law-abiding Filipinos to move their livestock and all household goods into towns controlled by the US Army. They were given two weeks to do so. Any able-bodied man found outside these protected areas without a pass would be arrested and locked up or shot if he tried to escape. Anyone suspected of helping the guerrillas would not be charged and tried. Instead, they would be arrested and detained for an indefinite period of time. His junior officers were told to use whatever methods they saw fit, anything that would make the Filipinos desire peace. On 13 December Bell declared that if any Americans were killed a prisoner or prominent member of the community would be shot in retaliation. Two days later he announced that any hostile acts would result in the starvation of prisoners. On 28 December Bell ordered that all rice and other food stuffs found outside the camp would be confiscated and destroyed, wells would be poisoned and all farm animals slaughtered.

On 1 January 1901, just after Sydney and the rest of the 6th US Cavalry arrived back in Manila, searches began throughout the whole of Batangas and neighbouring provinces. A total of 2,500 men in columns of 50 set out to destroy everything and everyone in their path.

In April 1901 the Americans began major operations in Northern Luzon. Whole villages were burned and storehouses and crops were destroyed. This led one anonymous Congressman to remark that there was never any trouble in Northern Luzon because there was nobody left there to rebel. There were no prisoners taken and no records kept. At Sorsogen American soldiers testified that approximately 1,100 Filipino prisoners were made to dig their own graves in groups of 20 and were then shot. The War Department dismissed the claims as they did with any rumours of atrocities.

To finish off the insurgency 4,000 soldiers were sent into the Batangas region, their orders to search each valley, mountain and ravine and destroy any crops and insurgents they came across. Numerous atrocities ensued.

Eventually, there were upwards of 300,000 people in the concentration zones. This had the desired effect of cutting off the guerrillas from their supporters and supplies. By the time Bell had finished American government official statistics estimated that at least 100,000 people had been killed in Batangas province alone as a result of the scorched earth policy. This was a reduction in the population of a third, a figure that was reflected in the census. Like Sydney, many of the soldiers were horrified by what they saw and what they were expected to do. Their concerns were echoed by the American civil governor of Tabayas who was concerned that the policy was so brutal it was likely to breed endless years of revolution.

But the pressure finally paid off and by the end of 1901 most of Malvar's fellow generals had surrendered. Malvar fought on a little longer but eventually decided he could no longer continue to put his men through hardship.

On 16 April 1902, General Malvar surrendered. There was no more organised resistance on Luzon, although there would continue to be problems on outlying islands of Mindanao and Jolo, both of which had fierce Muslim populations.

However, American victory came at a high price. Between 1898 and 1902 126,468 American soldiers had served there, although numbers were limited to 69,000 at a time. US Forces had lost 4,234 dead and 2,818 wounded and claimed to have killed 16,000 Filipinos in battle. As many as 200,000 civilians had also died from disease, famine and the harsh policies of both sides; 11,000 citizens from Batangas died in the concentration camps from disease, poor sanitation, malnutrition and various other health problems. Many died from cholera and malaria epidemics which the Americans were unable to prevent or stop. Having considered themselves morally superior to Europeans, it was a shock to many Americans back home to find out that their own military forces had used similar tactics to supress the insurgents.

On 4 July 1902 President Roosevelt declared that the Philippine emergency was over. All Filipino political prisoners were given an amnesty and civilian government established across the islands. Sydney was relieved it was over. He had seen and experienced things that had sickened him and while he enjoyed the life of a soldier he needed a break. It was time for him to find something else to do.

Chapter Ten

Back Home

Sydney was discharged from the Philippines in 1902. After that it is not entirely clear what he did. Anecdotal evidence, backed up by the photo opposite, suggests he joined one of the Canadian Reserve Forces (possibly the 10th Regiment Royal Grenadiers) for a brief time after he was discharged from the American Forces. He returned to Great Britain sometime in the next couple of years. Later documents state him having mining interests in Canada and the USA, possibly set up when he was in

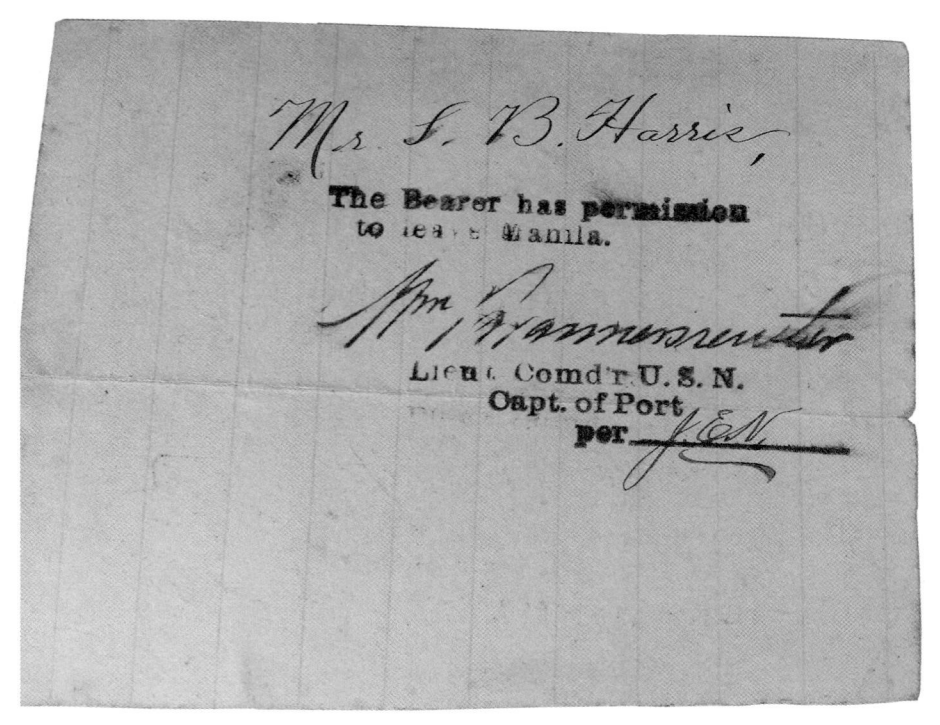

Sydney's discharge from the Philippines.

the Yukon, so this may account for his movements in the interim. The next definite date for Sydney is his marriage to Elsa de Verde Verder.

Elsa de Verde Verder was born on 5 August 1880 in Vermont, USA to Herbert and Nellie Verder (née O'Brien). Herbert Leslie Verder was born in Vermont in 1845 and Nellie O'Brien was also born in Vermont seven years later in 1852. Herbert and Nellie were married on 26 June 1878 in Castleton, Vermont. Elsa was a twin and her sister's name was Edith Mandana Verder.

On 18 April 1882 her mother gave birth to a boy, Herbert Wendell Verder, generally known as Wendell Verder. In 1884, Herbert Leslie Verder was listed in the Gazetteer and Business Directory of Vermont County as 'Verder H, L & Co. (Herbert L V and Thos J Lyon) steam baker and dealers in confectionery, 46 Centre cor Wales'. He was also listed in the same publication as 'sec of Rigby Combination Car Wheel Co, h 12 Prospect'.

In November 1887 Nellie again gave birth to twins, this time a boy and a girl.

There is anecdotal evidence that Sydney joined the Canadian Forces briefly before returning to Britain but despite several experts looking at this photograph we have been unable to identify which regiment. Sydney is on the right.

Elsa's family home in Vermont.

Sadly, both infants were stillborn and never named. To add to the tragedy, on 7 December Nellie died from childbed fever. Elsa and Edith became wards of their mother's sister, Hattie O'Brien, and moved to 53 Prospect Street, Rutland, Vermont. Hattie was listed on the 1900 US Federal Census as a governess. In 1900 their brother Herbert, who was by this time 18, was listed as living in Albany, New York as a boarder.

Elsa and her twin, Edith, as babies.

Elsa's mother, Nellie O'Brien.

Elsa's school in Rutland, Vermont.

In the Vermont Area Directories from 1889 and 1891 Elsa's father Herbert is still listed as living at 12 Prospect Street and in 1892 he had branched out into real estate. Sadly, Herbert died on 16 August 1892 leaving his children quite a lot of money. Some of the money appears to have come from Elsa's grandfather, Daniel, who owned land in Rutland. Elsa and Edith seemed to have travelled around quite a bit. Although I cannot find any record of her arriving in England, Elsa left Liverpool on 10 January 1903 and returned to New York on 18 January 1903 on the *Lucania*. For some obscure reason she is listed as male on the UK outward passenger lists yet as female on arrival! Furthermore, she does not appear to have applied for a passport until 13 November 1903 when she returned to England. Edith returned to Boston on 13 August 1902 on the *Ivernia*, however, it is not clear where she came from. There is anecdotal evidence that Edith became a nun so maybe it was something to do with that.

On 8 August 1903, at the age of 23, Edith died of hip-joint disease caused by interstitial nephritis, a disease of the kidneys. Apart from her brother Herbert, who was known as Wendell, Elsa was now alone.

Elsa and Edith, aged around 14. Elsa is on the left.

Elsa, 2 August 1897.

96 From Colonial Warrior to Western Front Flyer

A family party in Vermont, August 1899.

Elsa was very proud of her family history, her Irish roots and her connection to the Winthrops and Prudence Cummings. John Winthrop was born in Suffolk in 1588 and studied law at Cambridge. He became a Puritan and in March 1630 he and a large party of Puritans sailed to Salem, Massachusetts in the *Arbella*, arriving in June that year. He went on to settle in Boston. He was Governor of Massachusetts Colony twelve times and in 1634/5 he put the colony on defence against coercion from England. He defended Massachusetts against interference from England again in 1645/6 and died in office in 1649. He was married four times and had several children.

Prudence Cummings was a heroine of the War of Independence. Born in 1740, she married David Wright of Pepperell, Massachusetts in December 1761. They could trace their bloodline back to John Wright, who was one of the immigrant settlers of 1640. There were two parties in the colonies: the Whigs or Patriots, who wanted representation for the colonies and were sympathetic to the ideals of democracy, and the Tories who supported the church, establishment and the King. Massachusetts was considered to be the most rebellious of all the colonies and Pepperell was a Patriot town and had Minutemen who were part of a network of signals, messengers, committees and volunteer soldiers designed to continue

Elsa, 1899.

Elsa, 1902.

Elsa enjoyed dressing up and acting with her friends.

communicating with each other after Boston was occupied and town meetings closed.

On 19 April 1775 news reached the town that the Redcoats were coming, and the Colonel of the local militia left orders to the Pepperell men to mass at Groton.

Prudence was a Patriot but two of her brothers were Tories. While at her mother's house in Hollis she overheard them making plans to pass messages from the British to the north and those in Boston via the direct road which ran straight through Pepperell. Prudence immediately sent word for the thirty to forty women in the town to meet at Jewett's Bridge over the River Nashua which anyone travelling north to Boston would have to cross. The women dressed as men with old muskets, tools and pitchforks and lay in wait at the bridge. When the two dispatch riders arrived Prudence confronted them and the other women grabbed the reins of the horses. One of the men was Prudence's favourite brother, Samuel Cummings. The men were handed over to the Committee of Safety the following day and their papers sent to Charlestown. They were released on the understanding they never returned. Prudence lived until 2 December 1823 and she and her husband, David, had eleven children. Elsa, through her father's side, is related to the bloodline of Liberty Wright, Prudence and David's tenth child and fourth son, born on 30 May 1778; he died in 1877.

It's unclear where Sydney and Elsa met. There is anecdotal evidence from one part of the family that this happened sometime in London at the height of the Edwardian gaiety era and that Elsa was on the stage. However, this version is disputed by Elsa's granddaughter, Jane, who was very close to her grandmother. Her view was that Elsa did not come from the kind of family who would appear on a public stage, and she certainly would not have needed to earn a living. Jane is sure that they met in the USA, presumably when Sydney came back from the Philippines. The other possibility is that they did meet in London. Elsa came from a wealthy family and like many rich, young American ladies of the time she did the Grand Tour of Europe, probably with her sister. There are many photos of Elsa in various costumes and poses but, at that time, it was common in wealthy families for members to dress up and perform plays as part of their normal family entertainment and it might be this that has given rise to the suggestion of her being on the stage.

What is known is that Elsa and Sydney were married on 12 November 1904 with Mary Ellen Chenoweth and George William Paine as witnesses. On the

Elsa, 1902.

Elsa's bedroom in Rutland, 1902.

marriage certificate they were both listed as living at 6 Endsleigh Gardens, Euston Road and Sydney states his occupation as an insurance inspector. It was common practice for single people to rent rooms in Edwardian times and it's possible they met here. Their witnesses also lived at the same address.

Elsa's brother Wendell, now an Episcopalian bishop, and his wife, Susannah, were also in England at this time, leaving on 4 November to return to the USA. On 30 January 1905 Sydney and Elsa sailed to New York on the *Minneapolis*, returning to Dover on 27 February 1905 on the *Finland*. Their first child, Sydney Herbert Verder Harris, was born in the summer of 1905. Shortly after his birth his father joined the King's Colonials Imperial Yeomanry, later to be renamed the King Edward's Horse.

The King Edward's Horse (KEH) was formed in 1901, largely at the instigation of George Hamilton (later to become Lieutenant Colonel) who suggested that there was room in the home defences for a unit raised purely from the oversees element who were living in Britain. George Hamilton was

Elsa in Rutland, 1903.　　　　　　　Sydney, 1903.

a member of the Committee of the Colonial Club in London and envisaged something along similar lines. The Boer War had attracted considerable patriotic feeling throughout the empire and citizens from Australia, Canada, New Zealand and some local Afrikaner forces had joined up to fight with Lord Roberts' Army.

At the time, Lord Middleton, The Hon. St John Brodrick, who was then Secretary of State for War, was engaged in the reorganisation and enlargement of the Yeomanry. George Hamilton was a solicitor who had little knowledge of how the military functioned, but he used his legal mind to anticipate any obstacles that might be placed in his way. His first action was to enlist the help of an ex-regular soldier, Lieutenant Colonel N. Willoughby-Wallace, who was also a member of the Committee. He then proceeded to speak to all the colonial representatives in London.[1] All were in favour except the Agent General for New Zealand, the Hon. W.P. Reeves, although most had doubts as to whether there were enough colonials living in the country.

During the summer of 1900 an advert was placed in the London newspapers to see whether there was enough interest to make it a viable proposition. This proved successful with more than seventy men enlisting in a short time. The next step was to take it before Lord Middleton, Lord Roberts, Commander in Chief, Major General Sir Alfred Turner, Director General of Auxiliary Forces and Colonel Sir Edward Ward, Permanent Under Secretary who all agreed with the proposal. However, it was not until November 1901 that the King's Colonials, as the KEH was originally named, were officially sanctioned. The Duke of Fife, Lord Lieutenant of London volunteered to be the Regiment's Colonel in Chief and in December 1901 HRH the Prince of Wales, Duke of Cornwall and York KG became the Honorary Colonel of the regiment. Also at the end of 1901, Lieutenant Colonel Nesbit Willoughby Wallace, late of the King's Royal Rifle Corps, became the Commanding Officer. R.R. Thompson, late of the Australian Horse, was appointed Adjutant and Captain Sir Robert Baillie (Australia) and Mr John Howard (Canada) were appointed as Captains and George Hamilton (South Africa and Chile) and A.G Berry (Australia) as Lieutenants.

Their first HQ was at 30 Charing Cross Road with their Drill Hall and Recreation Rooms situated at 304 King's Road, Chelsea. Their uniform was a khaki serge tunic with a double collar with two narrow scarlet stripes on and four vertical scarlet stripes with gilt buttons on the cuffs. The trousers were khaki cord with double scarlet stripes down the seam, brown boots and leather equipment to match. The khaki was the green/brown mixture subsequently adopted as the general Army Service Dress and worn during the First World War.

The original intention had been for each squadron to represent an overseas dominion. Thus each squadron had its own badge which differed from that of the regimental badge. The proposed divisions were: 1st – British Asian Squadron, elephant badge; 2nd – Canadian Squadron, beaver and maple leaf badge; 3rd – Australian Squadron, kangaroo and a tree fern badge[2]; and 4th South African Squadron, an ostrich in front of a rising sun badge. As there was no special squadron for New Zealand, nationals from this country were able to wear a badge of a tree fern to indicate their nationality. The regimental badge had the letters 'K C' entwined under the Prince of Wales feathers with the regimental motto, '*Regi adsumus coloni*' underneath.[3] The individual badges were replaced by one regimental badge when the regiment changed its name to the King Edward's Horse in 1911.

Recruitment was brisk to start with and the first muster was held at the Drill Hall on 11 February 1902. However, the initial rush to enlist soon dropped off leaving the regiment short of strength. In order to ensure recruitment continued it was necessary to keep the regiment in the public eye. They were helped in this by King Edward whose coronation year it was and who intimated that if recruitment dropped he would summon it for inspection, thus bringing it back to the attention of the public.

On 9 April the regiment had reached a strength of 190 and paraded at King's Road HQ with its newly formed band. It was then inspected by Colonel Sir Edward Ward, Permanent Under Secretary of State for War. By the time of the Coronation Review there were still not enough men to form a regiment, but they were able to put together a squadron which entrained for Aldershot on 12 June. From the minute they arrived it did not stop raining leaving the lines hock deep in mud. To make matters worse two days before the ceremony they were issued with brand new saddlery and Mounted Infantry Cobs which were unbroken and untrained. Despite this the squadron marched past the saluting base in a satisfactory way, giving the salute to a stand-in as King Edward had been rushed into hospital with appendicitis.

The Review Squadron joined the rest of the regiment at Sidcup and had also been issued with the same type of Mounted Infantry Cobs. Their problems were exacerbated by the Commanding Officer at Sidcup who had little knowledge of mounted units.

The postponed Coronation of King Edward finally took place on 9 August and the regiment was represented by a mounted party of one NCO and eight men under the command of Lieutenant George Hamilton. They were brigaded with other detachments from the Yeomanry.

Lack of money was a source of preoccupation throughout the first couple of years. It was hoped that wealthy colonials who were living in Great Britain would support the regiment and although they did, it was not enough. Lieutenant Colonel Wallace, expecting large sums of money to flow in, had been rather extravagant with expenses and the regiment was only saved from bankruptcy by the intervention of a donor from Cheltenham, who gave them £5,000. The regiment was still under strength, something that would continue through its existence until the First World War.

Because of the problems of training at Sidcup the regiment was delighted to be given Latimer Park for this purpose in 1903. Owned by Lord Chesham, it was situated about half a mile east of Latimer House and provided an excellent training ground for the now 202 other ranks and 18 officers of the regiment. It was divided into four squadrons:

- 'A' (British Asian) Squadron with 1st Troop (Asian), 2nd Troop (Asian) and 3rd Troop (Australian),
- 'B' (Canadian) Squadron with 1st Troop (Canadian), the 2nd Troop (Canadian) and 3rd Troop (Australian),
- 'C' (Australasian) Squadron with 1st Troops (NS Wales), 2nd Troop (NS Wales) and 3rd Troop (Victoria),
- 'D' (South African) Squadron with 1st Troop (African), 2nd Troop (African) and 3rd Troop (New Zealand).

Lieutenant Colonel Willoughby Wallace retired on 19 April 1904 and command passed to Lieutenant Colonel Hon. H.A. Lawrence, late of the 17th Lancers. He came fresh from South Africa and his vision introduced a new standard of excellence that would bear fruit during the First World War when the 550 men from the KEH were commissioned as officers.

In 1904 the Regimental HQ was moved to Gloucester Terrace and arrangements were made with the officers commanding Cavalry regiments at Colchester to use their horses during the Easter and Whitsun holidays. This became

Sydney, St Peter's, Cliftonville, Kent, July 1904.

Sydney, Elsa and Verder, 1905.

Jeanette Harris (née Bywater), Sydney's mother, 1905.

an annual event until 1914. Although the regiment had been raised as the King's Colonials, for official purposes it was referred to as the 4th County of London (King's Colonials) Imperial Yeomanry. The 'Colonials' considered this to be an insult because it appeared to reduce them in name to nothing more than an English county unit. Eventually, the officials relented and the regiment became known as the King's Colonials, Imperial Yeomanry.

On 18 October 1905 Sydney's youngest brother, Percival, married Katherine Gertrude Cook in Holborn, and in the same year Sydney enlisted in 'B' Squadron, the Canadian Squadron, as a Trooper and was proud

Sydney in the King's Colonials.

Sydney in the King Edward's Horse (KEH).

to wear the badge with its beaver and maple leaf. With his experience in the American and Canadian armies his skill as a marksman was soon spotted and he added the crossed rifles to his uniform sleeve. That same year the regiment provided Guards of Honour for various functions of overseas significance. By this time their full dress uniform had been modified, especially the high crowned felt hat with scarlet plume and several cap-lines and badges. Its height had been reduced and black cock feathers had replaced the red and all the cap-lines and badges had been removed except one. The regiment opened the Colonial and Imperial Exhibition at Crystal Palace and provided the Guard of Honour when the Prince of Wales unveiled a memorial to the Colonial troops who had died in South Africa in St Paul's Cathedral.

In 1906 the regiment was enlarged with the formation of Liverpool Troop, a troop of Liverpool men who were Colonials. They were attached to 'A' Squadron for training and housed in the HQ of the Liverpool Scottish, courtesy of Brigadier General Macfie of the Liverpool Scottish.

On 23 June 1907 Sydney's first daughter, Edith Herberta Verder, was born. Sydney decided he needed more money coming in to support his growing family. The regiment was now a territorial unit reducing his income, so he joined Sun Alliance as a full-time Insurance Worker.

In 1908 there were many changes to the Army structure including the establishment of an Army Council and Imperial General Staff. The previous year Lord Haldane had produced a Territorial Scheme which had led to the Territorial and Reserve Forces Act. The King's Colonials came under this Act, however, they were a Colonial force and the Territorial and Services Act was designed for home-defence purposes. The War Office therefore proposed that in the event of the regiment being called upon under the Act it would not serve 'at home' but would serve as an emergency unit who would travel anywhere. This meant the regiment was separated from the Administration of the County of London Territorial Force Association and placed under an association of its own.

In 1909 a Masonic Lodge was established under the title the King's Colonials' Lodge and Sydney joined almost immediately. On 19 May the same year his second daughter, Margaret Elsa Verder Harris, was born.

On 6 May 1910 King Edward VII died. The state funeral took place on 20 May and the regiment furnished a dismounted detachment to line the route and also a small party to march in the procession.

By 1911 there was a general consensus that the term 'Colonial' was demeaning to the status and dignity of the self-governing Dominions and a new name was sought for the regiment. The King Edward's Horse (the King's Overseas Dominions Regiment) was born and at the same time the stringent criteria for enlistment was changed. On 29 March 1911 Sydney celebrated the birth of another daughter, Constance Mary Verder. Constance was baptised on 23 April 1911. Sydney was listed on the 1911 census as a District Inspector and Insurance worker. The family were living at The Gables, Purley, Surrey and they had one general domestic servant, Sarah Girling, who was 36. The census was taken on 2 April 1911, only four days after the birth of Constance, so also living there were Edith Pryor, nurse girl, who was 18 and a nurse, Susannah M. Coley, aged 35.

A Guard of Honour formed by the KEH when the Prince of Wales unveiled a memorial to the Colonial troops who had died in South Africa in St Paul's Cathedral.

On 16 May 1911 the ceremonial parades to mark the Coronation of George V began with the unveiling of a memorial to Queen Victoria in front of Buckingham Palace. The eight officers and twenty-four other ranks were split into small groups that denoted their Dominion status and posted by the foot of the six columns that flanked the entrance to the memorial, while the Commanding Officer and remaining men were stationed at the memorial itself.

Elsa with Margaret on a bike.

Elsa with Margaret in Ilford.

The Coronation took place on 22 June 1911 and twenty-five NCOs including Sydney plus the other ranks under Major George Hamilton lined the route at Charing Cross.

Two years later, on 20 February 1913, Sydney, Elsa, Constance and eldest son Verder (Sydney Herbert Verder Harris) went to New York on the *Celtic*. Elsa and Verder returned on 3 May 1913 on the *Oceanic*, leaving Sydney in the USA, presumably attending to his mining interests. The following year Sydney, Elsa and Verder again travelled to the USA this time returning home together in July 1914.

Sydney remained with the KEH until 1915. When the First World War started in August 1914 the KEH was mobilised in London and remained

Elsa in her new car, a 1914 Darracq Roadster.

there until April 1915. The regiment was then dispersed into separate squadrons and sent to France with different divisions. The decision to break up the regiment may have had some influence on Sydney's decision to apply to join the Royal Flying Corps (RFC). On the other hand, it was new and exciting and pilots were considered to be glamorous and adventurous. Sydney loved to be in the thick of the action and he certainly wasn't averse to female attention. He may also have longed for the excitement he'd felt while fighting in China and the Philippines. He was also getting older, something the adventurer in him would have hated. Flying high above the ground, risking his life every day, would allow him to prove to himself that he was still the same young man who had travelled halfway round the world to make his fortune.

Chapter Eleven

Royal Flying Corps

In the years leading up to the First World War Britain had lagged behind the other European powers in aviation. Although the Wright brothers had flown the Kittyhawk in 1903, the real beginnings of aviation came after 1909 when French engineers designed the rotary engine. Before this engines had been plagued by over-heating problems leading to engine failure. But the invention of the rotary engine introduced a more efficient cooling method by fixing the crankshaft, rearranging the cylinders and rotating them round its axis. The revolving engine also produced more torque so the engine ran more smoothly and it also reduced the power to weight ratio. These engines were soon being produced round the world under licence and British manufacturers became dependant on them. They were also reliant on German magnetos.

In 1910 the Chief of the Imperial General Staff declared aviation a 'useless and expensive fad', while the First Sea Lord decided that the navy only needed two aircraft. Cavalrymen considered their only use to be scaring the horses and even French General Ferdinand Foch thought they were worthless as far as war was concerned.

The turning point came after W. Sefton Brancker flew as an observer during military operations in India. The information he provided about troop movements was so accurate that the Chief of General Staff in India, Douglas Haig, was very impressed. On 28 February 1911, after public pressure, an army order established an Air Battalion of the Royal Engineers to come into effect from 1 April. It started with 14 officers and 150 other ranks, their task to train men in handling kites, balloons and aircrafts. They could recruit officers from any regular branch of the service and other ranks would be selected from the Royal Corps of Engineers. However, the pilots had to pay for their own Royal Aero Club certificate, normally £75, which was reimbursed if the candidate passed.

The Balloon Factory at Farnborough became the Army Aircraft Factory, yet Britain still lagged behind its French counterparts who now had more than 200 aircraft in service. British officers visited France to observe French Army manoeuvres in 1911 and watched as their aircraft were used for reconnaissance and also control of artillery and aerial photography. Even the Germans, who preferred to specialise in airships, set up a corps of military and naval aviation to train pilots and observers in reconnaissance.

In October 1911 aerial reconnaissance and bombardment were used for the first time in war in the skirmish between Italy and Turkey in Tripoli. However, the bombardment from the air attracted considerable protests on moral grounds even though it was apparently alright to bombard Turkish targets with artillery and from warships. However, this did focus attention on the potential of aerial warfare and for the first time questions were asked about whether it would be necessary to seek command of the air as well as the sea in any future conflicts.

Herbert Asquith and the Cabinet reluctantly appointed a Committee of Imperial Defence to consider future policy. One of the key contributors to the committee was Bertram Dickson, an early Army flying pioneer, who warned that any future European war was likely to have formations of aircraft all collecting information about the enemy and trying to hide its own movements. This would inevitably lead to armed aircraft as each fought for supremacy of the skies, something that would be of great importance.

A new flying corps was recommended with two wings, one army and the other navy. A Central Flying School would be established at Upavon on Salisbury Plain and the Army Aircraft Factory would now become the Royal Aircraft Factory. The Royal Flying Corps was finally established under Royal Warrant on 13 April 1912.

The Navy, as the senior service, were not happy about being made subservient to the Army, so, without any authority, developed its own training centre at Eastchurch and declared the birth of the Royal Naval Air Service (RNAS). No one challenged this and it was officially recognised on 1 July 1914. The main effect of this was that two separate agencies were now fighting over the same meagre resources. The War Office, trying to save money, had wanted both military and naval wings of the RFC to build their own aircrafts at the Royal Aircraft Factory, but the Admiralty ignored this and turned to private enterprise. This stimulated growth in firms like A.V. Roe, Shorts, Sopwiths, Vickers and Handley Page whose designs eventually overtook those of the RFC. This encouraged the growth of both a civilian and military aircraft industry, something that was to prove advantageous later.

After being approved by King George V, Army Order 40 was published in February 1913 and this introduced the pilot's insignia. This was a pair of swift's wings stitched in white silk with the letters RFC encircled by a brown laurel wreath surmounted by a crown and on a backing of 4in black cloth. It was worn centrally above the left breast pocket and medals on the service dress. On the full dress uniform it took the form of a gilt metal brooch with a larger span than the woven version. It was designed by Brigadier General Sir David Henderson, the RFC's first Commanding Officer, and his deputy in charge of the Military Wing, Major (later to be General) Sir Frederick Sykes.

Lord Kitchener was recalled to the War Office the day after war was declared and he immediately ordered five more air squadrons. The man in sole charge of the Military Aeronautics Directorate was Major W. Sefton Brancker and during his second interview with Kitchener he nervously suggested they would need at least fifty squadrons to provide air support to the enormous armies that were being planned. Kitchener immediately doubled that figure.

Brancker had three main urgent requirements that all needed to be addressed. The first was for the design and production of aircraft and aero engines. The second was for recruitment and training for pilots as well as air mechanics and an administrative branch. The third necessity was to establish airfields and training facilities. Poor pre-war planning had left the RFC reliant on the Royal Aircraft Factory to produce its aircrafts. There was a need to standardise the design of a single-purpose type to ease production, servicing and training. At the time the requirement was for a stable two-seater reconnaissance aircraft that was easy to fly so that pilot and observer could concentrate their time on their allotted tasks of observation and supporting the artillery. The only real choice was the BE2c, designed by Geoffrey de Havilland. It had been modified to give it additional stability and a 90hp engine, the RAF1, had made it faster. But it was still a slow, cumbersome aircraft that carried no defensive armaments and was difficult to arm. Brancker objected saying that both the Henri and Maurice Farman, although more primitive, did at least have both the pilot and observer sitting in front of the engine giving them a good arc of forward fire. He lost the argument, but was later blamed for the decision. The factory was unable to make the aircraft in sufficient quantities so civilian firms stepped in.

Meanwhile, the civilian firms who had shown an interest were busy supplying the Admiralty's orders. The only other aircraft the RFC were likely to receive were the FE2 (De Havilland) and the Vickers FB5 fighter, both of which owed their existence to the RNAS, not the RFC.

Fortunately, recruiting for pilots, fitters, riggers and mechanics proved less troublesome. The good wages on offer attracted 1,100 of the best mechanics to the squadrons. The initial source of pilots was from civilian training schools. The original intention was to recruit civilian flying instructors as sergeant pilots but because the RNAS were commissioning all their pilots the RFC had no option but to follow suit or they would have been unable to compete.

All the professional pilots they employed had to sign a declaration to state they would not perform any stunts including looping, while flying RFC aircraft. To increase the number of trainee pilots the pre-war policy of making them pay for their own instruction was abolished and courses were started at the Central Flying School at Upavon and other civilian air fields that had been requisitioned.

The idea of learning to fly for nothing appealed to many young men who were looking for adventure and they had little trouble recruiting. The fact that training was so dangerous you could kill yourself only seemed to add to its attraction.

New recruits were always asked why they wanted to join the RFC and then if they could ride. The idea that prospective pilots could be filtered in this way seems slightly ludicrous but having a good sense of balance and the self-confidence to control a horse was a good a way as any to see who might be up to the challenge. Unsuitable pupils would soon be weeded out as the training progressed, if they didn't kill themselves first of course.

The RFC tunic was referred to the 'maternity jacket'. It was a high-collared khaki jacket without external buttons in case they became caught on the wires or struts of the aircraft structure. It resembled a cloth breastplate. When the Military Wing was first formed the corps wore peaked caps, but these were soon replaced with forage caps that could be pulled down and tied under the chin.

All ranks wore similar clothing: Bedford cord breeches and puttees, either khaki or fawn. Some of the officers wore rising boots or long socks. Officers also wore epaulettes with metal or woven pips to denote their rank, and the Sam Browne which went over one shoulder, under the collar and which had a holster for a gun on one side and a sword on the other.

NCOs and other ranks wore a crescent-shaped piece of black cloth with the words 'Royal Flying Corps' in white stitching on the upper part of their sleeves. The word 'Corps' was underneath the others on an integral rectangle beneath the arc.

Because the RFC only had twenty-six months of peace before war broke out very few full dress uniforms ever existed. These were dark blue with high mandarin collars for both officers and men. For the men these were scarlet with a wide blue border and an RFC gilt badge set back from the fastening. On their shoulders they wore epaulets with RFC on and a button at the opposite end. The cuffs were deep scarlet cloth ending in a half-inch wide inverted chevron of Petersham and the tunic was fastened in the front with seven buttons.

Officers' full dress uniform was basically the same with a 2in-wide red stripe down the outer seam of the overalls and the tunic was fastened with eight buttons down to a sash which was also the belt. This was a darker blue than the uniform and made of 3-in-wide Petersham fastened by three gilded wire toggles. There was scarlet piping along the front fastening and the collar was similar to the men's, but the blue edging was narrower. Officers' gilt badges were worn nearer the fastening. The cuffs were also similar but with an upper edge of narrow blue Petersham piped in red. However, their epaulettes were completely different with three loops of gold cord. The back had an RFC button immediately below the sash. Their headwear was a dark blue cap with a black patent leather peak, a scarlet headband and a gilt badge in the centre.

Mess dress was a dark-blue jacket finishing just below the waist with scarlet lapels and pointed cuffs. Rank badges were worn on blue cloth shoulder straps and gilt collar badges. The overalls were as for full dress and the waistcoat or vest was also blue cloth.

Army Order 327 in September 1915 introduced another flying badge. This was the observer's stitched half wing on the left of the letter 'O' which was worn on the left. Initially, this was only given to officers, but Army Order 404 extended it to Warrant Officers, NCOs and men. It was worn by the observers of both aircraft and observation balloons.

Sydney transferred to the RFC at the start of the war and was promoted to Second Lieutenant in the Royal Flying Corps, Special Reserve of Officers on 9 March 1915. He listed his civilian employment as mining engineer and surveyor with mining interests in Canada and the USA. The records also show that he had fought with the US Army for two-and-a-half years and spent nine years with the KEH. His younger brother, Percival, followed him from the King Edward's Horse and also joined the RFC.

According to his records, Sydney was initially appointed as an Assistant Equipment Officer on probation. On 16 April 1915 he moved to Shoreham airfield where 14 Squadron had been formed on 3 February that year. The first military aircraft based there were Maurice Farman S11s, a French reconnaissance and light bomber aircraft

The cover of Sydney's aviator's certificate.

Sydney in his RFC uniform, 1915.

Sydney's aviator's certificate.

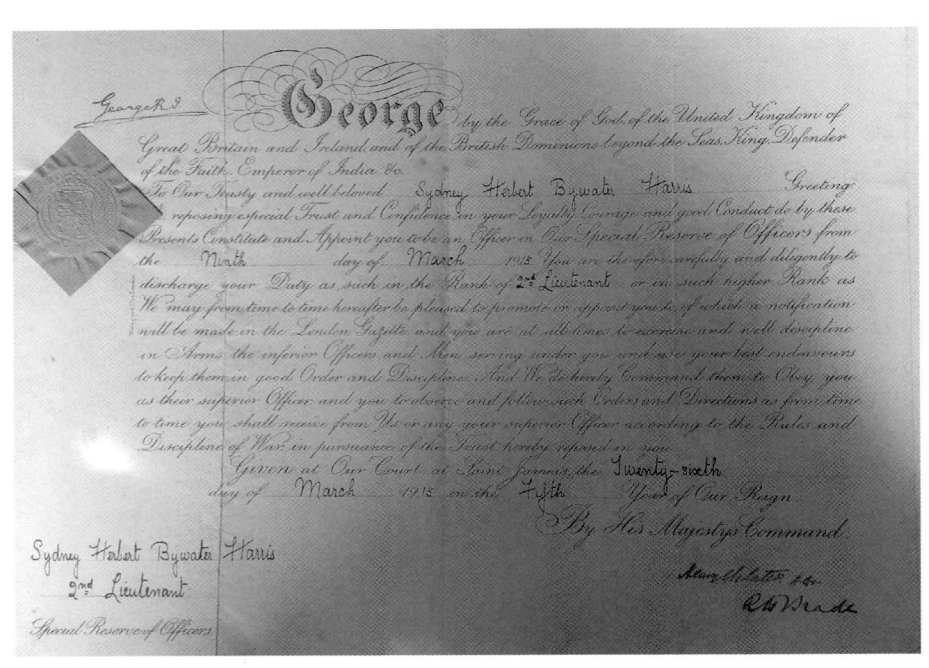

Sydney's Commission, 1915.

Sydney's Aviator's Certificate in its wallet, 1915.

which was withdrawn from service by the British early in 1915, and the BE2 aircraft, reliable but with a serious design fault that would eventually make it unusable. The pilot in the BE2 was seated in the rear of the aircraft so that the centre of gravity would not be affected by the absence of an observer. The observer's seat was surrounded by struts and cables between the wings. At the beginning of the war military aircraft were unarmed. After the Fokker E1[1] appeared in 1915 this changed, but the design of the BE2 made it almost impossible to arm. The pilot had the better view while the

Sydney in RFC uniform, 1915.

observer had his view obstructed by the wing. When they did arm them the guns could be placed in four positions, but the observer had to lift the gun out of one socket and place it in another and he had to stand up to do it.

By mid-autumn the two-seat FE2 and single-seat DH2 had begun to appear and these helped to reduce German air superiority. They were generally known by the Germans as 'Vickers' and they had a machine gun mounted forward with a good arc of fire.

Meanwhile, Sydney had progressed rapidly through the ranks. On 28 April his promotion to Second Lieutenant was confirmed. By 7 May he was Second Lieutenant EO3 and by 29 June 1915 he was a full Lieutenant. He would now begin his training to be a pilot. Normally, officers flew aircraft while other ranks either became riggers who tended the airframes and fitters

Sergeant Pilot Thomas Mottershead VC, DCM

Thomas enlisted in the Royal Flying Corps as a mechanic on 10 August 1914. Having obtained his Flying Certificate in June 1916, he was posted to 25 Squadron at St Omer where he flew the FE2b. On 22 September 1916 he carried out a low-level bombing raid on the railway station at Samain, successfully destroying an ammunition train. He and his observer, Second Lieutenant C. Street, were attacked by a Fokker and it was thanks to Mottershead's skilful flying that they were able to shoot down the enemy aircraft. He was awarded the DCM for this and other brave actions and promoted to Flight Sergeant.

On 7 January 1917 he was on patrol in a FE2d with observer Lieutenant W.E. Gower when he was attacked by two Albatros DIIIs of Jasta 8. Lieutenant Gower hit one and put it out of action but the second aircraft was flown by Leutenant Walter Göttsch, a German air ace with twenty victories to his credit. He hit Mottershead's petrol tank and set the machine on fire. Thomas was engulfed in flames which the observer was unable to put out. However, he managed to fly back to Allied lines and make a force landing. The undercarriage collapsed as the aircraft came into land, throwing the observer clear but trapping Thomas in the cockpit. Although he was rescued, he died of his burns five days later. He was awarded the VC, the only one ever awarded to a non-commissioned RFC officer during the First World War.

A selection of photographs of Elsa and Sydney, 1915.

who looked after the engines or observers and gunners. However, there were also sergeant pilots.

Training was a dangerous time. Of the 14,166 pilots who were killed in the First World War over half lost their lives while training. But for Sydney and the other young men who trained with him, the thrill of looking down on the world from 20,000ft far outweighed the possible dangers.

He began his training at Upavon on a Maurice Farman. These came in two versions, the Shorthorn and the Longhorn which had pronounced outriggers giving it the appearance of a breed of cattle. Both were ungainly having sixteen wooden struts joining the upper and lower wings together interwoven with a tangle of wires. Their advantage was that they were dual control, meaning both the instructor and pupil had a set of controls and were in front of one another, theoretically meaning the pupil should be safer while learning. The Maurice Farman Shorthorn was also known as a 'Rumpity' or a birdcage as the joke was that the easiest way to see if any of its wires were missing was to put a canary between the wings. If it managed to escape then a wire was missing. Sydney listened intently as the instructor informed them that if the machine went into a spin it could not escape from it and if it dived its wings were liable to fall off. But somehow this did not put him off, if anything it made him even more determined. Another joke that circulated was that it was better not to give the pilots too much mechanical knowledge about the aircraft or tell them too much about how it worked. After all the pilot would probably have to 'throw' the aircraft around quite a bit and if he knew how close it was to its breaking point he might lose his nerve!

Their next instructions were about the practicalities of flying the aircraft. The main control was a single lever called the joystick. It was rather like the gears on a car but it moved in four directions. Because it would be an instinctive movement to lean forward if you wanted the aircraft to go down when the pilot pushed the joystick forward the nose of the machine would point down. In the same way, if he pulled the joystick back the nose would point upwards and the aircraft would rise upwards. To turn it was necessary to bank the machine or it would skid outwards, but it was important not to bank too much. The joystick controlled banking. The pilot would have both feet on the rudder bar, holding the joystick with his right hand. With his left hand he controlled the engine by holding the throttle in his hand. If he was flying single-handed and he wanted to fire the gun he simply moved his thumb along the joystick and pressed the lever which pulled the trigger.

After a few more instructions it was time for their first lesson. Before they left the hangar the instructor reminded them once again that if they didn't like it they could return to their original Army units. No one said anything. Most had waited a long time to be transferred to the RFC and in any case no one was about to show fear or signs of nervousness in front of the other trainees. The RFC made the most of the long summer daylight hours so it was still very early morning as they made their way from the hangar to the field where the few training aircraft were lined up ready for them. As the mechanics stood around watching, Sydney put on his flying cap and goggles and followed the instructor to his aircraft. He was the oldest trainee there so he was determined not to show himself up. The sun was climbing high in an almost cloudless blue sky and there was very little wind. Above the rapid pounding of his heart he was vaguely aware of his instructor muttering something about it being a perfect flying day and then he was standing in front of the aircraft. It looked much larger close up and he marvelled at its intricate design. Then he realised the instructor was already on board and yelling at him to do the same.

The first hurdle was climbing into the cockpit. Sydney looked closely at the aircraft and successfully ignored his first impulse which was to put his foot on the wing and use the wires to pull himself up. He was just about to ask for help when he spotted the foot holes designed to help him climb in. He pulled himself up and then hesitated as he tried to work out the best way to get into the cockpit which seemed alarmingly small. Somehow he managed to squeeze in and once seated in front of his instructor he was shouted at to strap himself in. Before he could do that, however, the propeller began to spin. Frantically, he reached for the two parts of the unwieldy leather belt on either side of him and tried unsuccessfully to buckle them together. Realising he was sitting on part of the belt he struggled to free himself and then the aircraft began to move. With little time to spare he breathed a sigh of relief as he finally did the belt up. He felt the familiar ripple of excitement course through his body as the aircraft taxied slowly down the field and gained speed. He grabbed the sides of the aircraft instinctively as it lurched slightly and then the engine surged and they were off the ground and in the air. Sydney was transfixed as the aircraft slowly climbed up to the cloudless sky. Behind him the airfield grew smaller and smaller and within moments he was looking at a patchwork quilt of fields and lanes spread out below him. As the aircraft flew on he twisted round in his seat, trying to get his bearings. He couldn't believe how small everything looked and he couldn't wait to take the controls himself. As if he had heard him he suddenly felt the instructor tapping him on the shoulder. There was no other means of communication other than shouting and gestures so

Sydney twisted to face him and nodded as the instructor indicated it was his turn.

The next few moments were some of the most exciting of his life so far as the aircraft banked alarmingly and began to dive. He managed to level it out and then it banked again and dropped disturbingly. He quickly pulled the joystick back and the aircraft began to lift but the air speed indicator showed he was climbing too rapidly and in danger of stalling it. This time he eased the joystick forward gently and the aircraft slowly levelled out. Feeling more confident, slowly he began to relax until the aircraft flew over a wood, hit an air pocket and dropped suddenly. Sydney felt as if his heart had leapt into his mouth and for a split second he panicked. But he was beginning to understand the controls now and within seconds the aircraft was flying level again and he breathed a sigh of relief.

They flew on, sometimes he held the aircraft level for ages, at other times it banked and reared like a bucking bronco. As he fought the controls he finally understood the instructor's words 'It's like controlling a bucking horse'. The aircraft seemed determined to break away from him as it struggled through the air, buffeted by the wind as it howled through the struts and cables that held the aircraft together. It was hard work but it was also incredibly exhilarating. Sydney found he wanted to stay up there for ever, far away from his problems and earthly concerns. It was like being free, free of all the restrictions life had placed on his shoulders. He felt like he had when he'd first boarded the ship to Canada, as if the world was his and nothing could stop him succeeding.

He was so busy feeling ecstatic that it was several moments before he realised the instructor was shouting something at him. To his disappointment his first lesson was over and it was time to go back. Reluctantly, he let the instructor take back control and he sat back as the aircraft slowed and gradually lowered itself towards the field. The ground seemed to come at them at a terrific speed and then there was a gentle bump and they were down. Although the effects of the rarefied air soon wore off, the rapid changes in elevation sometimes meant the men needed assistance to get out of the machines when they landed. But not Sydney. He smiled to himself. He couldn't wait for the next lesson. The sooner he was flying solo the better.

Chapter Twelve

Off to France

Lessons varied from pupil to pupil but on average they would have at least two to three hours of lessons before being allowed to fly solo. However, as they could only fly in certain weather conditions, these lessons could be concentrated into a few days or over the space of two or three weeks. Once they had finished their lessons they would normally be encouraged to fly solo as soon as possible, but if the weather was bad it could sometimes be a week later before they were allowed to do this.

Sydney was a confident man and had proved an apt pupil and he did not have to wait long before it was time for him to fly solo. Half way through one of his lessons the instructor suddenly directed him to land the aircraft as he would now be allowed to fly solo for the first time.

As they taxied gracefully into land, the instructor reminded him not to come in too quickly and then told him he was ready to fly on his own. He then climbed out leaving Sydney in charge of the aircraft. He didn't hesitate. Waiting until the instructor was clear, he thrust the throttle open and wrenched the joystick back. The aircraft lurched forward, the nose lifted alarmingly as the tail dropped and he began to career towards the hangars. Ignoring the impulse to panic, Sydney quickly eased the joystick forward slightly and reduced the pressure on the throttle. Within seconds the aircraft was back in his control and he took a deep breath and relaxed slightly. It really wouldn't do to crash the aircraft in the process of taking off. Having straightened it out he opened the throttle again and

Verder on his bike, possibly at Shoreham airfield, 1915.

Sydney's flying certificate, September 1915.

this time eased the joystick back gently. To his surprise the aircraft lifted lightly off the ground and he rose gracefully into the grey cloudy sky.

The instructor had told him to be no longer than 10 minutes, but once he was up in the sky time lost its meaning. He rose higher and higher until he was suddenly engulfed in the low clouds. It was surprisingly cold and damp in the clouds, visibility was poor and his immediate thought was to drop back down again. But Sydney was by nature a risk taker and he couldn't resist trying to rise above the clouds to see if it was sunny. So, wiping his goggles with his gloved hand, he continued to rise until suddenly he broke through into the blue sky above. It was like being in another world. The sun felt warm on his head and as it glistened on the wings of the aircraft, Sydney felt a rush of exhilaration. He flew on a little way enjoying the freedom, then reluctantly decided it must be time to go back.

He banked away to the left and dropped slowly down through the clouds. They seemed thicker now and he had to keep wiping his googles to see though the rain splatters. It was also much colder and he shivered as the temperature around him fell rapidly. It seemed to be taking a long time to break through the clouds and he started to feel uneasy. It was also beginning to rain quite heavily, but somehow he resisted the impulse to thrust the joystick sharply forward. Instead, he continued to lose altitude slowly although he did begin to pray.

Suddenly, he was through and he breathed a sigh of relief which quickly turned to panic as he realised he had no idea where he was. He reached down for his map and then tried to make out a landmark that he could use to pinpoint his position. But there was nothing. He flew on a little further and then spotted a railway line. Hoping he was going in the right direction he began to follow it and then suddenly, in the distance, he spotted something that looked like the airfield. He turned north and headed towards it. He no longer cared whether it was the right airfield, only that it was somewhere he could land and, if necessary, ask directions. But luck was with him and as he flew closer he began to recognise the countryside. Now all he had to worry about was being in trouble for being considerably longer than 10 minutes. As he landed the heavens opened and the rain fell in torrents. Within moments the field became a quagmire but now Sydney was down safely the panic of being lost had gone. He could only remember the exhilaration of flying solo and he couldn't wait for his next flight.

Having survived their first solo flight, pilots would normally have to complete about 2½ hours of solo flying and then an hour-long flying examination before being accepted into the elite RFC club.

Sydney was granted his Aviator's Certificate on 18 August 1915, although he did not appear to receive it until 25 September. He was then posted to the Advanced School of Flying at Gosport to prepare for flying in action. Here he joined 23 Squadron. Sydney was now 34 and considerably older than all the other pilots so it wasn't long before he became affectionately known as 'Pops'.

Captain Louis Arbon Strange was posted to Fort Grange, Gosport on 1 September, his job to form 23 Squadron from the material left over by 14 Squadron which was about to go overseas. The aim was for 23 Squadron to be ready by 1 January 1916. Strange was an experienced officer who had flown with 5 Squadron throughout 1914 and the early part of 1915 before being posted to 6 Squadron. He had taken part in the battles of Marne, Aisne, Loos and the First and Second Battles of Ypres, twelve months of continuous flying before being ordered home to form 23 Squadron. On his arrival he was met by the Station Commander who was not expecting him and knew nothing about 23 Squadron. This would soon change as by 29 September a total of forty-four men of all ranks had arrived and training was progressing well. Strange used four of his best pilots as instructors and traded two of his Bleriots for one-and-a-half BE2cs from 22 Squadron, also newly formed. He bombarded RFC HQ with requests for machines, tools and spares, but then lost an entire flight because they were needed to form 16 Reserve Squadron. He was continually losing pilots and mechanics to replace casualties overseas and because his pilots could also fly at night some were commandeered for the home defence against the Zeppelins.

Despite these setbacks by Christmas the squadron was ready to go, but it still had no operational aircraft. On 10 January 1916 Strange collected the first FE2b from Farnborough. FE stood for Farman Experimental. The FE2b was designed as a fighter from the beginning. It could also carry bombs with a maximum load of 350lb. However, when fully loaded with bombs its speed fell to between 60 and 70mph and it would take about 10 minutes to climb to 3,000ft. It had a wing span of 47ft 9in and weighed 3,307lb. The upper section was nearly 16ft wide and its horizontal stabiliser was the same size as a wing. This created quite a lot of drag meaning its normal cruising speed was somewhere between 70 and 75mph.

By 18 January 23 Squadron was finally ready to go overseas. Two days later they were told to hold themselves in readiness to deploy. To celebrate the fact they were ready before 22 Squadron they challenged their rivals to a game of rugby. But by dinner neither team was satisfied with the outcome so they replayed the match after dinner on the airfield by the lights of their car lamps. Unfortunately for Major Strange (he had been promoted in November 1915) he was rushed to Cosham Military Hospital with appendicitis. To make matters worse, a swab was left inside him and he spent the next fourteen weeks in hospital. Instead of leading his squadron overseas, he was forced to watch them depart from his hospital bed.

Instead, Major R.E.T. Hogg took command of the squadron and they arrived in France on 16 March 1916. However, it wasn't quite as simple as it sounded. The day they were due to fly to Dover, the first leg of the flight to France, they were told that formation flying had recently been adopted. Therefore they should proceed in formation to Dover. No one had flown in formation before so only four aircraft from B Flight actually made it safely to Dover that day. The next leg was to Fienvillers and this time no attempt was made to fly in formation. To ensure they arrived safely across the Channel most climbed up to their ceiling of 10,000ft. This took about an hour but ensured that if they had engine failure they would be able to glide the rest of the way to France or, if necessary, back to Britain.

The squadron eventually arrived safely at Fienvillers, although one or two lost their way over France and had to land to get directions. Sydney and his observer, Second Lieutenant E.B. Harvey, flying in FE2b serial number 6353 had a more eventful journey. As they flew over Arras they came under heavy anti-aircraft fire. As the shells burst all around them the aircraft rocked alarmingly. Puffs of smoke indicated the progress of the aircraft across the sky and the shells came steadily closer. Sydney tried his best to avoid the increasingly accurate burst of shell fire but eventually his luck ran out and the aircraft took a direct hit. Sydney fought desperately to control the aircraft as he remembered his tutor's words about not letting it go into a spin. But preventing the aircraft from spinning was not his only problem. A fire had started on the tail. He began to search

Sydney in the pilot's seat of an FE2b.

frantically for somewhere to put the aircraft down, but everywhere he looked there were trenches. The anti-aircraft guns were still firing at them, the aircraft rocking dangerously as the shells burst around them. As they sank lower they became an easier target and Sydney wondered if this was it. His only option was to find somewhere to land and he needed to do it quickly. They did not have parachutes and if they did not put down soon they would be engulfed in fire. Instinctively, he reached down to check he had his pistol. Better to shoot himself than burn to death.

The engine spluttered and coughed, but somehow kept going. Each minute they remained in the air was taking them closer to the British lines. They finally reached no-man's-land, but the anti-aircraft fire continued. Both he and Second Lieutenant Harvey were frantically looking for some flat land when he suddenly spotted what looked like a race course. It was only just in time. The damage to the aircraft was making it even slower and a much easier target and the gunners had finally found their range. There was no time for the niceties of landing, as soon as the wheels were on the ground they both scrambled out leaving the aircraft eventually to judder to a halt several feet away. Seconds later it took a direct hit and burst into flames that totally consumed it.

As the fire gradually burnt itself out the shelling also eased off. Eventually Sydney judged it safe to stand up. He was relieved to see that Second

An FE2b.

Lieutenant Harvey was also unharmed and a wry smile crossed his face as he realised that they'd had a lucky escape. The fire was soon out and as Second Lieutenant Harvey had managed to rescue the camera he took a quick picture of the burnt out wreck. Then the two men began to walk to the nearest British post where they were given a lift to Fienvillers.

Two days later they flew on to their permanent base at Le Hameau. Sydney had been given another FE2b, serial number 6364, and he had a new observer, Second Lieutenant Powell. Here they became part of the newly formed 13th Wing of III Brigade. This brigade was operating with the Third Army which was holding the line from Gommecourt to Curlu. They would later fight on the Somme.

The day after arrival they began flying operational sorties, their orders to fly a constant two aircraft patrol. The weather for Sydney's first sortie was sunny and clear with good visibility. As he crossed the grass towards his aircraft he felt the familiar frisson of excitement. It was incredibly noisy as all the aircraft were out of their hangars and being tested and he could hardly hear himself think. He climbed into his aircraft and waited for the mechanic to shout 'contact'. 'Contact' he repeated loudly and then pressed

One of the planes Sydney flew, serial number 6364. (Courtesy of Cross and Cockade International)

the electric ignition switch, the propeller was given a sharp swing over and the engine started with a roar. It coughed a couple of times and then settled into its rhythm. Sydney throttled down until the engine was purring and signalled the ground crew to remove the chocks from under the wheels. The aircraft moved slowly forward under its own steam and taxied onto the field. The grass felt bumpy after the hard standing but Sydney carried on until the aircraft was facing into the wind. He opened the throttle wide and the machine rushed forward increasing speed all the time and then he was off the ground. He circled the airfield until he had gained enough height then set off towards 'Hunland'. Although they were meant to designate German aircraft as 'enemy aircraft' in their reports, they invariably thought of them as the 'Hun' and the German held territory as 'Hunland'.[1]

As they approached enemy territory the first flashes of crimson fire and black smoke appeared. 'Archie', the name the pilots gave to the anti-aircraft cannon, would follow them all along the lines. The more experienced pilots learned to anticipate its path and would manoeuvre accordingly but this was only Sydney's second time and it took him a while to adjust.

Sydney remembered what he had been told about flying sorties, either alone or with others. The difficulty was putting it into practice. He knew it was vitally important for the pilot to be constantly looking around, turning in his seat, manoeuvring the machine left and right and at the same time looking above, below and all around. But it was very tiring, especially for less-experienced pilots and he was almost relieved when he reached the German lines. Once they reached their target tactics changed and he had to fly a straight and level course for long enough to allow the observer to take accurate photos.

Sydney with one of his observers.

During the war there were some 650,000 prints of aerial views of the Western Front, the majority for reconnaissance to assist the commanders of the field forces on the ground. When the British Fourth Army took over the Somme Front in March 1916 aerial photographic reconnaissance increased rapidly as every attempt was made to photograph the German trench system meticulously. On 25 March Sydney and his observer set off to take some photographs of the German trenches.

The 'A'-type camera was the first official RFC camera and was first used early in 1915. It weighed 10lb and was encased in mahogany. It was difficult to use as the observer would have to hold the camera and lean over the side of the aircraft to take a photo. However, the photos were distorted by the angle at which the camera was held. Eventually, to the relief of the observers, the camera was attached by leather straps to the outside of the aircraft. It was used for the first time over the German trenches during the Battle of Neuve-Chappelle where it produced a photographic map of the whole of the German trench system. This was used successfully by the infantry to help them identify their objectives. Unfortunately, the camera had its drawbacks. It only took six plates and each one had to be changed by hand. When the aircraft returned to land the observer would rush the plates to be checked and to make sure they were clear enough or had been taken of the right place.

By the summer a new camera was introduced. This was called the 'C'-type and it could take eighteen successive photographs. The observer would take the first photo by pulling a piece of cord. He then turned a handle to push the exposed plate into a receiving magazine. Turning the handle back again brought the next plate into position and he was ready to take the next photo.

To take photos over enemy terrain Sydney had to fly low, and keep the aircraft as steady and level as possible but they were in full view of the German troops who

Sydney, 1916.

fired constantly at them. 'Archie' was very accurate and the pilots had to change course every 15 or 20 seconds or they would be shot down. The sky was thick with shell bursts and smoke which not only warned the enemy further along the trench that they were coming, it also served to highlight their position to any German aircraft.

The fixed camera was mounted to the side of the aircraft and under the control of the observer who did his best to take photos while the aircraft veered from side to side or was buffeted by the turbulence from the continual shelling. To take photos Sydney also had to fly quite slowly, about 70mph, which made them even more of a target. Although there was heavy steel armour plating mounted beneath the cockpits on the bottom of the nacelle, it was a different matter above. The pilots sat bolt upright in their yellow leather coats, fully exposed to the slipstream. The observers sat in what resembled a small hip bath with no respite from the constant crash of the shells, bursts of smoke and rocking from the turbulence.

As Sydney flew ponderously over the German lines and his observer took photos, a constant stream of anti-aircraft fire rocked the aircraft. Every now and then the gunners would get a direct hit and an aircraft would burst into flames or dive headfirst into the ground. The first time it happened Sydney twisted round in his seat to see if the pilot had survived but he soon realised that was not a good idea and veered left just in time to avoid a large shell that burst on his right deafening him and rocking the aircraft alarmingly. The next time an aircraft went down he continued on his way and tried not to think about which one of his friends would not make it back that day.

As they reached the end of the set photographic course Sydney breathed a sigh of relief. He banked sharply to the right and then began the long climb up into the sky. The idea was to fly back out of reach of the ground gunners, but the danger was far from over.

Alerted by the anti-aircraft fire, German aircraft were now waiting for them as they tried to get back to their own lines. Having finished taking photos, the observer could now concentrate his attention on defending the aircraft. He was in charge of the gun, a hollow steel rod anchored to a swivel mount in the front of the nacelle. Because of the three clips the gun was mounted on it could cover a huge field of fire. One clip allowed the gun to fire down, one was for firing to the right and the other for firing to the left.

When the observer fired the gun he had to put his knee against the mounting or the gun would blow out with the recoil. Between the observer and the pilot there was a second mounted gun. This was for firing over the FE2b's upper wings if the aircraft was under attack from the rear. To fire this gun the observer had to stand up exposing the whole of his body from the knees up. To adjust and shoot the gun he had to stand on the sides of the nacelle. There was no belt to hold him, the only thing that stood between him and falling out was his grip on the gun and the sides of the nacelle. He was in constant danger, not only of being shot but of falling out if the pilot made a wrong move. Eventually, British pilots would develop a defensive tactic of forming a circle which meant that no Fokker could get on the tail of a FE2b without coming under fire from another, but this had not yet been developed.

As they flew over Queant Sydney saw several Fokkers diving towards them and he took a sharp intake of breath. He leaned forward to shout to his observer but he had already seen them and was preparing to fire.

Chapter Thirteen

Action in the Sky

Sydney had not been in France long when the Fokker scourge took 23 Squadron's first victim. On 23 March an aircraft was shot down by the famous Max Immelmann, who gave his name to a flying manoeuvre.[1]

The tactics adopted by the Fokkers were revolutionary at the time and this made them very frightening to pilots who had received no fighter training. They would use their comparatively high ceiling to fly at a high altitude, ideally in the sun so they could not be seen. Then they would swoop down from above on their unsuspecting victim. The speed of their approach would give the enemy little time to mount much of a defence. Then to sustain the attack the pilot would dive past his target before pulling out of the dive into a loop. At the top of the loop he would perform a half roll which would leave him in an upright position ready to attack again. This was called the Immelmann turn. Another of his manoeuvres was to pull out of a dive into a steep climb that would almost stall the aircraft. Then he would kick on the rudder to turn sideways and dive at his opponent from the opposite direction.

The Fokker scourge had reached its height in 1915 and by late 1915 the Germans had gained aerial superiority which made it difficult and dangerous for the British to carry out aerial reconnaissance over German lines. But by the time Sydney arrived in France in spring 1916 the new British aircrafts, the FE2b and DH2, which were both pushers and could fire forwards, were beginning to reverse this.

The first bursts of fire missed the nearest Fokker and Sydney immediately took evasive action as it dived passed them. He needed to get behind the enemy aircraft quickly before it turned and resumed the attack. He flew high up in to the sky in an attempt to outmanoeuvre it, hoping to use the dive to increase his speed. In 1916 aerial combat was still considered by most pilots to

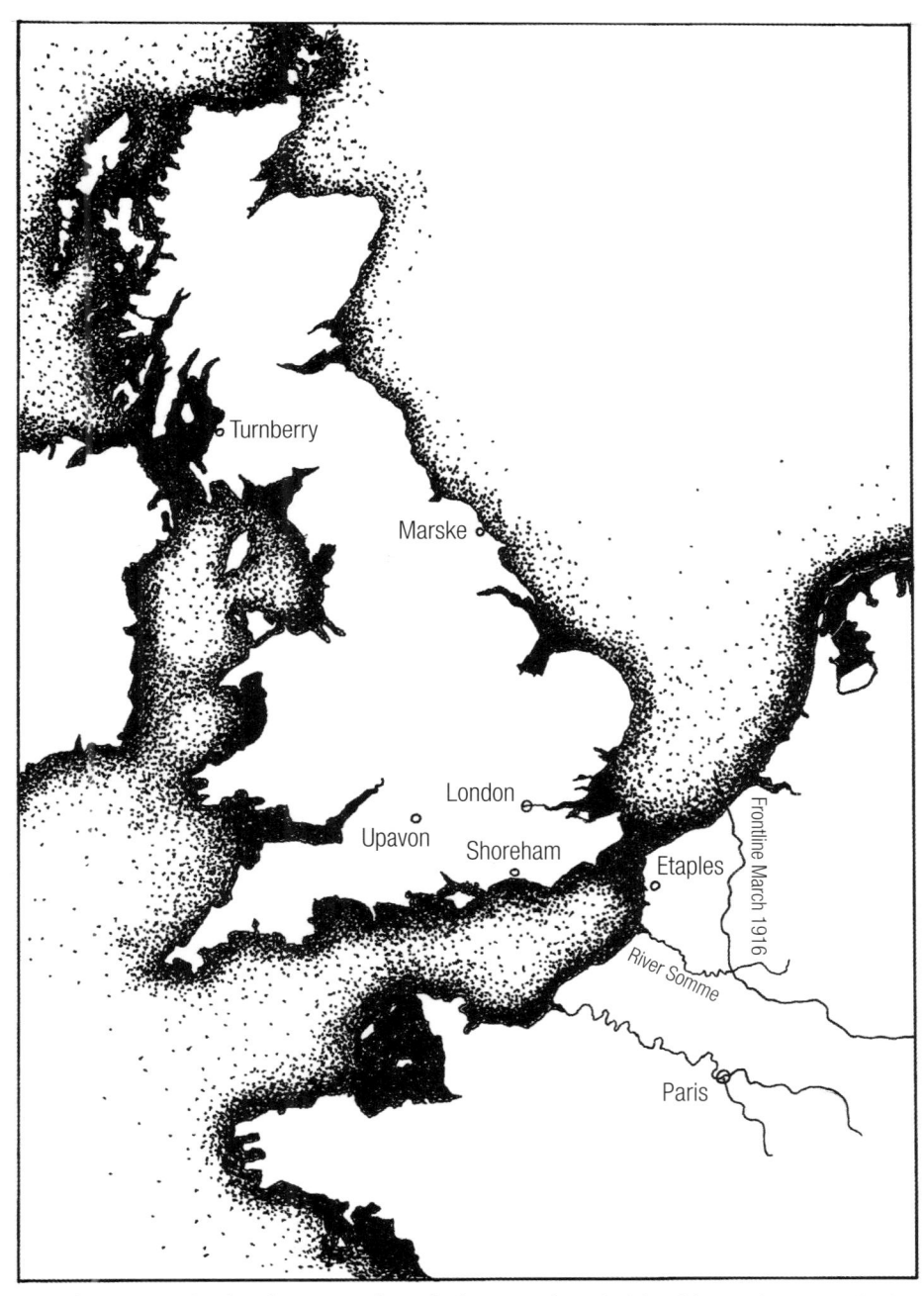

Locations in England and France where Sydney was based. After his previous travels the RFC was close to home.

A drawing of an aerial battle.

be quite chivalrous, and most saw it as being a duel in which they were not aiming to kill the pilots, but to shoot down the enemy machine. With the confidence and arrogance of someone who had already survived two wars Sydney had been quite looking forward to his first dog fight. But having been taught to fly straight and level, their noses firmly fixed on the horizon, he soon found that combat was something completely different.

It was like being in a sphere, there was no horizon. Aircrafts were like fish in a small tank, weaving fantastic patterns in the sky as they fought to place the nose of the aircraft where they could best shoot at the enemy. There was no manual that could teach Sydney the skills he needed to survive, only experience could do that. Lost in a melee of diving, climbing, looping, banking, spinning and turning aircrafts, Sydney lost all track of time and space. Pilots turned their aircrafts in tiny circles, often missing each other by inches, stood them almost upright or nose down, even flying distances on their backs, anything that would gain them an advantage and prevent the enemy from shooting them down. As Sydney fought to control the aircraft and steer clear of danger he was filled with a sense of exhilaration he had never felt before. At the same time he was conscious that all though he was surrounded by other aircraft he was very much on his own. Unlike the infantry who lived, fought and died together, he was very much an individual who only had his own reserves of courage to call on.

All these thoughts flashed through his head as the air around him filled with the rattle of machine-gun fire and tearing canvas. He heard rather than saw an aircraft to the left of him falter, its engine stalled as it spiralled helplessly towards the ground but there was no time to look. As his brain frantically tried to anticipate where the next danger would come from his observer was busy firing wildly at the enemy.

The battle grew in intensity as more aircraft joined the assault and then, as suddenly as it had begun, it was over. As they finally approached their own lines the last of the attackers flew off leaving him exhausted but ecstatic that he had survived.

He bought the aircraft into land and wearily climbed out. As he watched several other aircraft slowly returned and he noted their damage. Looked like he was the only one to come back unscathed. He turned back to look at his machine and congratulate himself and gasped. The aircraft had taken several bullets stretching from the tail along the whole structure and he realised that they were both lucky to be alive. For a split second he wondered how long his luck would last, then his natural optimism returned and he

One of Sydney's wrecked planes, probably the one he crashed during night-flying practice.

dismissed such thoughts from his mind. He turned to greet another pilot and chatting excitedly about the battle they headed back to the mess for some lunch.

Four days later Sydney and his observer, Second Lieutenant Powell, took part in a night practice flight. The Fee, as it was affectionately known, had a sturdy undercarriage that was well suited to harsh night landings. Its slow speed and good forward visibility worked in its favour and its slow speed didn't matter as much under cover of darkness.

Night flying was even more exciting as far as Sydney was concerned. The familiar objects and landmarks he knew by day seemed strange at night and while it was relatively easy to fly, it was much more difficult to land without hitting a tree or chimney stack. To aid the pilot in landing and taking off flares were laid on the ground. But while these guided the pilot in to land quite successfully, taking off past the flares had its own problems.

Sydney raced past the flares and then plunged into complete and total darkness. He had checked the landing ground before climbing into the aircraft and he knew he had a reasonable distance after the end of the flares before he hit anything but it still made his heart pound. Concentrating hard, he took off but he still had no night sight at all thanks to the flares and he could see absolutely nothing in front of him. He climbed higher into the sky and then levelled off. He flew straight ahead for a while concentrating his attention on the instruments in the aircraft which glowed brightly from the little electric bulbs. Above him the stars shone brightly but beneath him there was nothing but an inky blackness. Eventually, he faced the fact that it was time to turn back to the airfield and land. He had practised this several times at Gosport, but for some reason it seemed more difficult in France. Banking and turning during the day presented little difficulty but at night it felt like a very dangerous thing to do. This feeling of unease was exacerbated as he could not see the ground below at all or any horizon in the distance to ensure he was flying level. All he could do was to ignore his doubts and continue flying by instinct. But he couldn't keep flying indefinitely so he took a deep breath and banked away, turning the aircraft back the way it had come. To his intense relief, in the far distance, slightly to the left, he could see the flares burning away. He headed towards them and then when he was close enough he flew a big circle round the aerodrome and prepared to land.

He then realised he had completely miscalculated. Despite the chill of the night air he could feel the sweat forming on his upper lip as he flew round the airfield a second time before trying again. This time he had judged it better and made a good landing. Unfortunately, he had to repeat this several times, including flying to a certain height, before coming back in to land.

As he approached the flares for what seemed like the hundredth time Sydney allowed his concentration to wander and miscalculated the distance completely. The aircraft was now heading rapidly towards the ground and he was unable to control it. Within seconds the flares disappeared behind him and he was back in total darkness. He had no idea where the ground was but he knew he must be getting close. He was suddenly confronted by several trees which somehow he miraculously missed and then a field rose up to meet him and he instinctively closed his eyes and bought his arms up to cover his face.

The aircraft landed with a jolt which almost threw him out of his seat and then careered precariously along the bumpy field before gradually juddering to a halt and slowly tipping over on one side. Sydney slowly opened his eyes and his first thought was one of relief. He wasn't in any pain and he appeared unhurt. His next thought was that this was the second aircraft he had written off and he hadn't been in France a month yet.

The following day Sydney was given his third aircraft. This FE2b was serial number 6345[2] which had been delivered to 23 Squadron on 18 January 1916. Two days later it had been fitted with experimental exhaust pipes.

The British Fourth Army was formed in March 1916 and subsequently took over the Somme battlefront from the British Third Army between Fonquevillers and Maricourt on the Somme River. The proposal for a large offensive on the Somme had been put forward by General Joseph Joffre, the Commander in Chief of the French Armies, at the end of 1915, beginning of 1916. It was originally intended to be a joint Franco–British operation but the French had to reduce their role to that of support after the massive assault by the Germans on the Verdun Front in February 1916.

During April, May and June the British developed an operational plan for an offensive between Serre on the left wing and Maricourt on the right wing. The Third Army were to commit two infantry divisions for this attack at the same time as the main assault at Gommecourt on the Fourth Army's northern flank. This area was heavily fortified with five German front-line divisions and a further four in reserve or resting. Reconnaissance again took centre stage and photo sorties increased.

Major A. Ross-Hume from the Cameronians had assumed command of 23 Squadron in April 1916 and at the same time its role changed. The 'pusher' configuration of the FE2b with its excellent forward vision and armament capability had made it an ideal reconnaissance aircraft. But the advent of the more aggressive German tactics and their fighter aircraft, like the Fokker with guns fired through the propeller, meant new tactics had to be devised to protect the reconnaissance aircraft and the bombers. So up until June the aircraft was recast as a fighter cover aircraft, regularly escorting the BEs of 8, 12 and 13 Squadrons (12th Wing), the bombers and the artillery support aircrafts.

When the pilots and observers were not in the air they found several ways to amuse themselves. The very thing that made them good pilots, risk-taking innovators with a non-conformist attitude and a propensity to challenge every day norms often made them mavericks as far as the military were concerned. Whereas some took to gardening and growing flowers in the beds around the huts, others were more rebellious. One man brought a pack of hounds back with him when he returned from leave and was allowed to keep them. In 1917 Frederick Powell, CO of 41 Squadron, ordered some cement and created a roller skating rink for the officers to skate on when they weren't in the air. They also played badminton on the rink as well as rugby, although they did flood it first to minimise injuries. Another, Robert Loraine, CO of 41 Squadron, created a theatre. Others preferred solitude and would spend their rest periods reading books, painting pictures or writing poetry and letters home.

When the weather was bad and flying was not possible the men would often go into town. While some became tourists, visiting churches and places of interest in the towns and countryside near where they were based, others visited the local brothels. Many were barely out of school and had been brought up on Victorian ideas of virtue so a visit to 'the girls' was something they looked forward to. The girls were always pleased to see 'Les Anglais Aviateurs' as they were considered quite rich compared to their infantry counterparts. These meeting rooms smelt strongly of cheap perfume with a bare floor for dancing. In the corner there was usually an old piano and the walls were covered with pictures of nude women. They would be met by Madame who saw they all had a drink before clapping her hands and introducing them to the girls. The champagne flowed like water and the emphasis was on having fun, although many an airman came away with venereal diseases and others were so drunk they couldn't remember if they'd enjoyed themselves or not.

Alcohol played an important role in their lives allowing them to anaesthetise their feelings when yet another of their friends was killed. It also helped keep up morale and was a preferable alternative to crying. Fear was ever present and all but a few accepted that it was normal to be afraid. But it was something that was never talked about. Many used alcohol to help them hide their fears and give them courage. Unfortunately, it only offered short-term release. As soon as it wore off depression and anxiety returned as did the feelings of nausea and fear as they faced yet another sortie.

Although flying was very stressful, life on the air bases was considerably better than in the trenches. They had good mess rooms, nice billets and good food with no shortages. Most airmen had three meals a day. They breakfasted on eggs and bacon, had a hot meal, either a roast or steak and kidney pudding and vegetables, for lunch and cold meat and vegetables for high tea. Some squadrons even had their own bands.

The main flying uniform for the RFC was a brown knee-length, double-breasted chrome leather coat with three pockets. The RNAS had the same but in black. There was also a short version which was worn over an army greatcoat or together with a short fur jacket. The winter cold at altitude was such that the men would not put on extra clothing until just before flying because their sweat would freeze at high altitude. Urine also froze at high altitude so they would never drink more than one cup of tea before flying. This also applied to the dawn patrols. While the men only drank one cup of cocoa with their biscuits, the mechanics would frantically pour hot water into the engines in an attempt to warm them up. . Both pilot and observer were constantly exposed to castor oil and fumes from the engine which they breathed in. This gave them diarrhoea so they would often fly on an empty stomach.

Pilots also wore long undercoats with sleeves lined with camel fur and thigh-length fleece boots called 'fug boots', introduced by Lanoe Hawker

VC. As sorties became longer and the range of aircraft increased long coats began to be worn more often. Goggles were available in many forms and were so important pilots often took a spare pair with them. They could have tinted or untinted lenses and were worn with a face protector to give some protection against frostbite. Face protectors also came in many forms but they all covered the face leaving a small breathing hole and holes for the eyes and mouth. They were either made of leather or cloth with one type made of skin with the outer surface covered in fur. Pilots could also buy themselves a black chrome-dressed leather jacket with kapok lining or a floatation waistcoat to wear over everything in case of a crash landing in the sea. There were also some breathing devices to provide oxygen from as early as 1917.

Under their uniforms the men would wear their fibre identity tags on a length of string round their necks. The red one was 1⅜in in diameter and on both sides name, initial, religion and number were stamped. It had a single hole to one side. The other disk was octagonal grey-green, also with the personal details stamped on it and measured 1½in by 1¼in with two holes to the side opposite each other.

When not on duty the airmen made sure they were comfortably dressed, something not approved of by the Army High Command who looked somewhat askance at the casual clothes the men wore when they made official visits.

The RFC did not have parachutes on the aircrafts, although those on the observer balloons were issued with Spencer-type free-fall parachutes at the outbreak of war. There are differing opinions as to why this was. It would seem that there is no proof that General Trenchard discouraged the use of these by pilots and it is possible that it was more likely to be due to technical ignorance at the War Office.

As the weather improved and preparations for the big offensive planned for the Somme accelerated, photo sorties increased. Sydney now had a new observer, Second Lieutenant Arthur Norbury Solly. By 30 April they had flown several sorties together and had become good friends. The day dawned clear with blue skies and little cloud. Their orders were to fly low over the trenches near Ayette and take photos of the enemy gun emplacements. The sortie was just another mission and as Sydney and Arthur climbed into their aircraft, they had no idea how close they would come to death.

Chapter Fourteen

Gun Spotting

By April 1916 it was obvious to the Germans the British were building up to an attack but they didn't know when. German XIV Reserve Corps carried on as they had for the previous two years, entrenching on a large scale to improve and expand the sector. The weather was now warmer but there were also bursts of heavy rain. Their dugouts were deep and afforded them considerable protection against the long-range British artillery and bombing from aircraft. Although food was not as plentiful as it had been in the beginning, the meat ration increased for those on the front line and the warm weather improved the health of the soldiers. On 14 April Prince von Hohenzollern visited several regiments in XIV Reserve Corps and passed out medals to those members of RIR (Reserve Infanterie Regiment) 109 who had been recognised for bravery. RIR 99 received a new Commanding Officer on 15 April, Major Hans von Fabeck, and the Germans continued to extend their positions in anticipation of an attack.

By the end of April the use of German reconnaissance was increasingly restricted because of British aerial superiority. Numerous British aircraft swarmed above the German front line preventing ground traffic from moving around and German observation aircraft from crossing into the British lines. The Second Army did not possess enough fighter aircraft to stop the British having free reign over the German lines. They were also unable to obtain enough anti-aircraft guns or motorised guns to keep the aircraft at a distance. Large numbers of British observation balloons had also appeared along the line keeping a sharp watch on the German positions. Because of this German artillery was virtually paralysed so they didn't give away their positions. As British air superiority meant the German guns were relatively silent photo sorties were carried out at lower altitude and British pilots grew bolder, sometimes flying only 100m above the German positions. However low-flying aircraft were not immune to German fire and several were shot down.

Sydney flew towards the German trenches and dropped as low as he dared so that Arthur could take photos. It was a relatively windless day so it was easier than normal to keep the aircraft flying level. As he approached the trenches the first flashes of artillery fire burst in the sky around them causing some minor turbulence. Sydney steadied the aircraft and Arthur began taking photos.

As he flew further back into German territory the artillery fire strengthened, the aircraft rocked violently as he fought to control it and he heard the ominous sound of bullets tearing through the canvas and splinters flying off the struts as the bullets ricocheted off them. Sydney did his best to ignore the ripping sound as the fabric gave way and tried to concentrate on keeping the aircraft level.

The next pass was almost over when he suddenly felt a sharp pain in his chest. Glancing down he was horrified to see blood seeping through his coveralls. For a few seconds he watched fascinated as the red stain slowly spread and then his chest felt as if it was on fire.

He banked quickly to the left and turning the aircraft round he began the long journey back to the British lines. The sudden change in direction took Arthur by surprise and he turned back to question Sydney. One look at the blood clearly visible on his coveralls and the pain etched on Sydney's face was enough to answer his unspoken question and he turned back checking for enemy aircraft. Thankfully, there were none in sight. Their abrupt volte-face had probably confused the Germans as much as it had Arthur. Gradually, they moved away from the German lines and the white puffs of smoke and flashes and bangs of the enemy artillery faded away into the distance. The aircraft suddenly rocked violently and began to dive as Sydney lost concentration briefly. Just as it was about to go into a spiral instinct took over and he pulled it up and straightened out. Arthur hung nervously onto the sides and began to pray that Sydney would stay conscious long enough to land it safely.

He began to look round for somewhere they could land and finally spotted a large field ahead. He pointed it out but Sydney waved his hand and kept going. He was feeling too dizzy to shake his head and the pain in his chest and abdomen was growing but he knew his best chance of survival was to reach the airfield.

To his relief the airfield finally came into view but it was swaying in front of his eyes and seemed so far away. It was becoming increasingly hard to breathe. Every intake of breath caused such an excruciating pain in his chest that he was unable to complete it and the lack of oxygen to his body was causing pins and needles in his limbs. He wanted nothing more than to close his eyes and lie down but he knew he couldn't do that, not yet. Drawing on some inner instinct for self-preservation he somehow managed to land the aircraft before finally giving himself up to darkness as he lost consciousness.

When he woke up again it was several hours later. He was in hospital and covered in bandages. The sharp excruciating pain had been replaced by a dull ache and he felt groggy but he was alive. He had been badly wounded by artillery fire but he had survived.[1]

He would probably have been taken to a Base Hospital which was part of the evacuation chain. These were further back from the front line than the Casualty Clearing Stations and were manned by troops from the Royal Army Medical Corps supported by men attached from the Royal Engineers and Army Service Corps. They were usually located near the coast to enable quick evacuations back to England. They also needed to be close to railway lines. There were two types of Base Hospitals: Stationary and General and they were normally centred on pre-war buildings like seaside hotels.

It's possible the hospital Sydney went to was in Étaples, as that was probably the closest to Fienvillers. The Étaples Army Base Camp was a base for British, Canadian and Australian forces and the largest of its kind ever established overseas by the British, at its peak housing over 100,000 people. It was built along the railway adjacent to the town and was served by a network of railways, canals and roads. These connected the camp to the southern and eastern fields of battle in France and also to the ships carrying troops, supplies, guns, equipment and thousands of men and women across the English Channel. As well as a training base it was also a depot for supplies and a detention centre for prisoners. It was a centre for the sick and wounded and had sufficient hospitals to treat 22,000 people.

It's not clear whether Elsa would have travelled to see Sydney while he was in the Base Hospital. There were strict regulations about visiting and this would not have been possible for those who would have died before the relative could arrive, for those who would return to duty or those who were likely to be returned to Britain within three weeks or so. However, for those with money or the right connections these regulations may not have always applied. The evacuation system was quite efficient so it probably unlikely Elsa would have travelled to France. Although she did have money and was used to travelling, she also had young children to look after. Sydney would also have been evacuated back to England to convalesce so she probably remained at home.

According to his records, Sydney was considered unfit for service from 30 April until 30 October. On 17 June he received the good news that he had been promoted to Captain. By now he had returned home to hospital in England where he slowly began to recover. However, he did not spend all this time in hospital. On 12 July 1916 he was granted leave for three weeks and he returned home to his family until 31 July. Elsa and the children were still living at The Gables, Purley, Surrey and he was happy to back in their care.

Elsa and the children were delighted to see him and Sydney was pleased to be home for three whole weeks without someone trying to kill him. Although he had survived, it looked unlikely he would be able to fly in combat again and while his future was uncertain he knew that being injured had probably saved his life. Life expectancy for pilots was only a few weeks at best and he had survived six weeks, two crashes and being shot up.

The home Sydney returned to would have been quite different from the country he left several months earlier. The war was really beginning to affect the civilian population. They were beginning to suffer quite badly from the German U-boat campaign in the

Sydney's children ready to sink the German Navy. From left to right: Verder, Herberta, Margaret, Constance.

Atlantic. The Germans were so successful in sinking supply ships from the USA that by April 1916 there was only enough grain left for six weeks. Fuel was also in short supply and people were being encouraged to grow their own food. Conscription had been introduced at the beginning of the year but it's not clear what work outside the home Elsa did. As her children were still quite young it's probable she was looking after them. With food shortages and ever rising prices this was likely to have been a full-time job, even for someone of independent means. There was also the ever present menace of Zeppelin raids.

On 13 October 1915 Croydon had come under attack when Zeppelin L14 under Commander Böcker dropped bombs on Edridge Road, Beech House Road, Oval Road, hitting the school, Chatsworth Road, Morland Road and Stretton Road, killing nine people and injuring fifteen. But so far Purley had avoided the attentions of the Zeppelins, despite its proximity to Beddington Aerodrome, a small Royal Flying Corps airfield set up in December 1915 to protect London from the Zeppelins. It was later to become a training base. In 1918 National Aircraft Factory No. 1 was set up with Waddon airfield attached to it for test flying. In March 1920 these two airfields were joined together to become Croydon airport.

The total number of RFC aircraft lost between April and June 1916 was 198 – 134 of these were through accidents, 33 through deterioration and 31 through enemy action.

If he had not been wounded Sydney would almost definitely have been flying in the Battle of the Somme, which began on 1 July 1916 and lasted until November that year. The RFC took over 19,000 reconnaissance pictures, destroyed 164 enemy aircraft, drove 205 enemy aircraft down to land and dropped 17,600 bombs on the enemy. However, this came at a price – the Battle of the Somme claimed 782 aircrafts and the lives of 576 pilots.

As the news of casualties slowly filtered through to the home front Sydney knew he had been lucky. Even more so when he went with Elsa to watch the release of *The Battle of the Somme*, a documentary about the battle that appeared in picture houses in August 1916. For the first time those on the home front felt they understood what their men were going through on the Western Front and as they watched it together Elsa realised just how fortunate Sydney was to still be alive.

On 23 September Commander Mathy's L31 Zeppelin passed over Purley on his way to Mitcham, Streatham, Brixton, Kennington and Leyton. He dropped four 128lb test bombs which exploded in a straight line across Downscourt Road and Hall Way. Fortunately, three of them landed in gardens and one on the road so casualties were light, with an 18-year-old woman injured and an elderly lady treated for shock. Elsa and the children were unharmed, although they were shocked by the proximity of the bombing. By then Sydney had been declared fit again and was back on active service.

Chapter Fifteen

No. 2 School of Aerial Gunnery

Although still considered unfit for General Service by 11 September, on 22 September 1916 Sydney was posted to HQ of the 17th Wing for duty with general working parties. Formed at Gosport on 9 August 1916, 17th Wing's role was to control units at Gosport (ARS) and Beaulieu. It moved to Beaulieu on 2 August 1917 and joined 7 Group on 13 May 1918. It was disbanded on 12 August 1918.

On 3 October 1916 Sydney was sent to the School of Aerial Gunnery at Hythe where he was appointed as a Wing Instructor on probation. On 30 October he was finally passed his medical and was considered fit for General Service again. He then returned to 7th Wing on 9 December 1916 as a Wing Instructor in aerial gunnery in a supervisory role. On 14 December 1916 he was posted to 25th Wing as the Wing Instructor Aerial Gunnery. Here he remained until 31 December 1916 when he made his way to Scotland to take up the post, on 12 February 1917, of Chief Instructor at the 2nd Auxiliary School of Aerial Gunnery at Turnberry as a Temporary Major. It would seem he was also detached on special appointment to 39 Training Squadron (TS) briefly between 9 and 17 February as a Squadron Leader. On 28 August 1916 39 TS were formed and based at Carlton.[1]

Turnberry was on the coast, almost on a headland and was overlooked by hills to the east. The Marquess of Ailsa had built a small private golf course on his estate in 1902. In 1904 the Glasgow and Scottish Railway took it over and in 1906 they opened a hotel and railway station. It was requisitioned by

Another of the planes used to teach at Turnberry.

the Royal Flying Corps during the First World War and the RAF returned there during the Second World War.

It covered an area of 150 hectares, 1,645m by 1,143m. There were three runways, the main one (north–east/south–west) parallel to the hills. The other two were relatively short due to lack of space and the approach to these was either over the sea or down low over the hills. The bomb dump was sited on the hills overlooking the airfield. A number of local properties were also requisitioned. There were four aircraft hangars, a repair shed and a salvage shed. There were sixteen canvas Bessonneaux hangars as well as other workshops and training huts. The Officers' Mess was in the hotel while the other ranks were accommodated in twenty-five huts.

Sydney with wound stripe, 1916.

The hotel sat halfway up the hillside and looked out over the aerodrome and the sea. The officers lucky enough to have rooms at the front could see Ailsa Craig, a mass of rock sticking out of the water several miles away. All meals were served in the main dining room with many Scottish dishes on the menu: kippered herring with eggs and they had treacle on their cereal. The dining room was known as the 'Officers' Mess – St. 2 Auxiliary School of Aerial Gunnery, R.F.C.'

At the hotel they were treated like private visitors and only charged 3*s* 6*d* per day, although it was quite difficult to get a bath at night as they all wanted one. The hotel had a large palm court full of flowers and was a very luxurious and relaxing place to stay. There were no visitors at the hotel, all the guests were officers in the RFC. There were some 200 officers there and

Turnberry.

the aerodrome was situated on the seafront. They could also go to nearby Girvan, a seaside resort about 6 miles away. There were no trains so they would often walk. Because so many of the pupils were quite young the school was very strict with considerable red tape. Unfortunately, this made it rather boring for the pilots leading to excessive alcohol consumption by some.

At 3am on 17 August 1917 there was some excitement for the officers when the fire alarm went off because the cellars in the basement were on fire. Fortunately, the floor above the cellars was concrete and the fire was not able to spread. However, the rest of the hotel rapidly filled with smoke all the way to the top so the men were briefly evacuated while the fire was put out and the smoke cleared.

The golf course, complete with bunkers, traps and a brook that circled through the field, had been turned into the aerodrome. The prevailing wind came off the sea which was good for take-offs, but meant that to land the pilots had to come down the steep hillside where the hotel was and make a very short landing to avoid the brook and the other hazards.

On 22 March 1917 the *London Gazette* listed the following: 'Group Instructor in Gunnery (graded as an Equipment Officer, 1st Class). – Capt.

D. E. Ward, Lond. R. (T.F.), and to be seed., vice Lieut. (Temp. Capt.) S. H. B. Harris, S.R.; Feb. 17th.' In the same week this appeared in *Flight*: 'Lieut. (Temp. Capt.) S. H. B. Harris, S.R., a Flight-Comdr., and to retain his temp, rank whilst so employed.'

At Turnberry there were more than eighty machines and the men trained on a variety of aircraft, including Vickers FB9, Airco DH2, Armstrong Whitworth FK3, Maurice Farman F11 Shorthorn, BE2C, BE2E and BE2C.

Sydney also flew the SE5 and the DH9A. The SE5 first began service with No. 56 Squadron in March 1917 and was deployed in France in April. The SE5 was found to be underpowered so in June 1917 the RFC rolled out the SE5a. It possessed a 200hp Hispano-Suiza engine and soon became the standard version of the aircraft with 5,265 produced in all. Austin Motors produced 1,650, the Air Navigation and Engineering Company 560, Martinsyde 258, the Royal Aircraft Factory 200, Vickers 2,164 and Wolseley Motor Company 431.

No. 2 AG School, complete with original coffee stain.

A Second World War biplane.

It soon became a favourite with British pilots because of its good visibility, high-altitude performance and the fact that it was easier to fly than the Sopwith Camel. However, there were production problems with the engine and these were not resolved until a high-compression version of the engine (200hp Wolseley Viper) was introduced in late 1917. They did not reach the front in large numbers until early 1918 and were then used to equip twenty-one British and two American squadrons. It served until the end of the war and was one of the few aircraft not outclassed by the new Fokker DVII, which was introduced by the Germans in May 1918.

The DH9A entered RAF service in mid-1918 and was still being used in 1931. It was a development of the DH9 day bomber used by four squadrons (110, 18, 99 and 205). During the war the DH9A dropped a total of 10½ tons of bombs with relatively light losses. It was 30ft long with a wing span of 46ft, a height of 10ft 9in, had a maximum speed of 114mph, was powered by one 400hp Liberty 12A and could carry 450lb of bombs. It had one Vickers gun facing forward and a Lewis gun facing aft.

Other aircraft were equipped with two Vickers machine guns that fired through the propeller. During flying exercises about thirty aircraft went up together and the airfield resembled a beehive. The course was two weeks long and much of the learning was done in small wooden huts with uncomfortable backless benches and small tables or on the ranges. Towards the end of the course the last few days were spent flying. The course work consisted of a practical knowledge of the Vickers gun, the Aldis and ring sight and the CC or Cowper or SPAD interrupter gear. There was a practical demonstration of each of the points together with a series of important notes the students would be urged to keep. A lecture was given each evening on one of the three points. Once a student understood each point he was taken out to the firing range to put his knowledge into practice. It was very fortunate that the aerodrome was isolated as many had never fired guns before and their aim was rather inaccurate. With regards to the gun they needed a thorough knowledge of the parts and how to care for it and clean it. As well as general handling, it was necessary to know how to deal with the most common faults such as stoppages and defective ammunition. They also needed to know how to use and care for the sights, in particular their use for deflection and alignment. Finally, they had to understand how the gears worked.

All the teaching was about aerial gunnery and was carried out by corporals and sergeants. There was no instruction about land drill. They were also taught how the new form of gun interrupter gear, called Constantinesco gear, worked.

Once they had finished the course work they were taken outside ready to begin the aerial work. Each student was taken up with an instructor and at first they practised diving and firing at targets on the ground. These were aircraft silhouettes laid out on the beach away from the field. They also fired at rafts with targets on.

Once they had mastered that they moved onto the next instruction which was learning to clear stoppages in the guns with one hand while flying the machine. From here they progressed to deflection target practice. In this exercise there were camera guns in two machines and a 'fight' took place. The camera guns showed how close they were to making a hit. Once they had passed the course some progressed to Ayr and the School of Aerial Fighting, others were sent to France and some to Catterick.

Observers spent their days firing guns, either on the range or in the air. Again, when they had a 'scrap' with another aircraft a photo was taken and this allowed them to work out whether they would have hit the other aircraft. To start with the men went up with the instructors as observers to get used to taking photos but towards the end of the course they would fly the machines themselves and take the photographs as well as control the guns. They worked every day including Sundays with only Saturday afternoons and evenings off.

When the weather was fine the men spent most of the day shooting their weapons at moving targets from the air. If the weather was not good they were unfortunately restricted to practising firing their machine guns on the ground. If time was lost due to the weather they would often work up until the last few hours they were there in an attempt to get as much practice in the air as possible. At the end of the course they were also expected to pass a written exam. There was not normally time to take any leave after their course at Turnberry so most would have to wait until they arrived at their next posting before being able to go home.

Training was not without its risks and there were numerous accidents at Turnberry, some fatal. An Avro 504 of No. 1 Fighting School crashed into a hangar roof in 1918. On 11 April 1918 another pilot, Second Lieutenant Charles William Janes, was killed while flying a Sopwith Camel. He lost control at 200ft while practising firing at a raft target and hit submerged rocks. He was 23 years old.

On 17 August 1917 South African General Jan Smuts presented a report on the future of air power to the War Council. In it he recognised the potential for the destruction of industrial and population centres and as such recommended the formation of a new service, to be on a level with the Royal Navy and the army. There were at least two main advantages of this decision.

On 1 July 1914 the Naval Air Service had become the Royal Naval Air Service and the naval wing of the RFC. At the beginning of the war the RNAS had 93 aircraft, 6 airships and a staff of 720. The airships were based around the coasts of Britain to give early warning of the approach of enemy ships and submarines. On 1 August 1915 the Royal Naval Air Service became independent of the RFC and was under the sole control of the navy. Its main role was to patrol Britain's coastline and defend London from bombers and Zeppelins, but attacks on German coastal positions in Belgium did take place and it did have two squadrons fighting on the Western Front.

The Royal Flying Corps supported the army with photo reconnaissance, artillery spotting and increasingly with bombing enemy airfields and trenches. A new service which amalgamated the two would be able to bring the under used aircraft of the RNAS into the Western Front.

The other advantage was that it would remove the intense rivalry between the two which had at times affected aircraft procurement. On 1 April 1918 the RAF was born from the amalgamation of the RFC and the RNAS. The RAF was under the control of a new body called the Air Ministry.

In May 1918 No. 1 School of Aerial Fighting also moved to Turnberry. By the autumn of 1918 it was one of the biggest air stations in Scotland with 1,215 officers and other ranks, including 205 women, and there were 204 pilots under instruction. As well as several captured German aircraft for training purposes, there were also 96 aircraft, 24 Avro 504s, 8 Bristol Fighters, 16 DH4 or DH9, 30 Sopwith Camels, 12 SE5s and 12 Sopwith Dolphins.

Chapter Sixteen

In Charge

After the Americans entered the war on 6 April 1917 Elsa's brother was drafted for military service and attended West Point. On 8 November 1917, Sydney was posted to Marske (by-the-Sea), with the rank of Lieutenant Colonel, to form and command No. 2 Fighting School, previously No. 4 Auxiliary School of Aerial Gunnery. The rest of the manpower came from the surplus of staff caused by the amalgamation of the two stations from Turnberry and Ayr. The instructors, like Sydney, were usually pilots who had seen action on the front line so were able to pass on the tactics needed to survive and win in the air. Training was not an easy posting. Many instructors considered it more dangerous to train rooky pilots than being on active service.

Marske was opened in Northern Command on 1 November 1917 as home for 4 (Auxiliary) School of Aerial Gunnery. It came under the command of 4 Area from 1 April 1918. On 6 May 2 School of Aerial Fighting was moved from Eastbourne and together they formed No. 2 School of Aerial Fighting and Gunnery. On 29 May this was changed to 2 Fighting School (2FS) and came directly under area control.

The aircraft initially allocated to Marske were a mixture of refurbished machines and older training aircraft. It was originally intended to use 24 Avro and 8 Bristol Fighters plus 16 DH4/9 and 20 Camels, but there were also other aircraft there.[1] Some old aircraft hulks were used as targets and these were tied to anchored rafts in the sea or placed in the sand dunes.

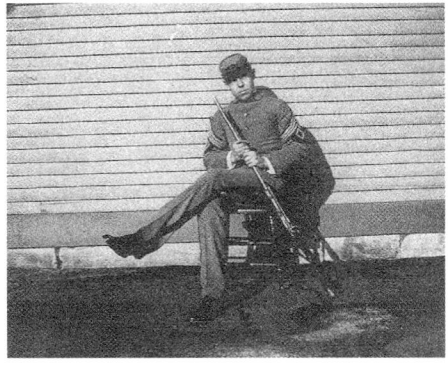

Elsa's brother, Wendell Herbert Verder, West Point, 1917.

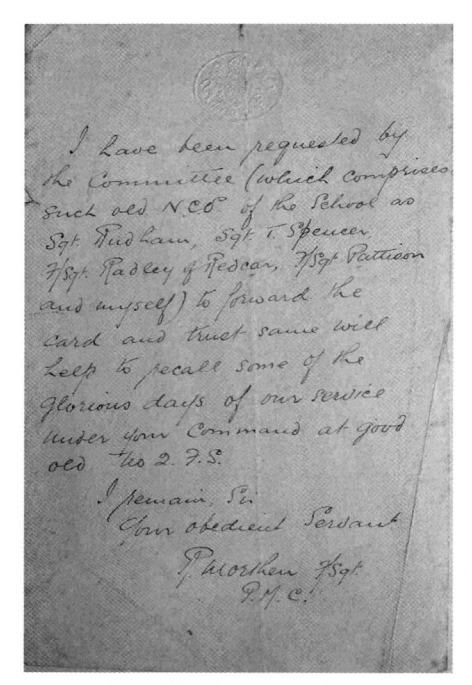

A letter from friends at No. 2 Aerial School of Gunnery.

A RFC menu.

2FS taught both single- and two-seat training. Pilots usually arrived there after 70 hours flying experience at a training depot station. If they completed the course successfully they would normally be promoted from Cadet to Second Lieutenant or full flying officer with the rank of Lieutenant. The course was run over two weeks after which the crews were posted to operational squadrons. Because the weather on the North East coast was not always good some of the courses took place without any flying at all.

The site for the aerodrome was in the large fields north of Ryehills Farm. The Redcar–Saltburn rail link ran alongside the fields and once the rail depot was set up men and equipment began to arrive. The RFC workforce, using the experience gained in France, began to set up the Armstrong huts which would be used for accommodation while the local farmers removed hedges and ditches. The aerodrome measured 1,000 by 900yd. There were seventeen temporary canvas Bessonneau hangars on the western boundary along Green Lane and four permanent hangars on the southern boundary.

These were four coupled 1917 pattern GS sheds measuring 170 x 200ft complete with folding wooden Esavian doors. Some of these would be used as temporary technical areas to erect and rig the aircraft as they arrived.

The telegraph wires to the north and west of the station were lowered, but the ones on the southwest were not. These would later cause an accident after a pilot crashed into them and was seriously injured. The air to ground firing range was on the east end of the aerodrome with targets set out on the cliffs. There were also several structures for the pilots to practise gunnery skills on. When they were being used red flags were hoisted at each end and guards posted to make sure people didn't stray into the area.

Up until 1917 damaging and writing off aircraft was frowned upon as it was cheaper to train pilots than replace aircraft. This meant many pilots went into action without the skills needed to survive as they were not allowed to push the aircraft to their limits or carry out any acrobatics. But the enormous loss of life and near annihilation of the RFC in the skies over France in April 1917 put an end to this. This attitude was challenged by Major Smith-Barry at Gosport Training School who actively encouraged his students to push their aircraft to the limit. New aerial manoeuvres were gradually developed and practised in two-seater aircraft with a communication device between student and instructor called the Gosport Tube.

The remains of a plane, possibly at Marske.

Gunnery practice.

By the end of 1917 plans had been drawn up for accommodation for the airmen and Marske began to play a pivotal role in the training of pilots. The training regime was very rigorous with pilots flying in conditions as close to combat as possible. This inevitably led to a high casualty rate, with almost half of all those who trained being killed or seriously injured. While many of the accidents were down to pilot error, a high percentage were due to engines stalling and machines breaking up as pilots took their aircrafts to the limits.

One of the most important things they were taught was the best tactics to utilise to put the Germans at a disadvantage. The element of surprise was of primary importance. If the pilot could get into a good position to shoot from before the enemy was aware of his presence it would narrow the opportunity for him to shoot back. But this was very difficult as the enemy was always on the lookout for opposing aircraft. The pilots soon learned that it was easier to surprise a formation of four or six than one or two.

The main tactic they learned was never to allow the enemy aircraft to get behind them, on their tail. If he succeeded it was very hard to throw him off because every time the pilot turned the enemy turned as well. Every move the pilot made the enemy made as well. But, they were told, that was exactly the position the pilot was aiming for. Once on the enemy's tail the pilot needed to line up and get into position to shoot him down as soon as possible. At the same time he was to continue keeping a look out for other enemy aircraft. It was emphasised that it was important that the pilot did not concentrate on the enemy for more than a few seconds or another Hun would be able to shoot at him without being in any danger himself. This was because it was very difficult to shoot an aircraft that was at right angles across the nose. It also required considerable judgement to know just how far ahead to aim. If the enemy aircraft was at right angles across the nose then the best option was to shoot the pilot and to make sure you got him in the upper part of the body. Igniting the aircraft was normally a matter of luck and usually meant some of the bullets had pierced the petrol tank and ignited the vapour escaping from it.

No. 2 AG School, Marske, from the air.

The cross shot was used mainly when combat was broken off for some reason, perhaps the gun had jammed or the engine was running badly and escape became necessary. While turning to flee the enemy was able to get a direct shot from behind. This was very dangerous and the answer was for the pilots to watch carefully over their shoulder and as soon as they judged that he was about to fire they should turn the machine quickly and fly at right angles to him. As the bullets passed behind them, the next tactic was to turn quickly to face him and open with cross fire.

It wasn't just when fighting alone they had to be careful. If they were fighting with other machines of their squadron they were told that not only did they need to watch very carefully to see where they were, but also whether other aircrafts in the squadron needed help as it was a matter of honour to go to the rescue of any other aircraft, however hopeless the task might seem.

Another key point was to think quickly because all battles differed and they would need to be able to react to circumstances and be adaptable. If large numbers of aircraft were involved they were taught that the best tactic was to try and be slightly higher than their opponent. This made manoeuvring easier. If that was not possible another tactic was to wait until the aircraft attempted to dive at or attack them and then pull the nose of the machine up and fire. It was often necessary to fly straight at an enemy machine as if they were going to crash head on, firing all the time. At the crucial moment one aircraft would swerve up, the other down, although there was always the danger they would both choose the same direction. The RFC prided themselves that they would never give way and that it was the Hun who would usually swerve away. However, this was not always the case and there were many mid-air collisions.

The American 25th Pursuit Squadron were stationed at Marske from 23 April to 7 August 1918 and Captain W.E. Johns, the author of the Biggles books, was also a flying instructor at Marske before being sent to 55 Squadron in France. Although he had no combat experience, it was not uncommon for the best new pilots to become flying instructors.

Captain Johns' first few days at Marske were not particularly successful. His initial flight in a Sopwith Camel ended with him ditching it in the sea. The following day the engine died in almost the same spot and although he managed to get back to shore, his wheels became caught in the sand dunes and turned over. Despite the fact that he fractured his nose and damaged his knee, the following day he took off again and this time did not even reach the sea. The engine died as he took off and he flew into a house on the edge of the airfield.

While many pilots passed their course without incident, others were accident prone. One, nicknamed 'Smasher', wrote off eight aircraft and still passed the course, crashed again in France and surprisingly survived the war. Another, who was unable to hit anything, adjusted his gun sight without informing his instructor and proceeded to pepper the bath-house with machine-gun bullets.

One of those injured at Marske was Captain Roy Brown, a Canadian pilot. Captain Brown shot down Manfred von Richtofen on 21 April 1918 for which he was awarded a Bar to his DSC and returned to England to be presented to the King. After suffering from various stomach complaints, probably caused by nerves and the constant ingestion of castor oil fumes and spray from the aircraft engines, he was posted to Marske on 6 July 1918 as an instructor. Nine days later he took off in a Sopwith Camel on what should have been a normal training flight. But the engine cut out at about 200ft. He struggled to control the aircraft but it stalled and nosedived into the ground from 60ft. Somehow Roy survived. It was touch and go as he had a crushed right lung, three broken ribs, a fractured right clavicle and concussion. He remained on the nominal role as an instructor until he was discharged from the RAF on 1 August 1919.

In March 1918 the Sidcot suit became widely available. The Sidcot suit was inspired by successful trials on oil-soaked cotton flying suits the previous year. It was made from light Burberry material, lined with fur and silk and with extra fur at the neck and the cuffs. It was worn with the Mk1 helmet which was also fur lined and had retained the cylindrical leather pads from earlier versions. These were in front of the ears to reduce wind noise. The helmet was lined with fleece of gabardine but if not lined it would be worn with a wool undercap.

Other courses in basic flying were also held at Marske and there was a constant stream of cadets learning the rudimentary elements of flying and gaining additional flying time.

But it was not all training. The newly formed RAF became involved in community events as well. On 3 May 1918 the Middlesbrough and District Chamber of Trade organised a big promotion to encourage the sale of War Bonds. These War Bonds were be on sale from the 6 to 11 May to raise money for the war. Bought for 15*s* 6*d*, they could be reclaimed after 5 years for £1. To help advertise this they organised an aerial display in the skies over Middlesbrough. The plan was for the aircraft to carry cards promoting the War Bonds and then drop them over the watching crowds. Those lucky

This photograph was taken at Marske. Sydney is sixth from the right, front row, next to the lady.

RNAS airship.

enough to collect them would find a voucher for a free War Bond. However, some of the flights had to be cancelled as the skies were hazy and there were reports in the newspapers the following day that people were seen fighting in Albert Park as they tried to find the free vouchers.

Although Sydney's room was quite basic in the Armstrong huts, he did manage to find room for his dog. The Officers' Saloon, however, was clean and airy with tablecloths, potted palms and two snooker tables.

A closer view of the RNAS airship.

According to his service records, on 5 July 1918 Sydney was promoted to Lieutenant Colonel as long as he carried on working in that capacity. But this was cancelled on 2 August 1918. This may be because the amalgamation of the two services into the new RAF meant the Army ranks no longer applied or that his services were no longer needed at that rank.

At the end of hostilities the aerodrome remained open and there were two pilots killed after the war finished. By the end of the war the RAF had 22,647 aircraft, 30,122 officers and 263,410 other ranks, but this was to reduce drastically as Britain slowly demilitarised. Between November 1918 and January 1920 26,087 officers, 21,259 cadets and 227,229 other ranks were demobilised. Aircraft were also sold off at knock-down prices. Top fighter aircraft such as the SE5a could be purchased for as little as £5 and many pilots did buy them. Some bought them because it would allow them to continue flying and others in the hope of making a living from flying after the war. In December 1918 Marske became

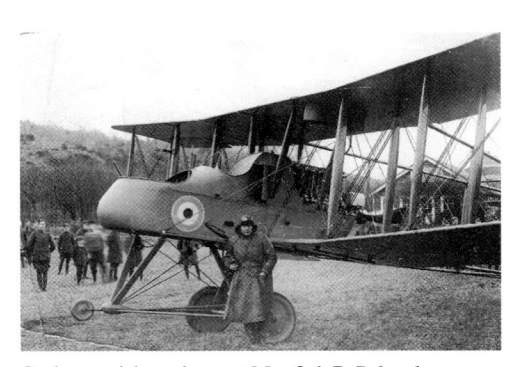

Sydney with a plane at No. 2 AG School.

Marske.

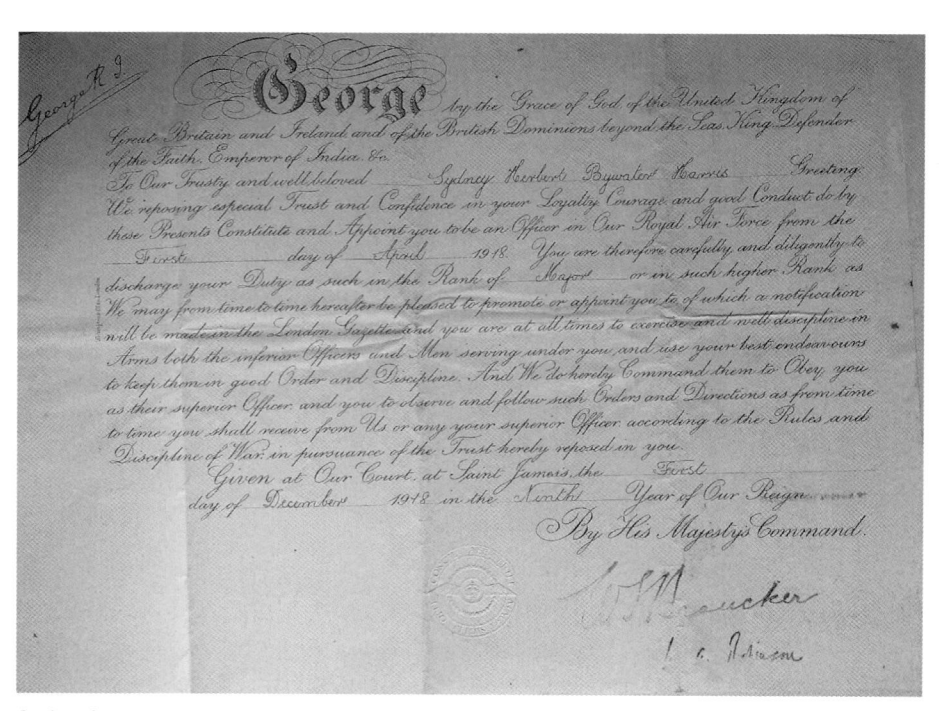

Sydney's promotion to Major in the newly formed RAF.

Sydney in his RAF uniform, 1918.

Sydney's daughters. From left to right: Constance, Margaret and Herberta.

the Headquarters for No. 8 Wing RAF with Wing Commander Guy De Dombasle, St George Cross, OBE as Commanding Officer.

Sydney was awarded the Air Force Cross on 3 June 1919, by which time the RAF had 150 Squadrons, 114,000 personnel and 4,000 combat aircraft. Aircraft speeds had increased to 130mph, they could dive at 200mph and were now able to attack with twin guns. It was not only speed that had increased, the flight ceiling, firepower and engines had also developed. Aircraft were no longer the passive observers they had been at the beginning of the war. Instead, they had evolved from a primitive means of fighting to a highly organised, large-formation, high-altitude controlled combat vehicle.

As the war ended it became apparent to all that in any future war aircraft would play a major part. In Britain, USA and Italy a theory developed that bombers would be all powerful, a theory that would tested by Hitler in the 1930s, first in Spain and then during the Second World War.

In June 1919, Sydney's fourth daughter and his fifth child, Patricia Nella Verda Harris, was born. From 1 May 1919 to 9 August 1919 Sydney was graded for pay and allowances as a Lieutenant Colonel because, even though he was a Major, he was employed as a Lieutenant Colonel. This was reported in the *London Gazette*, 23 September 1919: 'The undermentioned Majs. are graded for purposes of pay and allowances as Lt.-Cols. whilst empld. as Lt.-Cols. >(A. and iS.) : S. H. B. .Harris, A.F.C., from, 1st May 1919 to 9th Aug. 1919'. However, after 23 September 1919 his grade for payroll was once again reduced back to Major and his records seem to indicate this was backdated to May 1919. Yet, in the monthly Air Force List for August 1919 he is referred to as 'Wing Commander SHBH Harris'. This inconsistency, together with the need to support his ever growing family, may have contributed to his decision to leave the RAF in August 1919 and take up the offer of a new job as a branch manager for Sun Life Assurance Ltd.

Chapter Seventeen

From Aircraft to Trains

During the First World War and immediately afterwards the railways were removed from the control of private companies and were managed instead by the national government. During the war the NUR (National Union of Railwaymen) and ASLEF (Associated Society of Locomotive Engineers and Firemen) negotiated an increase in wages with the government, although these were below the rate of inflation. In March 1919 the government announced its plans to standardise and reduce the wartime rates of pay. For many this would be a reduction of 33*s* in their pay packets. Negotiations between the government and the unions failed so at midnight on 26 September the second national rail strike took place. One of the points raised by the NUR General Secretary was that sacrifices made during the war were not being acknowledged by the government.

During the strike Sydney drove a train for the Great Northern Railway Company, a railway company established under the Great Northern Railway Act of 1846. The main line ran from London's King's Cross via Hitchin, Peterborough and Granthan to York. There was a loop line from Peterborough to Bawtry via Boston and Lincoln and branch lines to Sheffield and Wakefield. The main line became part of the east coast main line when they amalgamated with the Midland Railway in 1893. This gave its two parent companies, the Midland Railway and the Great Northern Railway, access to the ports of East Anglia and the lucrative holiday revenue from the Midlands to the east coast resorts. At over 180 miles, it was the longest joint railway system in Britain.

The strikers were not happy that Sydney was driving their trains and several times he found himself under fire from rocks and stones. Having survived anti-aircraft fire and numerous bombings in the First World War, Sydney was completely undaunted by this and it just added to his determination to continue. At the same time his old aerodrome at Marske was also utilised as aircraft were used to deliver the mail instead.

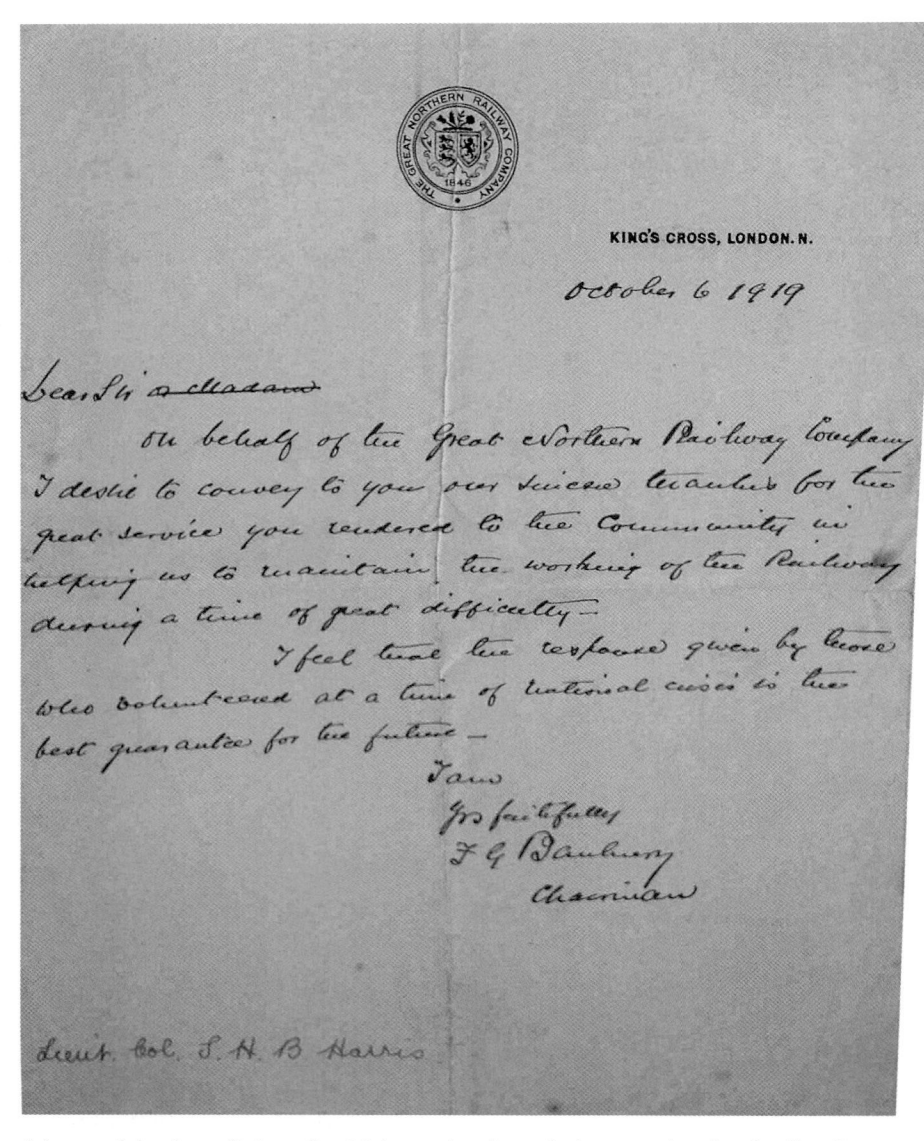

> KING'S CROSS, LONDON. N.
>
> October 6 1919
>
> Dear Sir or Madam
>
> On behalf of the Great Northern Railway Company I desire to convey to you our sincere thanks for the great service you rendered to the Community in helping us to maintain the working of the Railway during a time of great difficulty —
>
> I feel that the response given by those who volunteered at a time of national crisis is the best guarantee for the future —
>
> I am
> Yrs faithfully
> F G Banbury
> Chairman
>
> Lieut. Col. S. H. B Harris

A letter of thanks to Sydney for driving trains through the second national rail strike.

The strike continued for nine days and on 5 October the government agreed to extend the existing wage levels for another year. They further agreed a standardisation of wages across the railway companies and a maximum 8-hour day. Sydney returned reluctantly to his day job, but it would not be that long before he was called on again.

A family gathering, 1920s.

Sydney's children, 1919. From left to right: Baby Patricia with Herberta, Verder, Margaret and Constance.

Throughout the 1920s Sydney was still a member of the KEH Lodge and attended regularly. He also chaired the 21st Annual Dinner of the KEH in 1923. On 14 May in the same year Elsa and her youngest daughter, Patricia, now aged 3, went to Philadelphia, Pennsylvania, USA. They left on the ship *London Exchange* and didn't return until 17 September that year. Sydney appears to have remained in the family home, The Gables, Purley, Surrey.

His only son Verder had also joined the RAF and was presented with the Groves Memorial Prize in 1924 at

Verder flying a DH9A over Iraq, *c*. 1926.

Verder.

Cover of the invitation to the 21st Annual Dinner of the KEH, 1923.

A photograph of Sydney, then chairman, which featured inside the invitation to the 21st Annual Dinner of the KEH, 1923.

Cranwell for being the best pilot of his year. He was now a Pilot Officer with 55 Squadron RAF which was on policing duties in Iraq, where 55 Squadron had been based since August 1920. Verder was now having some adventures of his own, as the following letter to his father explained.

PO 55 Sqdn

23.3.26

My dear old Dad
Many thanks for your letter and the enclosed one from S/Ldr Beaulah.

I expect mother has been wondering why she hasn't heard from me during the past fortnight but I have been out in blue – the Adjutant sent you a chit I believe.

On Wednesday the 10th I left here as a passenger in a machine that had to go to Kirkuk so I could get to know the country. It was rather a thick day and we missed the way after passing Kifri. Kirkuk is a bit hard to hit on a bad day as it is more or less in the hills. We flew about a bit and then decided to try and get back to Kifri. Unfortunately the engine cut out and we had to try and land, down hill and against a cross wind – the country is very inhospitable all around there. The ground was covered with boulders, we hit one and went on our back but neither of us were any the worse for it. Some Kurds, armed to the teeth, soon rode up but were friendly. Neither of us knew any Kurdish and only a word or two of Arabic – very few of them understand it. We found out however that we were about a mile and a half from their village – Wasta Khedir in Kurdistan. We found out that we were 10 hours by horse for Kirkuk and 6 hours from Chamchamal. We thought at the time that they meant miles but apparently they always measure distance by the time it takes to ride it. The headman of the village, a very friendly old chap named Said Jakki, put an armed guard over the crash and took us back to his village and gave us food in his house. He wrote a note giving what we thought was our position etc and sent a horseman into Kermanshah with it.

It started to rain very heavily indeed and we slept in the village in the headman's house. Early the next morning we went down to the crash and started to take off the guns and instruments etc. In the afternoon an Assyrian officer with some national police and the son of the Qureshi Imam arrived as well. Kurdish class a Qureshi Imam as a Kurdish official who lives in Chamchamal.

No machines came on the Thursday and on the Friday so at midday on Friday I rode into Kermanshah arriving there at about 6 o'clock. There is a half company of Lahore and a British Officer stationed at Chamchamal and I got him to send a horseman into Kirkuk with a note to the Flight of 30 Squadron which is there.

Early on Saturday morning a couple of machines came over and dropped a note saying they were just going up to Sulaymaniyah on operations and couldn't stop and that some Lahore cavalry were on their way to the crash.

Owing to the heavy rain we were held up at Chamchamal until Thursday when two machines came over for us. We got back to Hinaidi on the Friday. I am very pleased I had the experience for it was very interesting, at least until the crash.

All the country around Wasti Khadi is wild and hilly. It is lucky we crashed near a friendly village for many of them are not, especially on the left bank of the Bassisah Alri – we crashed about two hundred yards on the right bank.

The food is very cheap and quite good. They use their fingers – picking up the food with pieces of chapatti which is uncooked bread and looks rather like a large cold dry pancake. They drink something which is made from goats milk which is refreshing but very bitter.

A pass for Sydney as a volunteer train driver at Wood Lane during the General Strike, May 1926.

Letter of thanks to Sydney for his assistance during the General Strike.

The third national railway strike took place during the General Strike in 1926 (4–12 May 1926). The TUC had called the strike to prevent wage reduction and worsening conditions for the miners. On 30 June 1925 mine owners had announced that they intended to reduce wages by ending the current wage agreement, abolishing the minimum wage principle and shorter hours and to go back to district agreement rather than the existing national agreement.

The General Council of the Trade Union Congress promised to support the miners in the dispute, but then the Conservative government intervened and provided the necessary money to bring miners' wages back up to previous levels. This event became known as Red Friday and a victory for working class solidarity. However, Stanley Baldwin, the Prime Minister, announced that the subsidy would only last nine months. In the meantime the government would set up a Royal Commission under Sir Herbert Samuel to look at the problems in the mining industry. In March 1926 the Samuel

Commission published its report which recognised that some reorganisation was necessary but rejected the idea of nationalisation. It also recommended that the government subsidy should be withdrawn and that miners' wages should be reduced.

While the Samuel Commission was publishing its report the mine owners decided to publish new terms of employment. These extended the 7-hour working day, reduced the wages of all miners and went back to district wage agreements. The effect on the average miner would be a 10–25 per cent cut in his wages. Anyone who did not agree to the terms by 1 May would be locked out of the pits.

The TUC held a conference on 1 May 1926 and subsequently announced that a General Strike in defence of miners' wages and hours would begin two days later. Not everyone supported the idea of a strike. The leaders of the TUC made frantic efforts to reach an agreement with the government and the mine owners. Ramsey MacDonald, leader of the Labour Party, also refused to support the strike, instead arguing that the best way to change things was through the ballot box, not through strikes. He considered the election of A.J. Cook as Miners' Secretary as the worst thing that had ever happened to the TUC.[1]

The TUC had called the strike on the understanding that they would take over the negotiations from the Miners Federation. Talks continued into Sunday night and they were almost close to agreement when Baldwin called off the talks. The reason behind this decision was that the printers at the *Daily Mail* had refused to publish an article attacking the strike. Although the TUC apologised for the printers' behaviour, Baldwin refused to continue the talks so the strike began the next day.

The TUC plan was first to bring out the workers in the key industries: the railwaymen, dockers, transport workers, printers, builders and iron and steel workers. This was a total of 3 million men, a fifth of the adult male population. The second phase would be to call out other trade-union members such as the shipyard workers and engineers.

The strike began peaceably enough. London's transport network was almost at a complete standstill. There were a few buses running driven by non-union labour and these were full as thousands of commuters tried to use them. The only news service running was the BBC because all the printers were on strike. The army and volunteers distributed food and other essentials and in Parliament the budget was passed with virtually no debate as the opposition only wanted to discuss the strike. The Prince of Wales came back from Paris and attended the debate.

The following day both sides published their version of events. The *British Worker* highlighted the strength of support for the strike and the solidarity of the British worker and stressed that the strike was an industrial dispute, not an attack on the constitution. The government published the *British Gazette*. It was edited by Winston Churchill and stressed that the aim was to overthrow the constitution. Because it also ridiculed the strikers the general public found it rather distasteful and treated it with suspicion. Although trams were running in most towns, a large hostile crowd gathered in London in an attempt to prevent them running. By using military staff and emergency powers the government finally managed to get some trains operating.

As before, Sydney immediately volunteered his services as a train driver. This time to the London Underground railways: Metropolitan District Railway, London Electric Railway, City and South London Railway and Central London Railway. There was less scope here for rocks and stones to be thrown at the cab but he still had to get to work.

A number of London buses were running, although the police had to escort them and there was wire mesh to protect the drivers. There were several buses attacked in London and some crowd trouble in Leeds and Nottingham.

By day three Sydney was not the only one driving the Underground trains in London and there was a skeleton service running. That night the railways announced that 1,700 trains had run, and over 80 buses had also run, but 50 had been damaged. The government began to take stronger measures to protect those who were not on strike and the volunteers who had replaced the strikers. Things were becoming much more heated. There were crowd problems in Edinburgh with civilians and police hurt. There were also disturbances in several parts of London, Leeds and Aberdeen.

By Friday, 7 May the government announced that strikers were planning to disrupt the temporary transport networks. Security was increased, another 50,000 special constables were recruited, but nothing happened. None of this really mattered to Sydney who was thoroughly enjoying himself. He hadn't felt so alive since the war and despite the widespread intimidation nothing would have convinced him to stop doing his bit to keep the country working. He had instructed Elsa and the children to stay indoors where they would be safe, but nothing would have induced him to do the same. The number of trains running was increasing and by the end of the day 2,400 had run.

The Archbishop of Canterbury appealed for a return to peaceful negotiation but this was not broadcast by the BBC until 11 May. The *British Gazette* did not publish it at all.

On Saturday, 8 May Stanley Baldwin broadcast on the BBC. He accused the unions of mounting an attack on the constitution and repeated that the government was not attacking the living standards of workers. The TUC responded by asking why the Prime Minister had only asked for the strike to end but had not appealed for the mine owner to end their lock-outs. Many businesses and shops that normally opened on a Saturday remained shut. Meanwhile, the Russian trade unions sent the TUC a large cheque, which it immediately returned, uncashed.

Although there was no violence and little ill-feeling, several lorries were prevented from leaving the docks in London so a 2-mile military convoy with sixteen armoured cars was used instead. Observers from the USA were heard to remark that minor strikes in their country caused more violence than the whole General Strike had so far.

By Sunday a small but steady stream of strikers were going back to work. Many of those on strike went to church where churchmen appealed for an end to the strike. Meanwhile, some Labour politicians protested when Cardinal Bourne, the head of the Catholic Church, called the strike a sin. The Home Secretary continued to appeal for new recruits to the Civil Constabulary and this received a good response.

By day 7, Monday, 10 May, over 3,677 trains ran and the government became more confident that the strike would soon collapse. Their emergency supply services had been successful and they were sure many of the strikers were returning to work. Behind the scenes Sir Herbert Samuel began trying to negotiate a settlement between the mine owners and the miners. The government made it clear that he was not doing so on their behalf and there were rumours they had tried to discourage him.

Without telling the miners the TUC negotiating committee met Sir Herbert Samuel and together they worked out a set of proposals to bring the strike to an end.

These included a minimum wage for all colliery workers, a national wages board with an independent chairman, alternative employment for workers who had lost jobs because of pit closures and the wages subsidy to be renewed while negotiations continued.

Meanwhile, the government was openly encouraging workers to return to work, promising to protect those who had not gone on strike or who returned from victimisation. In Manchester the Ship Canal was closed to wheat shipments as flour workers came out on strike and there were bitter exchanges between Labour and Conservative MPs in Parliament as Labour MPs complained about police violence towards strikers in Southwark.

On Tuesday, 11 May the TUC called out the engineering and ship-building workers and refused a request from print unions to allow some papers to be printed. Meanwhile, the National Sailor's Union and the Fireman's Union took court action to prevent union officials calling union members out on strike. High Court Judge Justice Asbury ruled that the General Strike was illegal and that the 1906 Trade Disputes Act did not protect those involved in a strike. There was still little violence in England but in Glasgow police had made between 300 and 400 arrests. The TUC General Committee also held a special meeting to discuss the results of their negotiating committee. Although Samuel had warned that wages might be reduced as a result of subsequent negotiations, the TUC decided to accept the terms he had proposed and call the strike off. These terms were rejected by the Miners' Federation.

On Wednesday, 12 May a TUC representative went to Downing Street and announced that the strike had been called off. At the same time they tried to persuade the government to support the proposals put forward by Samuel and to guarantee there would be no victimisation of strikers. However, the government refused.

On 21 June 1926 the government introduced a Bill suspending the Seven Hours Act for five years leaving miners to go back to an 8-hour day. The following month the mine owners introduced new terms of employment based on the 8-hour day. The miners were furious and although the General

Strike was over, the miners' strike continued until October 1926 when hardships began to force the men back to work. By November most had returned, but many were victimised and were unable to gain employment for several years. Those that did return were forced to accept longer hours, reduced pay and district agreements.

The following year, 1927, the government passed the Trade Disputes and Trade Union Act which made all sympathetic strikes illegal. It also ensured trade-union members had voluntarily to contract in to pay the political levy, made mass picketing illegal and forbade civil servant unions from affiliating with the TUC.

Sydney went back to working in the insurance industry, but he was still in contact with old friends, as the following letter demonstrates.

Headquarters
Air Defence of Great Britain
Royal Air Force
Hillingdon House
Uxbridge

31st August 1928

To:
Lieutenant Colonel SHB Harris. RFC.,
'Seacroft'
Kingsgate
Thanet

Dear Harris,
   Many thanks for the loan of 'War Birds' which I return herewith. It is most interesting and bears the unquestioned hall-mark of truth and was obviously not written with ultimate publication in mind.
   One is bound to notice how whilst he is France with the RFC the whole business begins to get on his nerves and goes on doing so more and more, until I should think that the poor fellow was in a pretty bad way by the time he went off on his last patrol.
   The book is of particular interest to me; pages 59–83 cover the period during which this fellow was at London Colney, January 1st 1918 to the end of February; at

that time I was Station Adjutant of London Colney and also Adjutant of 56 TS. Most of the 4 incidents described during that period I remember well; his version of them is not always absolutely accurate due, of course, to the fact that American Cadets attached to an RFC Station would not have the Adjutant's inside view of things.

The description on page 61 of the trouble about Springs and the DeGamo going off on Pups I remember very well indeed, with the exception that I have no recollection of 'catching hell' for not carrying out orders! An amusing thing about this incident is that after this fellow had himself been off in a Pup on February 8th (page 75), he recorded in his diary on the next day that he would hate to think what would have happened to DeGamo and Springs if we had allowed them to go off on Pups when they arrived at London Colney! He even says that if in America they attempted to put pupils straight off Curtisses on to Pups it would be a source of satisfaction and profit to the undertakers.

I witnessed the unpleasant incident described on page 75. The whole Squadron, together with the attached Americans, were having their photographs taken, as he describes in his diary. As a matter of fact the photographer had uncovered the lens a very small fraction of a second before the two Avros collided and he gave a normal exposure before covering up again. I afterwards saw a print of the particular negative; every person in the photograph was looking up in the air with a fixed expression of genuine horror.

Stillman, the American who was not killed on the spot, saved himself by climbing out along the fuselage of the Avro clinging to the empanage. The two locked machines spun down quite slowly and as far as I can remember Stillman was hardly injured at all by the crash, but had sustained severe burns from the fire. On page 83 he tells us that Stillman is dead; he was going on extraordinary well and was to have been moved to a London hospital the next day when one of those clots that often form in the blood vessels in cases of bad burns got to his head and put him out like a snuffed candle.

I hope you will take my assurances that the statement of page 60 that 'there is no discipline' at London Colney certainly did not apply to the RFC personnel there, though it might have done to a certain extent to the Americans!

You will notice that on page 62, G R Elliot, (the CO), and I are dubbed non flyers. That is really a bit 'ard!

Roderick Leopold Keller, who is quite well described on page 69, fulfilled our friend's prediction that if he wasn't careful as well as lucky he was going to push the golden gate too hard and get in. A few months later he was killed at London Colney flying the first Snipe that had been seen at the Station; it had been brought over by a visiting officer and he had obtained permission to take it up.

Many thanks again for the loan of the book. Apart from the general aspect, it is a most interesting tribute from a foreigner to the Royal Flying Corps.

Kind Regards
Yours sincerely[2]

Having returned to work with Sun Life, Sydney remained a branch manager until 1929 when the ill-health that had plagued him since he'd been injured finally caused a breakdown and he retired on a pension. The next few months were difficult as Sydney tried to recover mentally and physically from the effects of the First World War.

Sydney and Elsa both continued to travel, although usually separately. At some point in 1930 Sydney appears to have decided to take a trip abroad and subsequently travelled to Indonesia, returning on 20 September 1930 to Southampton on the *Jan Pieterszoon Coen*. His address at this time was given as 80 Lyncroft Gardens, Hemel Hempstead, London NW5 and his occupation as a 'Retired Lieutenant Colonel'. Barely two months later, on 29 November 1930, Sydney is again travelling, this time on the *Manela* to Port Said, Egypt, his occupation listed as an 'Airways Official' and it is believed he was part of a project to set up new air routes.

Elsa also seems to have enjoyed travelling as she and Patricia visited Indonesia, albeit a year later. They returned on the *Marnix van Sint Aldegonde* on 7 July 1931. At this time she and Patricia were living somewhere in Italy where Elsa and Sydney had built a house. Unfortunately, there are no details about this.

Sydney and family at their home in Kingsgate, Kent, 1929. Back row, from left to right: Herberta, Betty, Margaret and Verder. Front row: Elsa, Patricia, Sydney.

From Aircraft to Trains   183

Elsa in her new car, 1930.

Elsa, 1930.

Sydney and Elsa, 1930.

By 1933 Sydney and Elsa are back in England and living at the same address again in 13 Devonshire Terrace, Lancaster Gate, London W2. They do not appear on the electoral registers for 1934 but in 1935 are still registered at the Devonshire Terrace address. During the next two years, 1936 and 1937, Elsa was still registered as living there with her daughters, Constance and Margaret. Sydney, however, is no longer there. In April 1937 he is registered as a Civilian Assistant for the RAF and living at The Cottage, Cranwell Village, Lincolnshire and due in court on 9 December at 10.30am in The Municiple Buildings Boston. The same year, in Edinburgh, he was declared bankrupt.

Patricia Verder Harris, 4 January 1931.

Sydney in Egypt, 1931.

Chapter Eighteen

The Spanish Civil War

Spain had been wracked by strife from opposing political extremists from right and left of the political spectrum since the 1920s. The Great Depression of 1929 made things worse and by 1931 the country's centrist republic was doomed. The left-wing Popular Front won the elections in 1936 and this led to a coup by right-wing military officers in Spanish Morocco. It was led by General Francisco Franco and was followed by revolts in mainland garrisons at Cadiz, Seville, Burgos, Saragossa, Huesca and other places. To start with the Republican government had the upper hand. They controlled the country's communication network, the capital city, Madrid, and most of the other large urban areas. Madrid also held the country's gold reserves. The main rebel force was stranded in Morocco and the rebellions in both Madrid and Barcelona were easily put down by the government between the 18 and 20 July. Facing defeat, the Nationalists appealed to Hitler and Mussolini for help. On 28 July they both, apparently independently, decided to provide transport to bring the main rebel force across the Straits of Gibraltar to Spain.

The Republican government had already appealed to Britain and France for military aid when the coup started. But neither country wanted to get involved and instead in September 1936 they signed a Non-Intervention Treaty. The thinking behind the treaty was that if the signatories failed to provide military aid the war in Spain would be contained. Germany and Italy also signed the treaty but then ignored it and continued to supply support to the Nationalists. France veered between support for the Republic and enforcing the ban, thus much of the aid sent by the Russians was often halted at the Spanish–French border. Britain was the only country to abide by the agreement.

There were reasons behind Britain and France's reticence to become involved. Most British and French politicians were determined to see that the horrors of the First World War were never repeated and they assumed the Germans and Italians felt the same. While the populations of Germany and Italy might have had little desire to fight another war, Hitler had no such reservations. Furthermore, Hitler and the senior members of his Nazi Party considered war a purifying element that would clear out the weakest members of their society. There were also many right-wing Conservative politicians in Britain and France who considered that a Republican Spain was no different to Soviet Russia, and as this was something they feared they had no desire to support the Republicans.

The Russians were in a quandary. They were militarily weak and Germany was making aggressive noises in their direction. There might be a point in the future when they would need support from Britain and France so they did not want to upset them. However, if they did nothing to help the Republican government in Spain, they ran the risk of losing credibility among European communists.

It soon became apparent that non-intervention was not working and by August 1936 the Nationalists had control of the south and the west of the country, although the Republicans had managed to prevent Madrid from falling. Stalin finally began sending tanks, weapons, aircraft and ammunition to help the Republicans. But in return he insisted that all Spain's gold reserves should be shipped to Russia for safekeeping and everything the Republicans bought from the Russians was charged at the top price.

Having spent some time living in Italy under Mussolini, it is perhaps not surprising that Sydney took the first opportunity offered to him to fight against fascism. Another factor that may have swayed him, given his straitened financial circumstances, was that there was money to be made. The Spanish Republican government were willing to pay for pilots. The exact amount is unclear but it appears to have been around £200 a month, paid in advance, plus expenses. To adventurers, idealists and those looking to earn some extra cash the opportunity to go to Spain was too good to be missed. Before long, pilots from all round the world were making their way to Spain, and others were busy procuring aircraft and flying them to Spain.

In August 1936 the Air Ministry became so concerned about the number of British civil aircraft finding their way to Spain they issued a 'Notice to Airmen' warning they faced having their licence either suspended or even cancelled if they made false declarations to Customs while attempting to deliver aircraft to either side in the war. This did not deter Sydney or many other pilots.

Having managed to halt the number of aircrafts being flown to Spain from Britain, the next threat came from adverts in the press calling for British pilots to fly aircrafts from France to Spain and to fly them against the insurgents. The Republican government had already accepted a number of mercenary pilots from various countries, including those fleeing the fascist regimes in Italy and Germany.

On 9 January 1937 the Cabinet decided to make the Foreign Enlistment Act of 1870 applicable to Spain. This made it illegal for any British people to take part in the Spanish Civil War. Those found guilty could be imprisoned for up to two years or be fined or both. On 20 February, the Non Intervention Committee enforced its ban on volunteers.

Because of this it has been impossible to discover exactly what Sydney, at the age of 55, was doing in Spain. What is known is that he went in support of the Republican government in 1936 and returned sometime before August in 1937. Because of his age it is unlikely he was flying in combat, although given his extensive experience and his love of danger, excitement and adventure it can't be completely ruled out. However, it is more likely he was either delivering aircrafts from Britain to Spain and/or training pilots in the International Brigades.

The authorities soon realised that the easiest way to stop people volunteering to fight for the International Brigades was to refuse to issue them passports thus preventing them leaving the country. This did not prevent volunteers who just went to Victoria train station and bought special weekend tickets to France as these did not require passports. However, it was not always completely straightforward. Sometimes Special Branch would confront the volunteers at the station and try to persuade them not to go, although they never appeared to arrest anyone.

On the train they were told not to draw attention to themselves and once in Calais they took the train to Paris and from there to Toulouse. The train to Toulouse was often full of volunteers from various nationalities, also going to fight for the Spanish Republic and there seemed to be little secrecy about where they were going. For a while there were even banners proudly proclaiming the Spanish revolutionary government's slogan, 'They shall not pass' ('No Pasarán'), being waved optimistically out of the windows. But as they came closer to the Spanish border they were normally told to take them down.

If the pilots were not flying aircrafts down from France they were taken by train to Port Bou on the Spanish border. Having crossed the border, they travelled by train to Barcelona and then Madrid. Here they were greeted with wild enthusiasm by the Spanish and given a hero's welcome. Virtually every male over the age of 15 in Madrid was armed, as were many young women. They also wore the militia uniform of blue, khaki or white overalls with forage caps on their heads and carried bandoliers of cartridges on their shoulders and pistols on their hips. The women invariably looked extremely smart in their uniforms as they wore them with full make-up.

Having arrived in Madrid, the pilots made their way to the Hotel Florida which was located in Madrid's Gran Via. The pilots from all nationalities who were flying with squadrons round the capital were based here. Once settled in they were taken to Getafe airfield, about 10 miles southwest of Madrid. Here they were given the uniforms of the Aviación Militar Español, blue overalls with gold star and wings and green tasselled field caps. They were joined by the Soviets who also sent their aircrafts, the Polikarpov 1.15 biaircraft, known as the Chato, and the Polikarpov 1.16 monoaircraft the Mosca.

The pilots based round Madrid flew in a mixed Nieuport-Breguet Squadron led by Antonio Martin Luna and the British pilots began by patrolling the Talavera Front to the west of Madrid. It was here that the fascists were advancing slowly on the city. The volunteers were usually given reconnaissance or bombing missions in whatever aircraft was available, however antiquated. They rarely stayed for more than a few months, horrified by the violence and carnage around them.

It wasn't just the Republican government who used volunteer fighters. Whole squadrons of Italian aviators in Fiat fighters were sent to support the thousands of Italian ground troops fighting on Franco's side. They were joined by the Luftwaffe pilots of the Condor Legion with Heinkel and Messerschmitt fighters and Stuka bombers. The Iberian Peninsula, with its deadly warfare over the snow-covered Guadarrama mountain range north of

Madrid, had become a trial ground for a future air war. Military observers from England, France, the USA, Germany and Italy watched closely, evaluating the effectiveness of the new bombers and fighters, and the merits of machine guns, bombing systems and fighter and formation tactics.

By the end of October 1936 all the surviving British pilots were back in Britain and in late October 1936 an attempt was made by ex-Flight Lieutenant Dougherty to arrange for Spanish Republican pilots to be trained at civil flying schools in England. Despite the pleas of the Spanish Ambassador, nothing came of this plan because the Foreign Office was opposed to it. Republican pilots were subsequently sent to the Soviet Union for training instead. Dougherty spent the next few months travelling between Britain and Spain, procuring aircraft and pilots. He was later forced to resign from the RAF Reserve Service because of his involvement in Spain, although in 1941 he was able to re-join as RAF aircrew. He stayed in the RAF throughout the war and left in October 1948 having reached the rank of Warrant Officer.

More new recruits were soon heading to Spain in November 1936 but as the months went on it became increasingly difficult for British pilots to procure civilian aircraft for the Republicans. In March 1937 the police were tipped off about a silver and red Armstrong Whitworth Atlas in a hangar on West Malling airfield in Kent. When they arrived they found it fully fuelled up and about to take off. It was dismantled and ownership traced to Eric Griffiths, a New Zealander, and Henry F. Harrington, a former employee of Imperial Airways and Air Dispatch Ltd.

There were several factions within the Republican army and as the support from the Soviet Union increased so did the number of communist officials, their role to investigate the loyalty of the Republicans to the communist cause. There were numerous incidents of these officials investigating those they considered to be suspect, of executions without trial and false accusations against those they considered to be threats to the communist cause. This came to a head in May 1937 with a communist take-over in Barcelona.

While the Republicans were busy fighting themselves, the fascists were steadily increasing their grip on the country, culminating in the bombing of Guernica.

Given the deteriorating situation in Spain, this may have been why Sydney decided to return home. By August 1937 he was back in England and

RAF Cranwell.

living in The Cottage, Cranwell Village, Lincolnshire. He was employed as a Civilian Assistant in the RAF.

The April 1938 electoral roll shows that Sydney was living with Elsa at Devonshire Terrace and in 1939 he joined the Royal Air Force Volunteer Reserve as a pilot officer on probation. The entry on his RAF records stated that from 27 March 1939 he was employed in the Special Duties Branch of the RAFVF.

Flight Archive 1141 4 April 1939. The following are granted commissions as Pilot Officers on probation (April 4): – D. A. Batwell, R. H. Budworth, H. Chambers, H. R. Davies, W. L. H. Davies, C. M. Davis, E. S. Farrand, C. D. Griffiths, **S. H. B. Harris, A.F.C.C**, H. A. Hince, E. H. Irving, J. T. Knight, the Marquess of Casa Maury, T. E. Pennington, E. L. Roberts, W. N. Sherlock, E. A. Simson, A.F.C., C. A. Shute, C.M.G., C.B.E., P. Y. H. Smith, C. F. Snowden-Gamble, C. Q.

Chapter Nineteen

Blitzkrieg

P rior to the start of the Second World War Great Britain and France had agreed that in case of war the light bomber force of the RAF would move to airfields within France. The distance from the British mainland would have severely restricted their ability to attack the enemy. Based in France, they would be able to operate against more targets in Nazi Germany. On 23 August 1939 the RAF received orders to mobilise unobtrusively. The following day green envelopes began to arrive on the

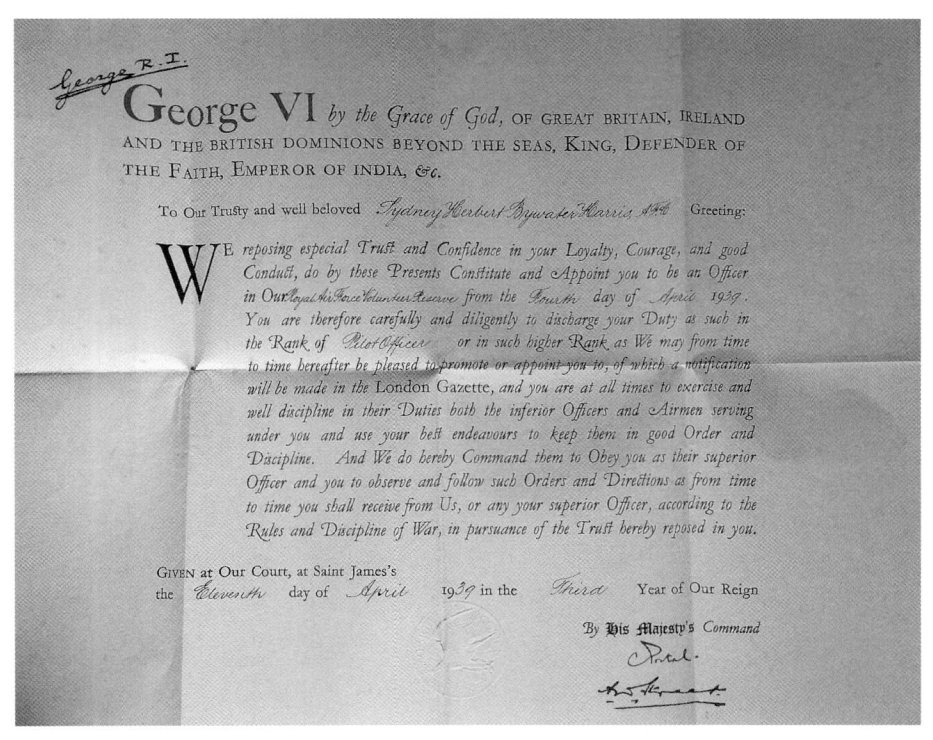

Sydney's Commission into the RAF, 1939.

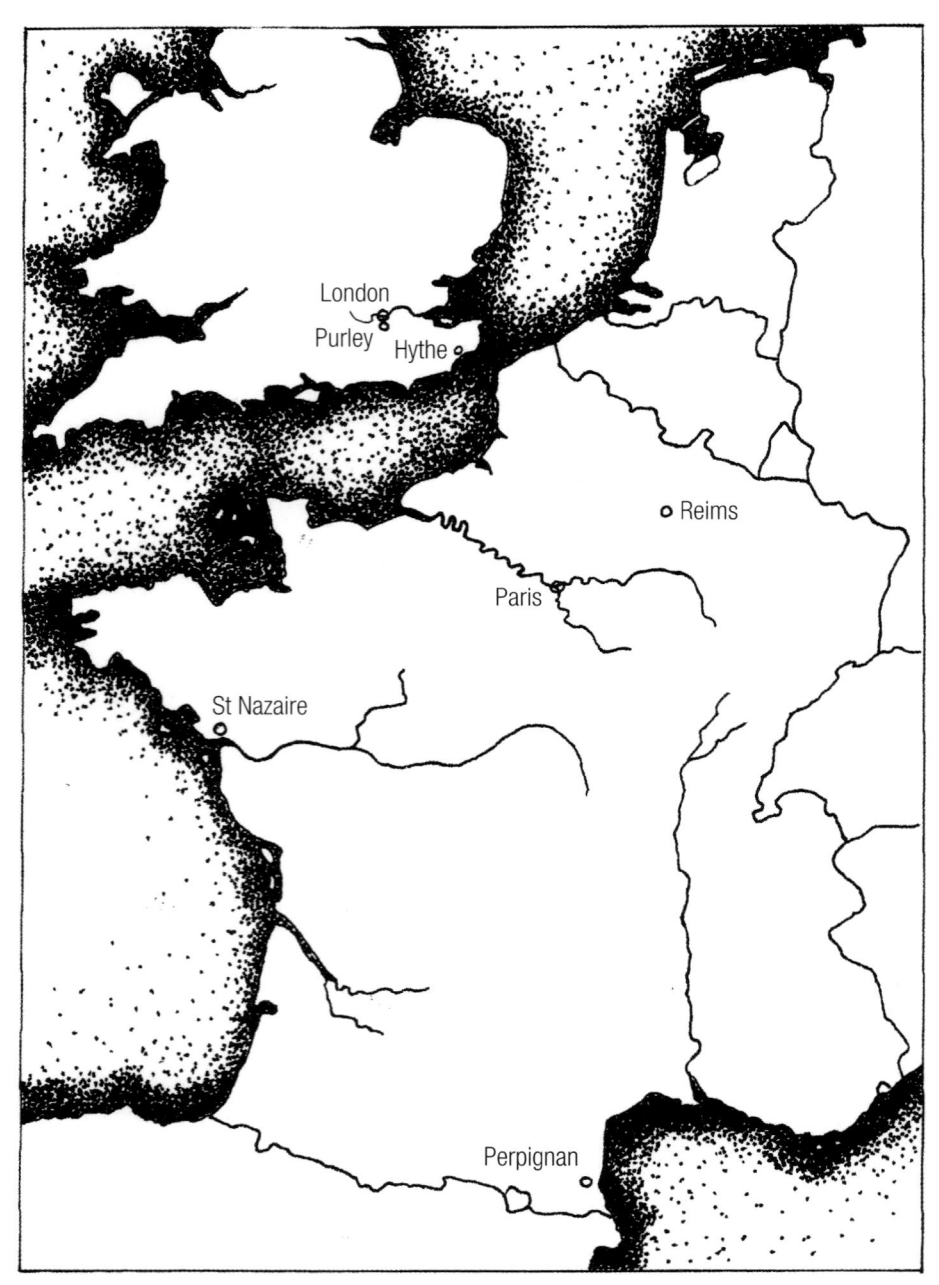

192 From Colonial Warrior to Western Front Flyer

Key locations for Sydney during the Second World War.

doorsteps of members of the Auxiliary Air Force and the 3,000 members of the Royal Air Force Volunteer Reserve. Sydney received his envelope and opened it in anticipation. It was not what he was expecting.

He had been ordered to report to RAF Turnhouse as Section Controller. RAF Turnhouse was the most northerly air defence base in the First World War. During the war 603 (City of Edinburgh) Squadron was housed there with DH9As, Westland Wapitis, Hawker Harts and Hawker Hind Light Bombers, all of which used grass to land on. In 1918 when the Royal Air Force was formed it was renamed RAF Turnhouse.

However, stuck in the north of Scotland was not Sydney's idea of war. Apart from the cold weather, which he disliked intensely as he grew older, he couldn't see the base being used for anything exciting. So, worried he might miss out, Sydney decided to call in some favours. He would see if he could be transferred to somewhere he was likely to see some action and hopefully some warmer weather. A few weeks after he left RAF Turnhouse fighter command took control of it and built a new 3,900ft runway to accommodate the new Vickers Supermarine Spitfire.

But Sydney didn't mind as his new posting was exactly what he had been looking for, as this letter to his son shows.

19th October 1939

My Dear Verder

I was so delighted to receive your letter of the 29th old son and as you say, this watch keeping racket was too much for me and I felt that if I was going to see this War from the aspect of a Section Controller at Turnhouse, it was no good to me, so I pushed off to the Air House and saw Philip Babbington who tried to teach me to aviate in 1915 and was with me at Cranwell when I was there, and I asked him to find me a job of work either in France or even Poland to get out of the rut, and he said I could go to Tangmere and go out as Adjutant to No 1 Squadron – so here I am and although I have to work all day and most of the night – I love the work and am as happy as a sandboy. You must forgive me for not answering your letter before but for 10 days prior to last Saturday I was on trek as O i/c of the Advance Party of the Squadron, which is one of the Units of the Air Striking Force and we have at last called a halt at a little village just behind the —— line. Am not allowed to state the name as although I do the censoring for the Squadron, the French open an odd letter here and there and mine would sure to be one of them.

Sydney and colleagues, 1940.

The RAF Advanced Air Striking Force (AASF) was formed on 24 August 1939 from No. 1 Group and on 2 September 1939 its ten squadrons of Fairey Battles were dispatched to airfields in the Reims area. The Battle was a single-engine aircraft that was considered advanced in its heyday but was now obsolete. It was slow, poorly defended, had a short range and was completely incapable of bombing Germany from England hence its dispatch to France. On arrival the squadron refuelled, bombed up and waited. Sydney arrived and took up his post, delighted to find the CO was an old friend. The weather was not much better than that in Scotland, but at least he was closer to the action. Happy with his lot, Sydney wrote to Verder to tell him all about his new post.

> It has been raining incessantly ever since we arrived and today the river has overflowed and the whole place is a quagmire, it is a dirty little village at the best of times but you can imagine what it is like now and we have had to issue rum rations to keep the spirits of the troops up, although it is not at all necessary as I never wish to be with a finer crowd of Officers & airmen than those we have in No 1 – they have got a big

reputation to keep up but they will do it – and some too. The CO is Sqdn Ldr Halahan who I knew when he was Adjutant to the Cadet College when I was at Cranwell and he is one of the best. Doesn't care two hoots for the Powers that Be but gets on with the job. He leaves me to attend to all the bumph in the Squadron and is continually in the air chasing the old Hun and does more hours aviating than any Officer in the Squadron – very different to my experience in the last show when the COs I served under never left the ground – still I suppose times have changed.

I have had to make contact with the French Commandants of the various aerodromes that we passed and was regaled with Champagne Lunches and speeches and Le Comandant Angleterre – or whatever you call him, was the big noise alright, although feeding and yapping was never much in my line. Still I seemed to go down alright and I suppose it was my ribbons that did it. I have a French interpreter at my elbow all the time and I have never heard so much yapping in my life – what would take an Englishman 2 shakes to explain, takes my French friend at least half an hour and then I am not always certain as to exactly what has been conveyed. The other day I had to get a French Labour Corps to dig some gun emplacements in a hurry and by the time the interpreter had explained it would have been quicker if I had dug them myself. But no more war talk – so let me know how the world is using you. Are you up at Pertrevie Castle for the duration or is there a chance of you getting out this way? I was in at HQs the other day and never met so many Wing Commanders in my life. I don't think one of them ever had a Squadron but they all looked very smart rushing about with a bit of paper and a pencil and when I had lunch with the AOC it was Squadron Leaders and Wing Commanders to the right and Flight Lieuts and under to the left. What a war.

How is Margot these days? I hope she enjoyed her visit to London and has come back full of revs. Give her my love and tell her I hope to be able to salute her husband when he comes out here as a full blown Wing Commander. Give my love to Mother & Betty and a clip on the ear for my little grandson.

With all the best
your affectionate Dad

By November Sydney was not enjoying his post quite so much and his age was beginning to catch up with him, although he would never have admitted it. He was also rather miffed that RAF Turnhouse, which he'd left because he'd thought it would be too quiet and removed from the action, was actually more involved in the war than where he had been posted to.

> Somewhere in France
> 19th November 1939

My dear old Verder

    I was so delighted to get your letter of the 30th and also yours of the 13th which I received yesterday and as, after warning everyone else on the station not to forget about putting their clocks back, I promptly forgot to put my own on I am going to put in the extra hour writing to you. You must forgive me for not writing you before but I have been very much under the weather as I picked up a bad cold and cannot seem to get shot of it. I had to stay 'put' on Docs orders for a few days as I developed a temperature but am on parade again now although I cannot seem to get rid of this coughing business. The weather is all against me as it has never missed a day without raining and everyone is getting a bit fed up with it. I was so bucked to hear of your promotion old son even if it is only for the duration, although I bet it is for keeps as you have earned it a thousand times more than some of the pip squeaks one meets out here with 3 bands up. Was interested to hear that you had been over to Turnhouse and met some of the crowd there, they are a good set of lads and have certainly seen more of this war that everyone is talking about than we have out here.

    I wish the balloon would start going up as it would probably put paid to all the bumph that comes in each day from HQ's – I expect you know the kind of things they ask – the number of empty petrol tins and the number of fingers an airman has on each hand. No – I have not heard from Herberta yet but expect a line anytime now – I think it was a jolly good effort going out there.

    I expect young Malcolm is quite the lad now and I can just imagine him into everything he can lay his hands on. Give him a clip on the ear from his Grand Dad and tell him to hurry up and grow up and he will be able to give us a hand out here. Give Margot my love and tell her I am still looking forward to that letter of hers, but I believe she is almost as bad as I am when it comes to letter writing.

               Must close now so with all the best from
                      Your affectionate Dad

At the beginning of the war Bomber Command began dropping leaflets on Germany and this had continued for several months. Early in 1940 they extended this to dropping leaflets over Prague and Vienna. Up until January 1940 the RAF Advanced Striking Force (RAFASF) reported directly to the

Air Ministry and were independent of the BEF. But this was considered to be inadequate so on 15 January they were placed under the command of the British Air Forces in France Head Quarters together with the air component of the BEF. British Air Forces in France were now all under the command of Air Vice Marshal 'Ugly' Barratt and the RAFASF was also drawn into leaflet dropping. However, five days later, on 20 January, all operations came to a halt as Europe became locked in the grip of an icy winter and several feet of snow. This lasted until 17 February 1940 and by the time air operations began again leaflet dropping was no longer the priority. The primary task now was for each Bomber Group to reconnoitre a different area of Germany in preparation for a large-scale mining campaign against German inland waterways and estuaries. However, they were still ordered to drop leaflets as this would help to allay the suspicions of the enemy and to continue the propaganda campaign.

The leaflet campaign continued until 6 April after which it was suspended by everyone except the RAFASF, which would not see action against the Germans until they attacked in the west in May 1940.

In March 1940 Margaret Elsa Verder Harris married Gordon Doubleday but Sydney was unable to attend. Instead his son Verder took his father's place, gave his sister away and made the necessary speeches.

Somewhere in France
19th March 1940

My dear old Verder'

You must forgive me for not having answered your letter before but I suddenly decided to get away to the South of France with Halahan for my spot of leave and since my return I have been away several times fixing things up for the Squadron – when we move, if we do? I thoroughly enjoyed my few days in the sunshine and we struck some delightful little villages.

We left ice and snow here and in 36 hours we were about without our overcoats and on the Sunday they wanted me to bathe but I thought it a bit too much at my age. We had a look at Nice but it was too much like Paris by the sea for my liking and I much preferred places like San Tropez and St Raphael – however it passed much too quickly and we had to come back to snow & ice again – the winter has been the very devil and what with the miserable living conditions I sometimes wonder how I have been able to stick it – on the top of all this when we move we have got to go under canvas and when I was there one of the inhabitants told me they always had a wet spring – so after carefully thinking about it I applied for a posting to No 1 ATS at Perpignan which is near the Mediterranean near the Spanish border and quite a good place to see the war from I believe. Shall be very sorry to quit the Squadron especially if the balloon really does goes up but having to turn out in the middle of the night to de-code signals asking how many pots of jam the troops consumed in the past week and such like – rather gets me down and I think a softer job will be more to my liking. Anyway we shall see what happens and even if I do get posted I expect the war will go on just the same.

    Yes – I was very disappointed not to be able to make it for Margaret's Wedding but I hear you did your stuff very well and had it all under control. I think Gordon is a very nice fellow and am very bucked to think he has joined up in the RNVF. Good luck to him and I hope he will have the chance of putting paid to a Hun sub – Margaret seems to be full of revs by her letters and I had an excellent photo of the bridal couple leaving the Church – have you got one of these they are really very good. Very many thanks for the cigarettes and I quite thought I had to let you know I had received them. They just came at the right time as we were very short of English cigarettes then. Have managed to cut down my smoking which is a good thing I think as they are only a habit. I expect young Malcolm is getting quite a lad by now – give him a kick in the pants from his Grandpa and tell him I shall want to have a go with the gloves when we next meet. Don't forget that snap when you have got it developed. How is Margot these days – full of beans I hope and keeping the Home Fires burning.

Much love to you both old son
Your affectionate, Dad

The idea of the Air Transport Auxiliary began in 1938 when the Director of British Airways, Gerard d'Erlanger, realised that if there was a war with Germany not only would many routes be suspended and aircrafts impounded, but many pilots would be out of work. The same thing would apply to the large number of amateur pilots as it was unlikely the British government would allow amateurs to fly for fun while there was a war on. It was therefore likely to impound their aircraft as well. Because of their age and physical limitations many of these pilots would not be considered suitable for the RAF despite their vast experience.

He envisaged that the war could provide an alternative role for pilots such as delivering mail, dispatches, supplies, medical officers, ambulance cases and the occasional VIP. He contacted Harold Balfour, the Parliamentary Under Secretary for Air, and Sir Francis Shelmerdine, the Director General of Civil Aviation, and suggested creating a pool of experienced civil pilots who could be used in time of war.

He was instructed to contact all those who held 'A' private licences and had a minimum of 250 flying hours. They would be interviewed and tested and then incorporated into a new organisation called the Air Transport Auxiliary. Out of the first 100 that came forward only 30 were selected and they were divided into 2 categories. First Officers were those with over 500 hours flying and the ability to pilot twin-engine aircraft. Second Officers were those with 250 hours of more and experience of only flying single-engine aircraft. The ATS had their own uniform consisting of dark-blue trousers, light-blue RAF shirt, black tie, forage cap and single-breasted jacket with the insignia ATA. This was a circlet enclosing the letters 'ATA' superimposed on a set of wings. Rank would be indicated by gold bars on the shoulders.

It was initially under the command of the National Air Communications and the Director General of Civil Aviation with the clerical, personnel and administration duties to be carried out by British Airways. But as the war geared up it became apparent that the RAF were unable to ferry enough aircrafts to the Operational Squadrons themselves and needed to free up pilots to fly operations. It was therefore decided to give ATA pilots crash conversion courses to allow them to fly Hurricanes and Spitfires and multi-engine types so they could deliver the aircraft instead. The training took place at the RAF Central Flying School at Upavon and control of the ATA was transferred to the Air Ministry, although British Airways was still responsible for clerical and administration matters matters.

As demand for their services increased the Under Secretary of State for Air suggested women should be allowed to join. But the ATA was now operating out of RAF bases and the RAF objected to women being posted to RAF units. Their arguments were that flying was no job for a woman and that women pilots would take away jobs from men.

There was considerable protest at these sentiments and one of the most vocal advocates of women pilots was Pauline Gower, a commercial pilot with over 2,000 hours flying experience. She had also trained and licensed civilian pilots as well as being a Commissioner in the Civil Air Guard. As the war situation deteriorated even more the RAF began to reconsider their position. In November 1939 eight women were chosen to ferry Tiger Moths, slow, small, single-engine open cockpit trainers. They would be based in Hatfield and their job was to ferry the aircrafts to destinations in the north of England and Scotland in the middle of winter. On 1 January the ATA officially accepted these women into service. Meanwhile, the 157 male pilots were busy ferrying aircrafts to operational bases and impounding civilian aircraft.

As the German armies swept through Europe in May 1940 the men of the ATA were given the urgent task of taking much-needed Fairey Battles to the RAF bases in France. On 12 May 1940 Flying Officer Russell H. Dingle RAF 39307 from Canada was ferrying a Fairey Battle, serial number L5289, to No. 1 ATS at Perpignan when he dived into the ground and was killed.

By the time others arrived in France things had deteriorated significantly. One group was stranded overnight and the next morning found themselves ferrying Hurricanes back to England with the Germans only 12 hours behind.

Chapter Twenty

The Long Road to Victory

The BEF had two main bases, the northern one was at Rennes and the southern one at Saint-Nazaire and Nantes. The main storage area for ammunition and frozen meat was at Saint-Nazaire while Nantes was used for motor transport and drivers.

The Germans opened their new offensive on 5 June 1940 and swept southwards. Although the RAF spared no effort to stem the flood, it was hampered by the inequality of the ground forces. Between 10 May and the end of the Dunkirk evacuation the RAF lost 432 Hurricanes and Spitfires. Despite the French demands for another twenty squadrons, the British government held firm. To continue with losses that great was impossible and would have endangered Britain's ability to defend itself in the event of France being overrun.

On 11 June Nos 17, 242 and 504 Fighter Squadrons were sent to France to reinforce the three fighter squadrons operating with the AASF. By then the Germans had reached Chartres and the French had withdrawn back to a line between Caen, Tours, Alençon and the Loire Valley. No. 1 Squadron, Sydney's previous Squadron, was at Chateaudun and still fighting. Close by 12 Squadron had lost its complete flying personnel twice over, a total of 72 pilots. They received reinforcements and carried on flying.

On the same day the Germans broke through the French positions on the Marne, Oise and Seine endangering all the RAF units. On 12 June Air Vice Marshal Sholto Douglas, the Deputy Chief of Air Staff, wrote to Air Marshal Sir Arthur S. Barratt warning him to be ready for a quick withdrawal from France. Barratt had already decided that this was the best course of action and had written to the Air Vice Marshal requesting permission to do that. The letters crossed.

On 13 June Churchill learnt that the French were pressing for an immediate armistice and asking to be released from their obligation not to make a separate agreement with the enemy. The RAF retreated to the west coast and secured fresh bases near Angers, Saumur, Rennes and Nantes. But the new airfields were becoming more congested by the hour as all the Allies withdrew towards the west. The all-Canadian 242 Squadron had already shot down twenty-eight enemy aircraft over Dunkirk. They moved back from Chateaudun and Le Mans to cover the evacuation of the AASF.

No. 1 Squadron arrived at Nantes and found so many aircraft already there it resembled Empire Day. It was crowded with aircraft from Britain, France and America, as well as numerous civil aircraft which had been commandeered by the RAF for communication purposes. Everyone was hurrying around trying to save equipment falling into German hands. But to retain so many aircraft in one place would be an open invitation to the Germans to destroy them on the ground, so Barratt decided to send his bombers back to Britain. It was left to the fighters of the AASF to protect the evacuation of the ground staff and the three main British divisions under Lieutenant General Alan Brooke.

On 13 June Paris was declared an open city and all French forces were evacuated from the capital. The following day French High Command withdrew back further, but the RAF were at the limit of their supply lines and ability to operate successfully. They could not pull back any further.

The RAF briefly considered retreating to aerodromes near Nantes and Rennes but then the Germans entered Paris. The French government withdrew from Tours to Bordeaux and considered moving to North Africa, but they were overruled by Laval.

On 15 June the Battle squadrons flew back to England after five days of desperate fighting. Barratt was left to defend seven ports with five squadrons. He needed to prioritise. The ports of La Pallice and La Rochelle would be used the least so he sent the anti-aircraft batteries to defend these. Saint-Nazaire and Nantes were the ports where the majority of troops would be evacuated from so he sent three squadrons, Nos 1, 73 and 242, to cover these. Nos 17 and 501 Squadrons were sent to Saint-Malo and Cherbourg. Fighter Command aircraft from Tangmere would also help to protect Cherbourg while Coastal Command would protect returning vessels. Barratt returned to England leaving the operation in the hands of his right hand man, Senior Air Staff Officer, Air Vice Marshal D.C.S. Evill.

In the early part of Operation Aerial 84,700 men were evacuated from Brest, Cherbourg and Saint-Malo and a further 21,300 from smaller ports. But there were still about 50,000 men in the area around Nantes and Saint-Nazaire at the mouth of the River Loire. While the garrison commander made arrangements to withdraw the men from France, plans were also formed to withdraw what was left of the 80 million francs the British had deposited with the Banque de France to cover their expenditure while garrisoned there.

Troops were already making their way across the French countryside in the hot sun. They had broken up their bases and destroyed all the stores, vehicles and equipment to prevent them falling into German hands. Sleeping in open fields, barns and village squares they made their way towards the western ports, hoping they would be lucky enough to be evacuated. They began arriving in Saint-Nazaire from 15 June and were directed to a nearby airfield that was still under construction. On their way they passed abandoned airfields with rows of burned out Blenheims and Battles, and deserted NAAFI stores where they helped themselves to cigarettes and tobacco from wooden crates that had been forced open.

Others had driven from port to port, always arriving too late to be evacuated. Saint-Nazaire was their last chance. There was no one giving orders at the airfield so most of the men took it upon themselves to make their way down to the harbour. Here they were tightly packed together as they waited for the French tenders to take them out to the ships that were moored out in the estuary. The queue stretched back for at least half a mile along the quay and movement was agonisingly slow. Every so often, in the skies above them enemy bombers appeared, dive-bombing the ships and raking the retreating forces with machine-gun fire. They dropped bombs by day and magnetic mines by night, but still the evacuation continued. The Hurricanes continued to patrol the skies above them, for the most part keeping the ships and men reasonably safe. But on 17 June the skies were covered in thick cloud and the Junkers Ju-88s from Kampfgeschwader 30 (KG30), newly based outside Louvain, east of Brussels, used the cloud cover to evade them.

From his position on the dock in Saint-Nazaire Sydney watched in horror as the Junkers broke its 300mph dive and released its bomb directly above the funnel of the ship. As the sound of the explosion ripped through the air he involuntarily closed his eyes. The blast was so intense he could almost feel it from where he was on the dock. There was a split second's silence then all hell let loose. On the *Lancastria* debris rained down on the survivors as the flames took hold. Those sheltering on the deck had been left stunned by the bombs and many were badly burned by the searing blast as the funnel exploded. A large crater appeared in the centre of the ship and men could be heard screaming from below. Those that could began jumping overboard. The men in the stern did not realise the seriousness of the explosion. To them it seemed like they'd had a lucky escape, then suddenly the ship lurched to port and the men knew something was seriously wrong. The corridors were packed with soldiers, their rifles slung over their shoulders, packs on the backs all fighting their way to the deck and then the lights went out before the ship lurched to starboard. Water was beginning to flow into the corridors and panic ensued. Within minutes the ship had begun to sink and the stern began to rise as the prow sank beneath the waves.

Sydney watched horrified as men continued to jump into the water, frantically trying to escape the sinking ship. There was nothing he could do as those who were too close were dragged down with the ship. Lifeboats, rafts, rescue boats and other ships did their best to rescue the men in the water, but they were hampered by the German aircraft attacking them and strafing the water with machine guns. Another ship was hit and sank as it tried to rescue them, the air was filled with thick, black, choking smoke, the sounds of machine guns, anti-aircraft fire and the screams and shouts of the injured and dying. The water was filled with lifeless corpses wearing life jackets and men clinging to whatever they could find to keep them afloat.

As the wounded came ashore Sydney did what he could to help but the images of that day would never leave him. Of the over 6,000 people on the *Lancastria* only about 2,500 survived.

As he watched the devastating scene unfolding he was relieved to hear the familiar sound of the Hurricanes above his head. The bomber that had sunk the ship was hit by a fighter from his old squadron, No. 1, and as the day progressed they managed to destroy fifteen more enemy aircraft.

The situation around him was now even more confusing and many troops left Saint-Nazaire and tried to find an alternative way home, others gave up and drank themselves into oblivion. Sydney and his companions were lucky, they found a collier the following day and were soon back in Plymouth. As they arrived back they were struck by the incongruity of being met by a band of the Royal Marines.

Evacuations continued through the port that day with a further 23,000 soldiers leaving for Plymouth on the 18th. As more troops converged there further ships were rushed out to bring them home and 2,000 Polish soldiers were bought out the following day. The Royal Navy continued to send ships for the next few days and by the 25th they had evacuated over 144,000 British and 50,000 Allied troops. Once Cherbourg had finished its evacuation Nos 242 and 17 Squadron flew home.

By the end of 18 June the ground forces in Saint-Nazaire had made good their escape and the fighter aircraft were free to leave. Many had flown six sorties on the previous day. After 73 Squadron had flown its final patrol the last of the Hurricanes left for Tangmere after setting fire to the unserviceable machines. The rear parties and operations crew left in the transport aircraft. They were only just in time as a few hours later German tanks entered Nantes. These fighter pilots were the last to leave with the enemy vanguard only a few miles away. As the last two ships left Cherbourg the final aircraft to patrol was that of Air Vice Marshal K.R. Park, which flew over the town and harbour before heading home. By the evening of 18 June all surviving British aircraft, including those based in Southern France, were back in Britain.

The sinking of the *Lancastria* was not made public for many years. It was considered to be too depressing for a public already reeling from the mass evacuation from Dunkirk. Although that was seen as a miraculous escape, the death of so many men so soon afterwards would have been bad for morale.

Unlike the survivors of Dunkirk who were greeted with adulation, the evacuees from Saint-Nazaire never received any recognition and most were ignored or treated with disdain, despite the fact that many had continued fighting for a further two weeks after Dunkirk. After the chaos and devastation of the past few days it was hard to accept they were finally safe, at least for the moment. With their ignominious departure from Europe and France's surrender Britain now stood alone and Sydney wondered what the future would hold. The RAF had lost a total of 477 aircraft in May and June

1940: the AASF 229, Fighter Command 219, the RAF component of the BEF 279, Bomber Command 166 and Coastal Command 66. There was an urgent need to replace these aircraft and the pilots and Sydney was sure that with his experience there was still something he could do, despite his age. There was also another reason Sydney wanted to carry on fighting.

To add to his despair on his arrival home Sydney learnt that his youngest brother, Percival, had been killed near Dunkirk on 28 May 1940. Sydney was devastated. He and Percival had been very close. But there was no time for grief. Britain now faced its biggest challenge and Sydney was posted to HQ 61 Group at RAF Kenley on 6 July for administrative duties. On 30 July he was transferred to 15 Group in St Eval in Cornwall.

RAF St Eval opened on 2 October 1939 after the local village was demolished to build the aerodrome, leaving only the church surviving.

In June 1940 RAF during the Battle of Britain, St Eval became a Fighter Command Sector HQ and Spitfires were stationed there. They were later joined by Hurricanes and Blenheims. After the Battle of Britain was over it reverted back to a Coastal Command airfield protecting the southwest approaches. It was often attacked by German aircraft and Lord Haw-Haw claimed several times that St Eval had been destroyed. On 21 August three Ju-88s bombed the airfield damaging two hangars and destroying three Blenheims. Hurricanes shot down two of the three German aircraft. The following day 14 HE bombs and 200 incendiaries were dropped but this time damage was light. There was a direct hit on a pyrotechnics store on 23 August and this caused an enormous explosion.

Three days later St Eval was again bombed at 2130hr and 2158hr and this time the enemy set fire to a false flare path and bombed it until the early hours of the morning. Although they left sixty-two craters, most of the damage was to the nearby heath. The rest of the month and most of September were more peaceful until 2300hr on 30 September when two HE bombs were dropped on the aerodrome and a further three outside, fortunately causing little damage. The attack on 3 October between 0655hr and 0710hr was more serious as two hangars were hit and two Spitfires and one Avro Anson were completely destroyed. At 2111hr on 14 October a further six HE bombs and twenty incendiaries were dropped on the station.

One way of protecting the airfield from the Luftwaffe was to display lights on the Denzell Downs which overlooked RAF St Eval. This fooled the Germans into thinking this was the airbase. The Home Guard were already active on the Downs and had dug slit trenches in preparation for any attempted invasion. Once the enemy had dropped their bombs on the Downs they lit oil fires, leading them to believe they had hit their target. Sydney remained at St Eval until 17 October. On this date his failing health meant he was no longer able to remain in the RAF and he was retired to the RAFVF on health grounds.

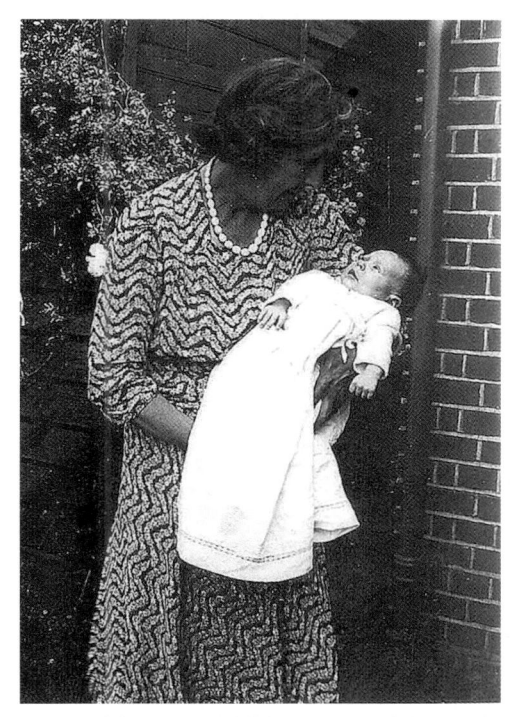

Elsa and her grandchild, Jane, aged 1 month, daughter of Margaret, 1941.

As the war progressed and Sydney grew older his injuries from the First World War and his adventurous lifestyle began to affect his health adversely. The snowshoes from the Yukon might still be hanging on the wall in Devonshire Terrace, but he no longer felt like the young man who'd travelled halfway round the world to make his fortune. June 1942 found him recently released from hospital in Epsom and staying with his cousin, Nena, while recovering from a prostate operation. As someone used to being active and living his life to the full, hospital life did not suit him at all, and neither did growing old, as the following letter to a friend shows.

Sydney's driving licence, 1941.

37 Glebe Road
Cheam
Surrey
22nd July 1942

My dear Billy

Thank you so much for your letter of the 16th which was forwarded on to me from the Epsom Cottage Hospital as two weeks ago I decided to have a breather and not have the other operation right away as they suggested – anyway I had a test which was not too good, and they wanted me to stay in hospital until it was ok but while I was waiting I thought I could have a spell here staying with my cousin Nena and her brother – who is also on the sick list – and we could compare notes together. His trouble by the way, is far worse than mine as he has been invalided out of the RAF suffering from TB and he is due to go into the King Edward VII Hospital at Midhurst to have his right lung removed. One can carry on without a prostate gland but I should not like the idea of only having one lung. So I've got something to be thankful for and once I get going and get the other operation over I shall soon pick up. At the present moment I feel like nothing on earth and anyone can have the lot for a bob. If I have known what they were going to do with me in the first instance – I would never have had the operation. As you know Billy it is not the first major operation that I have had but I have never suffered so much pain as I did for 4 days after having this one. I always thought that the hospitals job was to ease pain – but instead of giving me an injection to put me to sleep, the damned nurses just gathered round me and watched me go through it all. But enough of my troubles old son as I shall get through them alright – it's only just 'keep smiling' all the time.

I did so love reading all your news and you certainly are delivering the goods – but why so far away Billy. Alright in the summer but I should hate it in the winter and wonder how you were able to stick it. When this blasted war is over it's the South of France for me every time. One can starve in the sunshine quite comfortably but to starve in the cold. Not for me Billy in these trousers anyway. Was very interested to hear that you have still got old Mike – give him a pat for me and am glad to hear he is still full of life in spite of his 10 years.

Up to the time of my illness I have been very busy getting the garden in shape, also I have netted off the orchard and got 4 pullets who have been busy laying all summer. Then too I have gone in for keeping rabbits – we started with a Silver Fox doe and she produced 8 topping little youngsters and has just given us another kindle. We don't know how many there are as they are only just born and one must not look at them for the first few days.

Must close now as the District Nurse has just come to give me my daily wash out as I have to move about with a damned rubber tube in my belly and it's not too pleasant – take it from me.

Poor old Verder is having a hell of a time in Libya but I feel and know that he will come through and now that he has been made a Group Captain he will be kept busy at Headquarters and not go on those flying stunts. He has certainly earned his promotion and I give him full marks for being a G/Capt at the age of 37. I know of no other at his age and am hoping that he will not stop at this and I shall live to see him an Air Vice Marshall. We shall see!

About two months ago I went down to stay with Margaret and Gordon at Shrub Hill Farm and was delighted with my little grand daughter Jane. She is a little dear and one of the most contented little kiddies that I have ever seen. You must go and see her when you are next up in town. Gordon has a new job now – they are both very happy and I have got you to thank for this Billy as you certainly did your good turn when you introduced them to each other. I am very proud of my son in law and it was a damned good effort for him to join up when he did as being a farmer he could have easily got exemption.

Nurse says she is all ready to go now so have got to bring my harangue to a close. Again many thanks for your letter and I did so enjoy reading it – when you get the time write me again Billy and address it to the Epsom Cottage Hospital as I shall be going back there at the end of this week.

Much love old son and wishing you all the very best

Yours ever

Sydney HBH

As the war continued Sydney began spending more time with Nena. He might have been getting older but he was still as forceful as ever and not at all happy about his daughter's choice of name for his grandson.

37 Glebe Road
Cheam
Surrey
20th December 1943

Give my kind regards to the
Sister and Xmas Greetings,
Also wish Flora and Mrs Olly a cheery
Xmas and the best of luck in the New Year
My dearest Margaret,

Many thanks for your letter and I was so glad

To hear that you and my new grandson were making good progress and that you had *everything under control* to use an Air Force expression.

Just take it quietly and don't be in a hurry to get up as with the Sister there it's a good opportunity to take things easily.

No I don't approve of Andrew as the little chap's name and say what you like you cannot better John Doubleday as his name. I have always been very fond of the name John and it goes very well with Doubleday – so what? Still you have the final say but I should think it over carefully before you decide. I'll bet Jane is very thrilled with her little brother and by the way her Doll's House is really finished now and I took it up to the flat last week, it has to be carefully handled and it would not do to send it off by train so as to be there by Xmas so you must explain this to Jane and I will bring it along on the 31st, when I am coming with Mother as I should very much like to spend the weekend with you and see my little grandson. Many thanks and I can sleep on a camp bed in the living room so as not to crowd you out. Give my love to my Jane and I expect I shall find her to be quite a big girl when I see her, much love to yourself Margaret and wishing you the best of health, wealth and good cheer for Xmas and the coming year.

Your affectionate,
Dad

As usual, Sydney won the battle of the baby's name and he was named John. He was to grow up to become a famous sculptor. Gradually, the war drew to a close and Sydney remained in Cheam with his cousin.

Sydney, shortly before his death, with Margaret.

13 Devonshire Terrace
London W2
9th February 1944

My dear Billy

    Better late than never they say but I want to thank you and Margery for your kindly Xmas greetings enclosing the book 'Atlantic Torpedo' which I much appreciated as it came at the time I was laid up with an attack of influenza, so I could quietly read it whilst I was in bed. I wanted to write you before but did not know your address until I got it from Margot the other day.

    Yes I too was very sorry I missed you both when you were up at the flat but hope we may be able to meet in the near future. I hear from Margot that you are very much the farmer now and go it for poultry and keep the odd pig. Have you gone in for keeping any rabbits as when I was staying with my cousin Nena down at Cheam, we went in for these and bred quite a few Silver Foxes, for the fur and the meat – the pelts we sold for 15/- and the carcases fetched on average 6/6d each, so it seemed quite a paying proposition. I gave one of the does to Margaret and she has done quite well with them.

    Give my regards to Margery and say I hope I have the pleasure of meeting her when next you are up in London and with all good wishes to yourself and the best of health and happiness to you both.

    Your sincere friend
    Sydney Harris

Despite his ill-health Sydney was still in the RAF Reserve and as the war finished there was one more post awaiting him before retirement.

Sydney, November 1950.

The Long Road to Victory   213

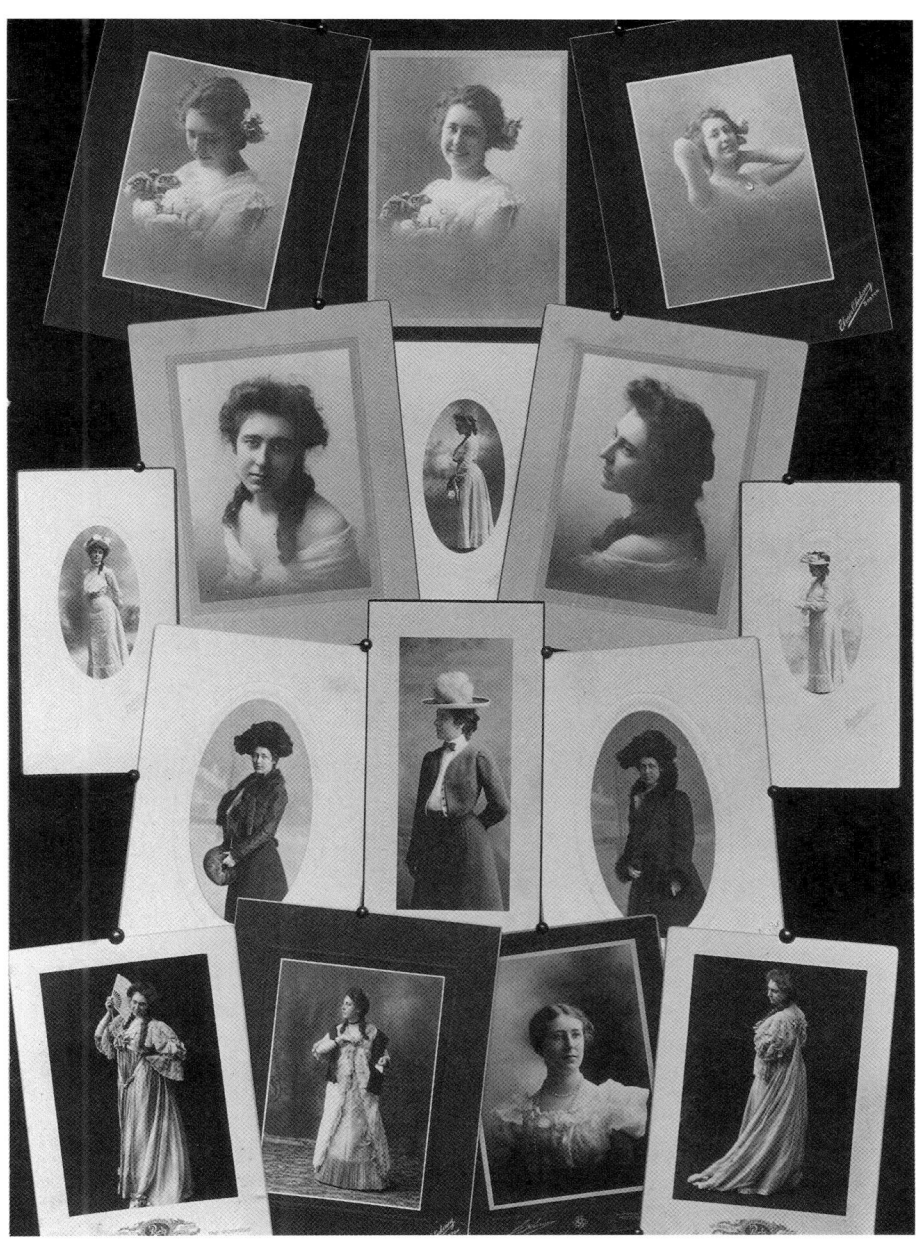

Elsa.

Chapter Twenty-one

Adventures End

On 3 May 1947 Elsa went back to America on the *Queen Elizabeth* and spent some time with her family. Although she had lived in England for many years, Elsa still considered herself an American and as she approached New York she always felt as if she was coming home. At the time she was still registered as living at 13 Devonshire Terrace, Lancaster Gate, London W2.

That same year Sydney became Commander at Marchwood Park near Hythe, a convalescent home for badly burned RAF pilots, run in conjunction with Sir Archibald McIndoe's Hospital at East Grinstead. Sydney remained at Marchwood Park for a year and then, at the age of 65, he retired from the RAF Reserve. In 1948 Sydney and Elsa were again both registered as living in the flat in London. But this was not to last as by the 1950s the English climate was too cold for him and he had made the decision to move to Spain with his cousin Nena. Elsa remained in London, and although her health was failing, she still found time to write to her granddaughter Jane who was now at boarding school.

London 11th October 1952

My Very Dear Jane
   Thank you very much for that nice card. I hear Mummy and Daddy had a very nice time on the Broads and that John was a very good boy. Grandpa has now gone off to Spain where it is much warmer than here. Aunt Herberta will soon be coming back from America where she is having a lovely time. I am keeping fairly well these days.
                            With love and kisses
                                  Grannie

Jane remembers her grandmother as a lovely gentle person who was adored by all the children and grandchildren, a strong woman who provided a stable home life and who obviously loved Sydney very much. While Jane was at boarding school it was Elsa who wrote to her more often than anyone else and who provided her link with home. A religious woman who loved high church services, Elsa was well educated and had a love of art which she passed on to her grandchildren.

6th November 1952

My very dear Jane

I enclose these 3 postcards for you to see and get familiar with the lovely pictures so that when you visit the art galleries you will take far more interest in them. You will soon want to visit the National Gallery and Tate Gallery.

The Annunciation is an exceptionally beautiful picture, the colouring is magnificent and the atmosphere of perfect serenity. If you don't see the original pictures there are often copies in London of the galleries. One can't start too early to take interest in art.

Mummy tells me she spent a very nice time with you on Saturday and that you were in very good form.

Lots of love and kisses to my Jane
From
Grannie

On 15 December 1952 Elsa died in London aged 71. She suffered badly from asthma in her later years and Jane remembers visiting Elsa and seeing the oxygen cylinder by the side of her chair. The smog in London at this time was dreadful and it was this pollution that finally caused Elsa's death. Elsa chose her daughter Patricia as executor of her will and left the sum of £662 14*s* and 1*d*. Her body was taken back to the USA for burial and she was interred next to her sister, Edith, in Vermont. Just two years later, on 17 October 1954, her brother Herbert died. He too was buried in Vermont.

Jane also feels that Sydney loved Elsa. Their family was a very close unit, they were married a long time and, up until the last few years, he always appears to have returned to her. After Elsa's death Sydney continued to live in Spain with his cousin Nena, of whom he was very fond and with whom he had spent much of his life after the Second World War. He finally returned to England where he died in hospital in Bath in September 1960, aged 79.

No. 2 School of Aerial Gunnery 1.

No. 2 School of Aerial Gunnery 2.

No. 2 School of Aerial Gunnery 3.

No. 2 School of Aerial Gunnery 4. This is the original proof of the picture that would have been sent to Sydney to approve.

Epilogue

The View of a Grandson
by John Doubleday

Memories of Sydney Herbert Bywater Harris are slipping into oblivion. The few of us who do remember him are divided between those who think of him mainly as a man of action and adventurer, while another, principally female, perspective is influenced by the implications of his lifestyle for his wife and family.

By any standards it was an extraordinary life. Some of his descendants see him as an exemplar of the personality type that projected Britain to the forefront of international affairs. His leaving home at 17 in 1898 to participate in the last of the great nineteenth-century gold rushes indicates impetuosity, courage and resolve. It is difficult to imagine the high hopes, demanding conditions and almost inevitable disappointments that would have accompanied the project. The gold rushes of the Victorian era almost amounted to mass hysteria.

His experiences of panning for gold and the arduous travelling which it entailed informed his character and remained something of a touchstone. Why else would he have his crossed snowshoes hanging up as decoration at the family home at Devonshire Terrace in London fifty years later? Or have kept the receipt for his mining equipment? His mining didn't make him rich. It imposed upon him the necessity of earning a living which he did by enlisting in the US Cavalry. It was with the US Cavalry that he was sent to Manila during the American actions to counter the Philippines Insurrection. From there he was sent on to China to participate in the siege of Peking (as it was then). All I ever knew from him of his time in the Far East were his tattoos, in particular the snake that coiled round his arm and ended with its head just above his wrist. I also remember the appalling fascination I had as a boy, hearing of the pigtail, kept as a morbid souvenir, which had been cut off a condemned prisoner prior to his beheading!

The View of a Grandson 219

The material that the author has brought together to write this account of his life enables me to see a fuller picture of the man. It should also allow others to gain a rounded view of Sydney. Certainly, his adventurous nature brought him a remarkable range of experiences which, in turn, enabled him to participate in the development of powered flight and contribute to the emergence of the RAF as a mature organisation. His eventful life started with an adventure into the unknown, which led to his enlisting as a trooper in the US Army 6th Cavalry and thence to the British Colonial Cavalry. At the end of the First World War he was stood down with the rank of a Wing Commander in the RAF. In the intervening years he was married, had five children, was severely wounded, decorated and became an outstanding pilot. He went on to involve himself in the General Strike, the Spanish Civil War and the Second World War.

As a child my recollection of him was of a man full of schemes and ideas, some practical, some less so. On the purely practical side, I remember the elaborate doll's house which he made for my sister, fully wired with lighting and a little Bakelite doorbell button with 'PRESS' written on it in white lettering. I also have the vivid memory of him wanting to teach his grandchildren to shoot. He had a target set up on a mulberry tree which gave him the opportunity of demonstrating his impressive proficiency. I remember the 'set to' which resulted from my refusal to participate. I had been indoctrinated by the anti-military rhetoric of our gardener, Dick Thurgood, who had gone through the First World War in the trenches. Dick had seen and experienced much and had come to the conclusion that warfare, at best, was a miserable necessity and for the most part solves little. I remember my mother took my part and rescued me from the impasse.

Sydney teaching his grandchildren to shoot. John Doubleday is in the immediate foreground and Malcolm is in the background, behind Sydney.

There was a reserve in the relationship between my mother

and her father which was in contrast to the closeness between my mother and Elsa, her mother. That bond stayed strong throughout her life. When faced with a dilemma my mother would often say: 'What would Mother do?'

Likewise, there was a strong matrilineal connection between my grandmother and her eldest granddaughter, Jane. She has fond recollections of her grandmother writing to her when she was at boarding school. She remembers her firm Christian faith and rather old-fashioned sentimentality and has always valued the special bond she had with her. Elsa died comparatively young of heart failure resulting from asthma, exacerbated by London smog. Her eldest granddaughter felt bereft. As a younger grandson, my recollection is of a more remote figure – ill and with an ever-present oxygen bottle.

The death of his wife does not seem to have much changed Sydney's restless lifestyle. He continued his habit of wintering in Spain and entries in my parents' Visitors Book show him living at a number of addresses up to the time that he moved to Essex in 1959. By this stage he was without assets and entirely dependent on his pensions. He stayed with us for a while until his need for 24-hour care precipitated his move to a nursing home nearby in Essex, at Althorne. Even then his restlessness persisted. He died of lung cancer in hospital at Bath. At the end, Sydney Herbert Bywater Harris, the man of action, dwindled away.

It is all too easy to judge things of the past by the standards of today. Some things, such as Sydney's implacable hatred of 'the Hun' would offend modern sensibilities; at the time it seemed normal. During the course of his married life the considerable inheritance of his wife was dissipated in the purchase of numerous houses, travel and a lifestyle beyond that capable of being supported by his income. The largely self-centred trajectory of his life imposed an undoubted burden on his marriage and children but that, likewise, was not so unusual at the time. Men on the whole pleased themselves and their wives had to deal with the consequences. Things may not be so different now but women are more independent too.

I look back on the life of my grandfather as a glimpse into a different world. It was a life of adventure and energy and his curiosity provided him with a kaleidoscope of experiences. He found meaning in challenge.

Notes

Chapter 1
1. Charles Constantine (13 November 1846–5 May 1912). He served in the Canadian Militia during the Red River Rebellion in 1870 and the Northwest Rebellion in 1885.

Chapter 2
1. In March 1899 the company became Beaver Line of Steamers (Elder, Depster and Co.). The *Lake Ontario*'s last voyage was from Liverpool to New Brunswick on 28 March 1903 and in 1905 it was scrapped in Italy.

Chapter 6
1. Adna Romaza Chaffee was born in Orwell, Ohio on 14 April 1842. He enlisted in the 6th US Cavalry as a private in the Union Army when the American Civil War broke out. He took part in the Peninsular Campaign and the Battle of Antietam. In September 1862 he was made First Sergeant of Company K and was commissioned as a Second Lieutenant in May 1863. On 3 July of the same year his 6th Cavalry attacked a Confederate Cavalry Regiment at Fairfield, just outside Gettysburg. After being wounded he was briefly held as a prisoner of war. He continued to serve with the 6th US Cavalry for the rest of the war despite being wounded on two more occasions. He was promoted to First Lieutenant in February 1865 and then brevetted Captain for his actions in the Battle of Dinwiddie Court House.

Chapter 8
1. Li Hung-chang (1823–1901) was a Chinese statesman and general who successfully put down the Taiping Rebellion. He was viceroy of the capital province of Zhili (1870–1895) and controlled Chinese foreign affairs for the Empress Dowager Tz'u-hsi. He was an experienced negotiator, having negotiated the Treaty of Shimonoseki (1895), which ended the First Sino-Japanese War and the treaty that granted Russia the right to build the Trans-Siberian RR across Northern Manchuria in 1896. When he was Viceroy of Guangzhou during the Boxer Uprising (1900) he protected foreigners.

Chapter 10
1. The Right Hon Lord Strathcona, GCMG, High Commissioner for Canada; Sir Andrew Clark, KCMG, Agent General for Victoria; Sir Philip Fysh, KCMG, Agent General for Tasmania; Sir Walter Pease, KCMG, Agent General for Natal; Sir David Tennant, KCMG, Agent General for Cape Colony; Sir Horace Tozer, KCMG, Agent General for Queensland; Sir John Cockburn, MD, KCMG, Agent General for South Australia; the Hon. E.H. Wittennoom, CMG, Agent General for Western Australia; the Hon. Henry Copland; the Hon. W.P. Reeves, CMG, Agent General for New Zealand; Mr C.A. Duff-Miller, CMG, Agent General for New Brunswick; Sir John Howard, Agent General for Nova Scotia.
2. In 1903 this became simply a kangaroo.
3. 'Colonials venture for the King'.

Chapter 11
1. The Fokker E1 was the first successful fighter aircraft, its sole purpose to intercept and shoot down enemy aircraft. Allied aircraft were designed for reconnaissance and light bombing and were unarmed so when the Fokker E1 appeared in mid-1915 it gave the Germans air superiority and proved devastating for the Allied aircraft. This period was known as the 'Fokker Scourge' and lasted until the Allies developed their own fighters.

Chapter 12
1. The term 'Hun' comes from the time of the Boxer Rebellion and a speech by the Kaiser who referred to the German troops waiting to leave for China as 'Huns'.

Chapter 13
1. Max Immelmann received the Blue Max in January 1916 from Kaiser Wilhelm. This was Prussia's highest military honour. He was known to be a fierce fighter pilot, and was called 'The Eagle of Lille' by his enemies. However, he was also known as a mamma's boy because she regularly sent him chocolates. He gave his name to the 'Immelmann Turn', a half-loop, half-roll manoeuvre, although there are doubts over whether he invented it. As with many 'heroes', there are conflicting accounts of his death.
2. This aircraft was eventually lost in action on recce escort near Cambrai on 31 May 1916. It was bought down by a German aircraft. Its pilot was Second Lieutenant A. Cairne-Duft and the observer was Corporal G. Maxwell, who was wounded and became a prisoner of war.

Chapter 14
1. 'Wounded. Lieutenant S. H. B. Harris, Royal Flying Corps.', the *Gazette*, 11 May 1916.

Chapter 15
1. 39 TS and 45 TS were both absorbed into No. 46 Training Depot Station at Rendcombe.

Chapter 16
1. Representative aeroaircrafts: Airco DH4 B5224, B5228, B7878; Airco DH9 B9341, C1161, C1182, C1183, C1184, C1185, C1273, C1274, D493, D1261, D7309, E610; Airco DH9A E9702, F952; Avro 504A/J/K B8617, B8700, C694, D4391, D6221, D6276, D6279, D6281, D7676, D7742, D7745, F8729, F8731, F8732; Bristol M1C C4954, C4995, C4996, C4998, C4999, C5000, C5001, C5002, C5003, C5005, C5006, C5025; Bristol F2B B1127, B1321, B8938, C752, C756, C822, C1009, C4675, C4692, C4694, C4695, C4800, E2550, E2631, F4286, F4315, F4326, F4522, F4657; Martinsyde F4 H7636, H7637, H7639; RAF RE8 B6619; RAF SE5a D397, D398, D399, D3943, D3952, E5837, E5844, E5930, F7965, F8991; SPAD SVII A8802; Sopwith Pup B6008, C271, C414; Sopwith Triaircraft N5912; Sopwith F1 Camel B2504, B5554, B5582, B7295, B7333, B7447, B7449, B7451, C82, C84, C87, C167, C175, C176, C177, C178, C179, C180, C190, C1662, D1880, D1881, D1882, D1932, D1933, D1934, D1936, D1937, D8225, D8227, E1401, E1455, E1456, E1532, E7295, F2094, H2712, H2717, H2720, H2730; Sopwith Dolphin C3765, C3854, C8090, D3765, D3773; Sopwith Snipe E6140, E6142, E6258, E8077, E8114, E8189, E8316; Sopwith Cuckoo N6952.

Chapter 17
1. Arthur James Cook was the son of a soldier. Born in Wookey in Somerset in 1883, he was raised as a Baptist and at the age of 16 was known as the 'boy preacher'. He was a teetotaller and saw socialism as a natural expression of his Christianity. He was a wild and hypnotic orator that drew large crowds and his speeches seemed to embody all the frustrations the miners felt.
2. Unreadable signature.

Index

AASF (RAF Advanced Air Striking Force), 194, 201, 206
Abanador, Valeriano, 87
aboriginals (Canada), 13–14
Addams, Jane, 41
Advanced School of Flying, Gosport, 125–126
aerial warfare
 aerial superiority, 134, 143
 battle tactics, 133–134, 136–137, 140, 160–162, 167, 189
 first use in military operations, 110–111
 gunnery skills, 154–155
Aguinaldo y Famy, Emilio, 38, 40, 43, 84, 86–87, 89
Air Battalion of the Royal Engineers, 110
Air Force Cross award, 167
Air Ministry, 156, 199
Air Navigation and Engineering Company, 152
Air Transport Auxiliary, 198–200
Airco aircraft
 DH2, 118, 134, 152
 DH4, 156–157
 DH9, 156–157
 DH9A, 152, *171*, 193
aircraft (civil), Spanish Civil War, 186–187
airships, 111, *164–165*
Alacrity (HMS), 51
Alaska (USA), *2*, 12, 12–13, 14–15, *see also* Yukon Gold Rush
American Forces *see* US Forces
American War of Independence, 96–98
Anderson, Col Thomas M., 12
Anderson, Lt, 89
anti-aircraft fire, 127–128, 130, 132, 143
Anti-Imperialist League (USA), 41–42

Archie, *see* anti-aircraft fire
Arctic Express, 34–37
Armstrong Whitworth Aircraft, 189, 152
Army Aircraft Factory, Farnborough, 111, *see also* Royal Aircraft Factory, Farnborough
Army Service Corps, 145
Asbury, Justice, 179
ASLEF (Associated Society of Locomotive Engineers and Firemen), 169
Asquith, Herbert, 111
Atlantic crossings, 17–22, 99, 108, 171, 214
Austin Motors, 152
Austrian forces, Boxer Rebellion, 49–50, 51–52, 57
Auxiliary School of Aerial Gunnery No. 2, Turnberry, 149–155
Auxiliary School of Aerial Gunnery No. 4 *see* Fighting School No. 2 (2FS), Marske
A.V. Roe and Co., 112, *see also* Avro aircraft
Aviación Militar Español, 188
aviation *see* aerial warfare or civil aviation
Avro aircraft, 155, 156–157, 181, *see also* A.V. Roe and Co.

Baillie, Sir Robert, 101
Balangiga (Philippines), 87–88
Baldwin, Stanley, 175, 176, 178
Balfour, Harold, 199
Balloon Factory, Farnborough, 111
balloons, 142, 143
Barcelona (Spain), 185, 188, 189
Barratt, Air Marshal Sir Arthur S. 'Ugly', 197, 201–202
Barrow, Gen, 57
Batangas (Philippines), 88–89, 90

Battle of Britain, 206–207
Battle of the Somme, The (film), 147
BE2 aircraft, 117
BE2C aircraft, 112, 125, 126, 152
BE2E aircraft, 152
Beaver Line, 17, 221
Bell, Brig Gen J. Franklin, 89, 90
Bengal Lancers (25th), 73–74
Bennett Lake and Klondike Navigation Company (BLKN), 34–35
Berry, A.G., 101
Biddle, Maj William, 56
Blenheim aircraft, 203, 206
Bleriot aircraft, 126
Blitzkrieg, vii, 200, 201–206
BLKN (Bennett Lake and Klondike Navigation Company), 34–35
Blocksom, Capt, 73–76
Böcker, Cdr, 147
bombing
 Croydon area, 147, 148
 Lancastria (HMT) at Saint Nazaire (France), ix–x, 203–204
 St Eval, Cornwall, 206–207
Bonifacio, Andreas, 38
Bookmillar, Capt, 88
border Canada and USA, 26, 28–29
 disputes, 12–13
Boxer Protocol (7 September 1901), 79
Boxer Rebellion, 48–52, 56–71
Boxer society, 45–48
Brancker, Maj W. Sefton, 110, 112–113
breathing devices for pilots, 142
Brest (France), 203
Bristol Fighters, 156, 157
British Airways, 198–199
British Expeditionary Force (BEF), vii–x, 197, 201–206

Index   225

British forces, Boxer Rebellion, 49–52, 56–63, 65, 67–68, 71, 73, 75–76
British Gazette, 177, 178
British Worker, 177
Brodrick, Hon St John, Lord Middleton, 100–101
Brooke, Lt Gen Alan, 202
Brooklyn (USS), 55
Brooks, Revd Sidney, 48
brothels, 32, 54, 140–141
Brown, Capt Roy, 163
Bruce, RAdm, 51
Buchan, Lt, 78–79

Cabell, Capt De Rosey C., 58, 66, 72, 80
Camels *see* Sopwith Aircraft, Camel
cameras (for aerial reconnaissance), 129, 131–132
Canada, 1–14, *2*, 22–37
Canadian mining laws, 9, 10, 12
Canadian Reserve Forces, 92
Carmack, George Washington, 3, 7–9, 11, 31
Carnegie, Andrew, 41
cavalry charges, 75–76
Cavite Province (Philippines), 38, 89
Central Flying School, Upavon, 111, 113, 119, 199
Centurion (HMS), 49
Chaffee, Gen Adna Romanza
 in China, 53, 55–58, 60–61, 65–66, 68–70
 early career, 221
 in the Philippines, 89
Chamchamal (Iraq), 173–174
Chaoli (China), 82
Chateaudun (France), 201, 202
Cherbourg (France), 202, 203, 205
Chien-men gate (Peking, China), 68–70
Chihli province (China), 46, 48, 51
Chilkoot Trail (USA to Canada), 12, 34
China, *39*
 Boxer Rebellion, 45–52, 56–71
 occupation, 72–83
China Relief Expedition, 53–56
Chinese Imperial Troops, 51, 73
Ching Dynasty, 82, 83

Christians
 rescue, 81–82
 treatment in China, 46, 48, 50
Churchill, Winston, 177
Civil Air Guard, 200
civil aviation, 186–187, 198–200
civil unrest in the General Strike, 177, 179
civilians in the First World War, 146–148
Clarendon Commission, 17
Cleaveland, Grover, 41
coal loading at Nagasaki, 54–55
Cobh (County Cork, Ireland), 22
Coltman, Robert, 77, 78
Communists, 186, 189
concentration camps, Philippines, 86, 90
Conger, Minister, 68
Connell, Capt Thomas, 87
Constantine, Inspector Charles, 12, 221
Constantinesco gears, 154
Cook, Arthur James, 176, 223
Coolidge, Lt Col Charles A., 56
coronation of Edward VII, 102
coronation of George V, 107–108
County of London (King's Colonials) Imperial Yeomanry (4th) *see* King Edward's Horse (KEH)
Craddock, Cdr C., 51
Cranwell Village, Lincolnshire, 184, 190
crashes (aircraft), 128–129, *137*, 138–139, 159, 162–163, 173
Croydon, Surrey, 147–148
Cummings, Prudence, 96–98
customs duties (Canadian), 12, 29

Daggett, Colonel A.S., 56
Daily Mail, 176
Dawson City (Canada), 13, 23, 29, 31–33
Daza, Capt Eugenio, 87
De Dombasle, Wg Cdr Guy, 167
De Havilland aircraft
 BE2, 117
 BE2c, 112, 125, 126, 152
 BE2e, 152
 DH2, 118, 134, 152
 DH4, 156–157
 DH9, 156–157
 DH9A, *171*, 193

Dead Horse Trail (Canada) *see* White Pass (USA to Canada)
demobilisation, 165
d'Erlanger, Gerard, 198–199
Dewey, Cdre George, 38, 40
DH2 aircraft, 118, 134, 152
DH4 aircraft, 156–157
DH9 aircraft, 156–157
DH9A aircraft, 152, 153, *171*, 193
Dickson, Bertram, 111
Dingle, Flg Off Russell H., 200
Director General of Civil Aviation, 199
discipline, of troops, 72–73
dogs, 36–37
Doubleday, Gordon (son-in-law), 197, 209–210
Doubleday, Jane (granddaughter), *207*, 209, 214–215
Doubleday, John (grandson), 210–211, 218–220
Doubleday, Margaret Elsa Verder (née Harris) (daughter), 106, 197, 209, 210, *211*
Dougherty, ex-Flt Lt, 189
Douglas, Air Vice Marshal Sholto, 201
Dunkirk (France), 205–206
Duran, Sgt Pedro, 87

Edward VII, 102, 106–107
Egypt, 182, *184*
Empress-Dowager Tz'u-hsi (China), 48, 49, 79, 82, 221
Epsom Cottage Hospital, 207–210
Étaples Army Base Camp (France), 145–146
ethnic divisions, Philippines, 38, 41, 44
evacuation from France, viii–x, 202–205
Evill, Air Vice Marshal D.C.S., 202

Fabeck, Maj Hans von, 143
Fairey Battle aircraft, 194, 200, 203
Fame (HMS), 52
Farman aircraft, 113, 152
 Maurice Farman aircraft, 119–120
 Maurice Farman S11s, 115
Farman Experimental Aircraft *see* FE2b aircraft
Favier, Pere, Bishop of Peking, 48

FE2 (De Havilland) aircraft, 113, 118
FE2b aircraft, 133, 134, 140
  flown by S.H.B. Harris, 126–130, 129, 139
Federal Volunteer Regiments (USA), 44
Fee *see* FE2 (De Havilland) aircraft
Fengtai (China), 47, 49
Fiat fighters, 188
Fienvilliers (France), 127, 129
Fife, Duke of, 101
Fifth Artillery, Light Battery, 55–56, 57, 60–62, 65, 68–70
Fighting School No. 2 (2FS), Marske, 157–166, *216–217*
Filipino Army, 40, 42–44, 84–89
Flintshire (USS), 56
Fokker aircraft, 133–134, 140
  DVII, 153
  E1, 117, 222
Fokker scourge, 134, 222
Forbidden City (Peking, China), 47, 73
Foreign Concession (Tientsin, China), 47
Foreign Enlistment Act (1870), 187
Foreign powers (China), occupation rights, 79
formation flying, 127
Forsyth, Capt (previously Lt), 73–76, 78–79, 81–82
Fort Constantine (Canada), 12
Fortymile (Canada), 5, 7, 9, 12
Fourth Army (British), 131, 139
France, vii–x, *135*, *192*, 193–205
Franco, Gen Francisco, 185, 188
Freemasons, 106, 171
French aviation, 111
French forces, Boxer Rebellion, 49–50, 51–52, 56–63, 66, 71
French High Command, 202
Frey, Gen, 57
Fukushima, Maj Gen, 57
Funston, Brig Gen Frederick, 86

Gamlin, Pte Adolph, 87–88
Gaselee, Lt Gen, 52, 57, 60
Gaussen, Lt, 73
General Orders 100 (GO 100), 85
General Strike (May 1926), 175–180
George V, 112
  coronation, 107–108

German forces, XIV Reserve Corps, 143
German forces, Boxer Rebellion, 49–50, 51–52, 56–63
German intervention in Spain, 185–186
Getafe airfield (Spain), 188
gold, discovery in the Yukon, 2–11
gold prospecting
  equipment, 1, 4, 26
  living conditions, 31–33
  panning, 6, 8, 34
gold reserves, Spanish, 186
gold rush (Yukon, Canada), 1–12, 14–15, 17, 22–31, 33–34
Gompers, Samuel, 41
Gosport, Advanced School of Flying, 126
Gosport Training School, 159
Gosport Tube, 159
Göttsch, Leutnant Walter, 118
Gower, Pauline, 200
Grant (USS), 53, 55, 56
Graves, Samuel H., 25
Great Northern Railway Company, 169
Griffiths, Eric, 189
Groves Memorial Prize 1924, 171
Guam, 41
guerilla war, Philippines, 84–89
Guiney, Lt, 66
Gulf of Pechihli (China), 47, 49
guns mounted in aircraft, 132–133, 153–155

Hales, Stephen, 17
Hamilton, Lt Col George, 99, 101, 102
Handley Page, 112
Harper, Papa, 5
Harper, Lt Roy B., 56
Harrington, Henry, 189
Harris, Constance Mary Verder (daughter), 107
Harris, Edith Herberta Verder (daughter), 106, 214
Harris, Elsa de Verde (née Verder, wife)
  early life and marriage, 93–100, *213*
  family life, *104, 107–108, 119*, 146, 182, *183*
  later life and death, *207*, 214–215

Harris, Frederick (brother), 16
Harris, Frederick W. (father), 16
Harris, Gordon (brother), 16
Harris, Harold (brother), 16
Harris, Jeanette (née Bywater), 16, *104*
Harris, Katherine Gertrude (née Cook, sister-in-law), 104
Harris, Margaret Elsa Verder *see* Doubleday, Margaret Elsa Verder (née Harris) (daughter)
Harris, Mildred (sister), 16
Harris, Patricia Nella Verda (daughter), 167, *184*
Harris, Percival (brother), 16, 104 115, 206
Harris, Sydney Herbert Bywater
  Air Force Cross award, 167
  bankruptcy, 184
  birth and early life, *1*, 16
  Canadian experience, 26–29, 33–34, 35–37, 92, *93*
  children, *104*, 106, 107, *146*, 167, *171*
  China experience, 53–56, 59–62, 64–66, 69–70, 72, 82
  civilian career, 99, *100, 103*, 106, 107, 168, 180, *184*
  death, 214
  family life, 99, 182, *183, 219*, 220, 146–148
  Japanese experience, 54–55
  King Edward's Horse (KEH), 104–106, *105*
  marriage, 93, 98–99
  mining interests, 92, 108
  Philippines experience, 85, 87, 89, 91
  retirement and old age, 182, 207–210, *211, 212*, 214
  Royal Air Force service, 157, 165, 167–168, 184, 194–196
  Royal Air Force Volunteer Reserve service, 190–191, 193, 207, 214
  Royal Flying Corps service, 115–133, 136–146, 149–155
  Spanish Civil War, 187, 189–190
  tattoos, 82
  train driver, 169–170, *174*, 177–178
  US Cavalry (6th) service, 44, 53–56, 59–62, 64–66

Index   227

Harris, Sydney Herbert Verder (Verder, son), 99, *123*, 193, 197, 209
  RAF career, 171–174
Harris, William (brother), 16
Hartsfield, Pte, 73
Harvey, 2Lt E.B., 127–129
Hasbrouck, Capt Alfred, 71
Hawker, Lanoe VC, 141
Hawker Harts, 193
Hawker Hind Light Bombers, 193
Heinkel fighters, 188
Henderson, Brig Gen Sir David, 112
Henderson, Robert, 3, 5–10, 11
Hilles, Sir Richard, 17
Hispano-Suiza engine, 152
Hitler, Adolph, 185–186
Hogg, Maj R.E.T., 127
Hohenzollern, Prince von, 143
Holtman, Robert, 79
Hong Kong (China), 40, 89
horses, treatment, 24, 25, 26
hospitals (Army), 145–146
Howard, John, 101
Hsuch-chuang-tsz, 80–81
Hun Ho (China), 77
Hunker, Andrew, 10
Huns, 130, 222
Hurricanes, viii, 199, 200, 201, 203, 204, 205, 206
Hutcheson, Adjutant General, Capt Grote, 56

Ho Chuan *see* Boxer society
Ilocano people (Philippines), 44, 85
Immelmann, Max, 134, 222
Imperial Airways and Air Dispatch Ltd, 189
Imperial City (Peking, China), 47, 69–70
Indian River (Canada), 5, 6
Indiana (USS), 55, 56
Indians (North American), 7, 8–9, 13–14
indigenous peoples (Canada), 13–14
Indonesia, 182
insurance career, 99, 106, 107, 168, 180
insurgents, Philippines, 84–89
International Brigades (Spain), 187–189
International Force, Boxer Rebellion, 51–52, 56–63, 73

interrupter gears, 154
Inuit people, 13
Iraq, 172–174
Irish emigration, 22
Italian forces, Boxer Rebellion, 49–50, 51–52, 57
Italian intervention in Spain, 185
Italy, 182

Janes, 2Lt Charles William, 155
Japanese forces, Boxer Rebellion, 49–50, 51–52, 56–67, 71, 75–76
jingals, 74, 76
Joffre, Gen Joseph, 139
John J. Healy's Trading Post, 23
Johns, Capt W.E., 162
Johnson, Charles, 10
Junkers Ju-88, ix–x, 203–204

Kaiser Wilhelm II, 52, 222
Kampfgeschwader 30 (KG30), 203
Kanochia-ju (China), 59
Kan-su troops, 49, 50
Karnes, Lt, 75
Katipunan Society, 85
Ketteler, Baron von, 51
King Edward's Horse (KEH), formerly King's Colonials Imperial Yeomanry, 97–104, 107–108, 115, 171–172
Kingsgate, Kent, 182
Kipling, Rudyard, 42
Kitchener, Lord, 112
Klondike Gold Rush *see* Yukon Gold Rush
Klondike River (Canada), 5, 7, 8, 10, 31
Kung-tsun (China), 48

La Pallice (France), 202
La Rochelle (France), 202
Laimee, Marguerite, 11
Lai-shui (China), 48
Lake Bennett (Canada), 12, 23, 24, 26, 29, 34
Lake Laberge (Canada), 30
Lake Lindemann (Canada), 12
Lake Ontario (SS), 17, 18–22, 221
Lancaster Gate, London, 184, 190, 207, 212, 214, 218
Lancastria (HMT), ix–x, 204–205
Langfang (China), 47, 50
Laude, Joseph (Joe), 5, 6
Lawrence, Lt Col Hon H.A., 103

Lawton, Maj Gen Henry, 84
Le Mans (France), 202
leaflet dropping, 196–197
Lee, Maj Jesse M., 57
Legation Quarter (Peking, China), 47–48, 49, 50–51, 52, 68–69
Lewis guns, 153
Li Hung-Chang, 79, 221
Light Battery, Fifth Artillery, 55–56, 57, 60–62, 65, 68–70
Lingayan Gulf (Philippines), 84
Little, Lt Louis M., 57
Liu-chia-pei (China), 59
Liverpool, 17, 18, 21
living conditions
  China, 72–73
  Dawson City (Canada), 31–33
  Fighting School, No. 2 (2FS), 165
  on board ship, 18–20
  Philippines, 43, 87
  RAF Advanced Striking Force (RAFASF), 197–198
  Royal Flying Corps in France, 140–141
  School of Aerial Gunnery (No. 2), 150–151
London, Lancaster Gate, 184, 190, 207, 212, 214, 218
London Colney, 180–181
London Mission Chapel, Kung-tsun (China), 48
London Underground Railways, 177–178
Loraine, Robert, 140
Lowry, Mr, 66, 78
Lucar, Emanuel, 17
Luftwaffe, 188
Lu-kou-chiao (China), 77
Luna, Antonio Martin, 188
Luna, Gen Antonio, 43–44
Luzon (Philippines), 43, 44, 84, 86, 88–90

Mabini, Apolinario, 43
Macabebe people (Philippines), 85, 86
MacArthur, Maj Gen Arthur, 84–85
Macaulay, Norman, 30
McClennan, McFeely and Co., 1, 4
MacDonald, Sir Claude, 49, 62
MacDonald, Ramsey, 176
Machiapu (China), 47

McKinley, President, 38, 41
Madrid (Spain), 185, 188
mail delivery (Lake Bennett to Skaguay), 34–37
Malalos Congress (Philippines), 43
Malvar, Gen Miguel, 88–89, 90
Manchu Bannermen, 51
Manchu Dynasty, 82, 83
Manila (Battle of), (1899), 38, 42–43
Manila (Philippines), 38, 40–41
March, Maj Peyton C., 84
Marchwood Park, Hythe, Kent, 214
Marinduque Islands (Philippines), 86
Marpak, Solomon, 10
Marshall, Lt, 75
Marske, North Yorkshire, 157–167, 169
martial law (Philippines), 85–91
Martinsyde, 152
Masons, 106, 171
Mathy, Cdr, 148
Maurice Farman aircraft *see* Farman aircraft
medical inspection, on board ship, 20–21
Merchant Taylors' School (London), 16–17
Messerschmitt fighters, 188
Métis people, 13
Middlesbrough, 163
Midland Railway, 169
Miles Canyon (Yukon, Canada), 29
Military Aeronautics Directorate, 112
Miner's Certificate, 1, *3*
Miners Federation, 176
miners' strike, 180
miners' working conditions, 175, 179–180
missionaries, 46–47, 48, 80
Montreal (Canada), 17, 22
Moore, Capt William, 23–24
Morocco, 185
Mottershead, Sgt Pilot Thomas, VC, DCM, 118
Mounties (Canadian Royal North-West Mounted Police), 12–13, 26, 28, 30

Nacionales, Casiana 'Geronima', 87
Nagasaki (Japan), 54–55
Nantes (France), 202, 203
National Air Communications, 199
National Assembly, Malalos (Philippines), 43
National Union of Railwaymen (NUR), 169
Nationalists (Spanish), 185
Naval Air Service *see* Royal Naval Air Service (RNAS)
Nena (cousin), 207–208, 210, 214–215
Neuve-Chappelle (Battle), 131
Newark (USS), 55
Nieh, Gen, 49
Nieuport-Breguet Squadron, Spain, 188
night flying, 138–139
No. 2 Auxiliary School of Aerial Gunnery, Turnberry, 149–155
No. 2 Fighting School (2FS), Marske, 157–166, *216–217*
Non-Intervention Committee, 187
Non-Intervention Treaty (1936), 185–186
Numbered Treaty Eight (1899), 13–14

O'Brien, Hattie, 93
observers (in aircraft), 117–119, 127–129, 130–133, 137–138
Ogilvie (Canada), 5
Olympia (USS), 40
Operation Aerial, 202–206
Otis, Maj Gen Elwell S., 42–43, 44, 85

Pact of Biak-na-Bato, 89
Paddock, Capt, 74, 76
Palanan (Philippines), 86
Panic of 1893, 17
parachutes, 128, 142
Paris, Treaty of (1898), 41
Park, Air Vice Marshal K.R., 205
Partido Federal, 85
Partridge, Otto, 34
Passenger Act (1855), 18
Pechili, 56
Pei-ho River China), 47, 50, 58, 71
Pei-t'ang Cathedral (Peking, China), 50, 70
Pei-Tsang (China), 57
assault on, 58–62

Peking (China), 47–51, 57–58, 73, 77
assault on, 62, 65–71
Pelly River (Canada), 5, 11
Philadelphia and Reading Railroad (USA), 17
Philippine Insurrection, 38–44, 84–91
photography, 131–132, 144, 154–155
pigtail (souvenir), 82, 218
Pilar, Brig Gen Gregorio del, 84
pilots
civilian, 198–200
life expectancy (Western Front), 146, 147
risks in training, 155, 160
Spanish Civil War, 186–189
training, 119–125, 158, 159–162
policing the Yukon, 12–13, 24, 25–26
Polikarpov aircraft, 188
Polish soldiers, 205
Popular Front (Spanish), 185
Port Albert (USS), 55
Powell, 2Lt, 129, 138
Powell, Frederick, 140
Prince of Wales, 101, 106
prospector's code, 6, 8
prostitution, 32, 54, 140–141
Public Schools Act (1868), 17
public transport, 177–178
Puerto Rica, 41
Purley, Surrey, 107, 146, 148, 171

Queen Elizabeth (SS), 214
Queenstown (County Cork, Ireland), 22

RAF *see* Royal Air Force
RAF Kenley, 206
RAF Turnhouse, 193, 195
RAF1 engine, 112
railroad speculation (USA), 17
railways, 169–170, 175
China, 47, 49–50, 51, 60, 77
General Strike (May 1926), 169, 170, 175
White Pass (Canada), 25, 26
rampart guns, 74, 76
reconnaissance activities
aerial, 117–119, 127–129, 131–132, 144
occupation of Peking, 73–82

Index 229

Red Friday, 175
Reilly, Capt Henry J., 55–56, 57, 60–62, 65, 68–70
Reims (France), 194
Relay Company (Canada), 35–37
Rennes (France), 201–202, 202
Republican Army (Spanish), 189
Republican government (Spanish), 185–187
RFC see Royal Flying Corps (RFC)
Richthofen, Baron von (Red Baron), 163
Roberts, Lord, 100, 101
Roosevelt, Theodore, 42, 91
Ross-Hume, Maj A., 140
rotary engines, 110
Royal Aero Club Certificate, 110
Royal Air Force Advanced Air Striking Force (AASF), 194, 201–203, 206
Royal Air Force Advanced Striking Force (RAFASF), 196–197
Royal Air Force Bomber Command, 206
Royal Air Force Coastal Command, 206
Royal Air Force Fighter Command, 206
Royal Air Force (RAF), 156, 165, 184, 191–193
Royal Air Force (RAF) Squadrons
  1, 202
  12, 201
  14, 115
  17, 201, 202, 205
  55, 162, 172
  73, 202, 205
  242, 201, 202, 205
  501, 202
  504, 201
  603 (City of Edinburgh), 193
Royal Air Force (RAF) Wings,
  8th, 167
Royal Air Force Volunteer Reserve, 190
Royal Aircraft Factory, Farnborough, 111–112, 152
Royal Army Medical Corps, 145
Royal Engineers, 145
Royal Engineers, 10th Regiment (Canada), 92
Royal Flying Corps (RFC), 109, 115, 147, 155–156, 159, 180–181

establishment, 111
uniforms, 114, 141–142
Royal Flying Corps (RFC) Groups, 7, 149
Royal Flying Corps (RFC) Squadrons
  8, 140
  12, 140
  13, 140
  14, 126
  22, 126
  23, 125–129, 134, 139–140
  25, 118
  41, 140
  56, 152
Royal Flying Corps (RFC) Training Squadrons, 39, 149
Royal Flying Corps (RFC) Wings
  7th, 149
  12th, 140
  13th (of III Brigade), 129
  17th, 149
  25th, 149
Royal Naval Air Service (RNAS), 111, 113, 155–156
Royal Navy, viii, 204–205
Rudy, Pte John, 80
Russian forces, Boxer Rebellion, 49–50, 51–52, 56–68, 71
Russian support for Spain, 185–186, 188

St Eval, Cornwall, 206–207
Saint-Malo (France), 202, 203
Saint-Nazaire (France), viii–x, 201–205
Samuel, Sir Herbert, 175–176, 178–179
Samuel Commission, 175–176
Samur campaign (Philippines), 88
Samur Island (Philippines), 87–88
San Francisco (USA), 37, 53–54
San Isidro (Northern Luzon, Philippines), 86
Scales, Lt, 74
Scarth, Inspector, 12
School of Aerial Fighting and Gunnery No. 2 see Fighting School No. 2 (2FS), Marske
School of Aerial Fighting, Ayr, 154, 157
School of Aerial Gunnery, Hythe, 149
School of Aerial Gunnery No. 1, 156

School of Aerial Gunnery No. 2 (Auxiliary) Turnberry, 149–155
School of Aerial Gunnery No. 4 (Auxiliary). see Fighting School No. 2 (2FS), Marske
School of Fighting 1, 155
scorched earth policy (Philippines), 88–90
SE5a aircraft, 152–153, 156, 165
Seattle (USA), 10, 11
Second Army (British), 143
Seven Hours Act (suspension, 1926), 179
Seymour, V Adm Sir Edward, 49
Seymour expedition, 50
Shang-shia (China), 64
Shan-his Province (China), 48
Shantung province (China), 46, 48
Shelmerdine, Sir Francis, 199
Shookum Jim, 9, 11
Shoreham, West Sussex, 115
Shorts (aircraft manufacturer), 112
Sickle, Pte Van, 75
Sidcot suit, 163
Singapore, 40
Sir Archibald McIndoe's Hospital, East Grinstead, 214
Siwashes see Indians (North American)
Skaguay (USA), 1, 12–13, 23–24, 26, 34–37
skirmishes
  Boxer Rebellion, 78, 80–81
  Philippines, 89
Smasher, 162–163
Smith, Gen 'Howlin' Jake', 88
Smith, Judge John, US Commissioner of Skaguay, 12–13
Smith-Barry, Maj, 159
Smuts, Gen Jan, 155
snipers, 70
Solace (USS), 56
Solly, 2Lt Arthur Norbury, 142, 144–145
Somme battlefront, 142–144
Sopwith aircraft
  Camel, 155, 156, 157, 162, 163
  Dolphin, 156
Sopwiths, 112
Sorsogen (Philippines), 90
Spain, 214–215
Spanish Army, 40–41

Spanish Civil War (1936–1939), 185–189
Spanish-American War (1898), 38–41
Spitfires, 199, 201, 206
Squaw Man *see* Carmack, George Washington
Steele, Inspector Sam, 12, 30
steerage class, 17–18, 19
Stessel, Maj Gen, 52
Strange, Maj Louis Arbon, 126–127
Street, 2Lt C., 118
Stuka bombers, viii, 188
stunt flying, 113
Sugiyama, Mr, 50
Summerall, Lt Charles P., 69
Sun Alliance, 106
Sun Life Assurance Ltd, 168, 182
Sykes, Maj Sir Frederick, 112

Taft, William Howard, 85
Tagalog people (Philippines), 38, 41, 44, 85
Tagish Charley, 9, 11
Tagish tribe, 7, 8
Taku (China), 47, 49, 51, 52, 55
Talavera Front (Spain), 188
Talisay (Batangas, Philippines), 88–89
Tang-chia-wan (China), 59
Tartar City (Peking, China), 47–48, 49, 62–70
tattoos, 82
Terrible (HMS), 51, 52
Third Army (British), 129, 139
Thompson, R.R., 101
Three (III) Brigade, 13th Wing, 129
Thron-diuk River *see* Klondike River (Canada)
Tientsin (China), 47, 51–52, 56–57, 62, 71, 76
Tiger Moths, 200
Tila Pass (Philippines), 84
Tillman, Senator 'Pitchfork Ben', 42
Tongku (China), 47, 51
Toulouse (France), 187
Trade Disputes Act (1906), 179
Trade Disputes and Trade Union Act (1927), 180
Trades Union Congress (TUC), 175–176, 178–180
trading posts, 5

training aircraft, 152, 156, 157
tramway, Yukon River (Canada), 30
Treaty Eight, 13–14
Treaty Six, 13–14
Trenchard, General, 142
Tsungli Yamen, 47, 48–49, 51
Tung-Chow (China), 48, 63–66, 67, 82
Tung Fu-hsiang, 49, 50
Tung-pien-men Gate (Peking, China), 65, 67–68
Turnberry (No. 2 Auxiliary School of Aerial Gunnery), 149–157
Turner, Maj Gen Sir Alfred, 101
Twain, Mark, 41

uniforms
 Air Transport Auxiliary, 199
 King's Colonials Imperial Yeomanry, 101–102, 106
 Royal Flying Corps (RFC), 112, 113–115, 141–142, 163
 Spanish militia, 188
 US Cavalry (6th), 53
Upavon *see* Central Flying School, Upavon
US 25th Pursuit Squadron, Marske, 162
US Asiatic Fleet, 38
US Cavalry (6th)
 China, 56–61, 65–67, 69–70
 occupation of China, 72–83
 Philippines, 53–54, 85, 87, 89
US Cavalry (7th), 56
US Forces
 Boxer Rebellion, 49–50, 51–52, 56–71, 72–83
 Philippines, 40–44, 84–91
US Infantry (9th) Regiment
 China, 55, 56, 58, 60–62, 68
 Philippines, 43, 87–88
US Infantry (14th) Regiment, 55, 56, 58, 60–62, 65–70, 77–79
US Infantry (33rd) Regiment, 84
US Marines, 56, 57, 60–62, 68–69, 71
US Navy, 86

Vancouver (Canada), 21, 22
Verder, Edith Mandana, 93, 94, 95, 215
Verder, Herbert Leslie, 93, 95

Verder, Herbert Wendell (Wendell), 93, 99, *157*, 215
Verder, Nellie (née O'Brien), 93, *94*
Vermont (USA), 93, *94*, *96*
 family home, *93*, *99*
Vickers, 112
Vickers aircraft
 FB5, 113
 FB9, 152
Vickers machine guns, 153–154
Victoria Cross, 118
Visayan Islands (Philippines), 86

Waldersee, Gen Albrecht Graf von, 52
Wallace, Lt Col Nesbit Willoughby, 100, 101, 102, 103
Waller, Maj Littleton W.T., 56, 58
Walsh, Maj J., Commissioner of the Yukon, 12, 25
War Birds, 180–181
War Bonds, 163, 165
Ward, Col Sir Edward, 101, 102
Wastz (China), 81
Westland Wapitis, 193
Wheaton, Brig Gen Lloyd, 84
White, Sir Thomas, 17
White Pass (USA to Canada), 12, 23–29
William, James, 41
Wint, Lt Col T.J., 58, 75–76
Winthrop, John, 96
Wolseley Motor Company, 152
Wolseley Viper Engine, 153
Wright, David, of Peperell, 96
Wright, Liberty, 98

Yamaguchi, Lt Gen, 52, 57
Yang-tsun (China), 50, 57
 assault on, 60–62
Yneya (China), 82
Yongkichon (China), 81
Young, Brig Gen Samuel M.B., 84
Yu-hsien, Governer of Shan-his, ex-Governer of Shantung, 48
Yukon Gold Rush, 1–12, 14–15, 17, 22–31, 33–34
Yukon River (Canada), *2*, 22, 24, 26, 29–31
Yu-lu, Viceroy of Chi-li, 48

Zeppelin raids, 147–148, 155